PRAISE F

THE RIPPLE EFFECT

"This book offers a unique systemic approach to health, integrating the biological, psychological, social, environmental, and spiritual dimensions of well-being. It acknowledges the interdependence of the major problems of our time, seeing them all as problems of health. The author lucidly demonstrates the deep interconnectedness of all life, the important links between individual and planetary health, and the critical relationship between well-being and sustainability. This is an inspiring and tremendously hopeful book."

—Fritjof Capra, coauthor of *The Systems View of Life*

"Once we understand the deep implications of the truism that 'we are all microcosms of the macrocosm' then we can begin the process of healing ourselves and healing the Earth. In her timely new book, *The Ripple Effect*, Dr Andrea Revell explains how, through systems thinking, we can relinquish the 'illusion of separation' and recognize that we can each play a creative role in this vitally important regenerative undertaking."

—Lorna Howarth, former editor of *The Resurgence and Ecologist* magazine and author of *Sandpaper for the Soul*

"*The Ripple Effect* is one of the most important books for optimizing the human experience. This is a clear and detailed guide of where we have gone wrong and how we can go right with living healthily and harmoniously on the planet. For anyone who cares about our world it's a must read."

—Tom Cronin, Founder of Zen Academy and bestselling author of *The Portal*

"*The Ripple Effect* is a breath of remarkably fresh air. Andrea shifts the paradigm from the treatment of illness to the pursuit of good health, and in doing so unfolds the connections between our personal health and our social interactions, the state of our planet, and our search for meaning and purpose."

—Shakti Saran, systems thinking consultant, Cornell University

"At first glance *The Ripple Effect* appears to be about two sets of crises which are defining the 21st century: environmental destruction and the rise of chronic disease. This book cogently expresses that, at their heart, they are symptoms of the same issue—the unhealthy relationship between the social and natural world. Drawing on the latest scientific evidence with insights from Eastern philosophy, Revell constructs an enlightening narrative which describes this relationship from the individual scale, where we are neglecting the four pillars of health, to the planetary scale, where we are exceeding planetary boundaries."

—Dr. Sam Hampton, Zero Emissions Enterprise, Oxford University

"*The Ripple Effect* is an impressively profound and wide-ranging examination of the interconnectedness of life on Earth and of the planet herself/itself. It offers advice on well-being at all levels and can be used as a reference book on multiple subjects. It is refreshing in that it combines fully referenced science with metaphysics in a concise and easy to understand way. Highly recommended.

—Sue Gross, former pain management consultant, St Thomas's Hospital

"As a medical doctor, I find the principles explored by Andrea to be both insightful and timely. The connection between obesity, chronic disease, and stress is something I encounter daily in my practice, and this book rightly emphasizes that these issues are not just personal health concerns but are deeply embedded in broader societal problems. The links drawn between our struggling healthcare systems, economic inequality, and the climate crisis offer a compelling argument for a more holistic approach to health.

—Nish Srikantha M.D, Portsmouth Hospitals University Trust

"Andrea is a pioneering thinker and brilliant writer. Evocative and thought-provoking, *The Ripple Effect* joins the dots on mind-body spirit health at the individual level, and planetary health at the macro level. While each chapter can be read as a standalone, the interconnectedness of life is cogently expressed throughout, concluded with impactful messages the world really needs to hear. It emphasizes that there are real solutions to the systemic problems we face, and that even the smallest lifestyle change can have a ripple effect which changes the planet. This book inspires hope for a much brighter future to come."

—Anu Garg, holistic health expert, founder of BeVajra.com

The Ripple Effect:
Healing Ourselves, Healing Our Planet
by Andrea Revell, PhD

© Copyright 2024 Andrea Revell, PhD

ISBN 979-8-88824-491-3

All rights reserved. No part of this publication may be reproduced, stored in a retrieval system, or transmitted in any form or by any means—electronic, mechanical, photocopy, recording, or any other—except for brief quotations in printed reviews, without the prior written permission of the author.

Published by

köehlerbooks™

3705 Shore Drive
Virginia Beach, VA 23455
800-435-4811
www.koehlerbooks.com

THE RIPPLE EFFECT

Healing Ourselves,
Healing Our Planet

ANDREA REVELL, PHD

VIRGINIA BEACH
CAPE CHARLES

Dedicated to the team at the Taymount clinic (Hertforshire, UK), without whom I would not have been able to write this book. Their pioneering microbiome transplant treatment (called "FMT") saved me from the rigors of an autoimmune condition that incapacitated me to do what I love most—write. I have nothing but gratitude for you all; I thank you from the bottom of my heart.

TABLE OF CONTENTS

Introduction 1

PART 1: A GLOBAL HEALTH CRISIS 3

   Chapter 1: Troubling Times 4

   Chapter 2: The Challenges of Modern Medicine 12

   Chapter 3: Reason For Hope?
   Recent Trends in Healthcare 26

PART 2: THE FOUR PILLARS OF HEALTH 37

   Chapter 4: Relaxation 39

   Chapter 5: Nutrition 54

   Chapter 6: Nutrition and Planetary Health 79

   Chapter 7: Sleep 100

   Chapter 8: Exercise 119

PART 3: THE FIFTH PILLAR OF HEALTH—
CONNECTION ... 131

Chapter 9: The Mind-Body Connection ... 133

Chapter 10: Mind-Body Medicine ... 150

Chapter 11: Social Connection ... 167

Chapter 12: Environmental Connection ... 189

Chapter 13: Spiritual Connection ... 212

Chapter 14: Spirituality, Ecology, and Health ... 234

Chapter 15: Conclusions—
Toward a Systems View of Health ... 254

Acknowledgments ... 271

Endnotes ... 273

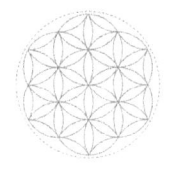

INTRODUCTION

Why is it that a billion people in the world are obese, and one in three people suffer from multiple chronic conditions? What is the link between stress and chronic disease? How are our struggling healthcare systems connected to the climate crisis or the growing gap between rich and poor? Is our diet cooking the planet? Can we prevent cancer by taking a walk in the woods, reduce heart attacks with positive thinking, or grow our brains by meditating?

This book answers these thought-provoking questions with a bird's-eye view on our global health and environmental crisis, exploring where we have gone wrong with our unsustainable way of life and what we can do about it. The explosion of disease we see in the world today is so intertwined with the climate crisis, global inequality, and humanity's disconnect with the natural world that we can no longer use our normal reductionist lens to find the health solutions we so desperately need. What is required is a "systems view"— looking holistically at the interplay of our lifestyle habits, mindsets, social relationships, environmental actions, and spiritual (dis)connection—to highlight where potential answers might lie. Influenced by *The Systems View of Life* by acclaimed physicist and systems theorist Fritjof Capra, this book encourages joined-up thinking on how to heal ourselves and our planet.

The chapters are evidence-based, detailing the latest science behind the four pillars of health: nutrition, sleep, exercise, and relaxation. Because of its systemic remit, a fifth pillar of connection has been added, including mind-body-spirit, social, and environmental connection, which are all fundamental to human health and well-being. While the story that runs through this book is of a joined-up view of health, each chapter can also be read as a stand-alone, succinctly summarizing the wealth of information on each subject so that the reader can use this as a reference and a guide, as well as a treatise on holistic well-being.

The Ripple Effect has a sustainability focus, so there is considerable commentary on the way our environmental actions impact our health. The pages are not about doom and gloom, however, nor are they scaremongering about humanity's health concerns. This book is full of hope, illuminating the scope of the challenge but also inspiring faith with simple solutions that we can all act upon right now. The systemic worldview emerging out of the dualistic conceptions of the past is one that emphasizes unity—which means we all have a role to play in healing ourselves and this beautiful blue planet of ours.

One of the most heartening things about the interconnectedness of life is that because we are all microcosms of the macrocosm, every healthy lifestyle choice we make at the individual level has a ripple effect. These ripples reverberate throughout the system to become big waves, until a critical point is reached where previously inconceivable transformations occur, such as the fall of the Berlin Wall or the sudden end of apartheid in South Africa. We have at our disposal all we need to change—our creative minds, our intelligent bodies, and our ineffable spirit. Our illusory sense of separation from the natural world comes from our collective amnesia about its sacred nature, which is also our own nature. When we feel our profound connection with all things, we can create a healthy, sustainable society where humanity flourishes in dynamic harmony with the entire web of life on the planet.

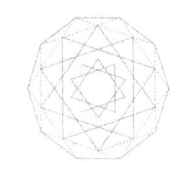

PART 1

A GLOBAL HEALTH CRISIS

He who has health, has hope. And he who has hope, has everything
—Arabian Proverb

This introductory section outlines the latest statistics on the global health crisis, taking a bird's-eye view on how our unsustainable lifestyles have created systemic problems for ourselves and our planet. The numbers are sobering, and our healthcare systems are struggling to cope, with skyrocketing costs threatening to bankrupt governments. The fault lines in conventional medicine are becoming increasingly evident as the pharmaceutical approach to health continues to focus on treating the symptoms of our lifestyle diseases rather than the underlying causes.

Fortunately, pioneering new models of well-being are emerging to take up the slack, and there is now considerable interest in preventive, functional, and integrative medicine, all of which take a more holistic approach. Coinciding with these perceptual shifts in healthcare is the burgeoning popularity of complementary and alternative medicine, which is encouraging a much broader perspective of what it means to be well. Part I concludes that at the frontiers of medicine, a systems view of health is emerging with the potential to navigate us through the stormy seas ahead, providing much hope for a healthier, more sustainable future.

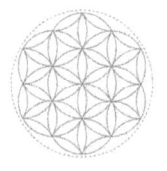

CHAPTER 1

TROUBLING TIMES

It is health that is real wealth and not pieces of silver
—Mahatma Gandi

The year 2020 will go down in history as the beginning of the COVID-19 pandemic. While both our biology and our ecology had been in a state of crisis for a long while by then, it took on a special urgency at this critical time. COVID caused such enormous upheaval and global transformation that it became much more than a pandemic; it put all of humanity's woes in the spotlight, like the eye of Sauron casting its gaze on the great troubles of the world. While this book focuses on the root causes of chronic disease rather than infectious ones, the pandemic highlighted so many of the same systemic issues that it became increasingly clear how everything in the world is connected. COVID mortality went hand in hand with underlying health issues, highlighting how infectious diseases are intimately connected with chronic ones. In the same vein, chronic diseases are linked with our unhealthy, unsustainable modern lifestyles and the ecological stress that starts the spread of infectious diseases. We cannot think of any of the world's problems in isolation; all are interrelated.

COVID showed us that it is not just our world order that is fragile, but our physical health. Humanity is a sick species. There seems to be almost as many people with chronic health conditions as not, and half the population in the developed world is either overweight or obese, with the developing world catching up fast. The statistics are horrifying, as the following section reveals. Chronic disease did indeed become the elephant in the room of the COVID-19 pandemic.

THE STATISTICS

According to the World Health Organization's 2020 report, chronic disease now accounts for a staggering seven out of the world's top ten causes of death.[1] Aging populations are the most obvious reason for this upsurge, but in fact, almost half the people dying from degenerative diseases are below the age of seventy. This explosion of ill-health is affecting every age group in every nation, across all socio-economic strata, over gender and racial divides. Chronic disease is now more than twice as deadly as all infectious illnesses in the world combined.[2]

According to the WHO, heart disease is in pole position, increasing four-fold since 2000, followed by stroke, cancer, and chronic obstructive pulmonary disease (COPD). Alzheimer's and diabetes are in the top ten for the first time. Western lifestyles are a key factor, with a staggering 60 percent of all Americans[3] suffering from chronic disease, along with more than a third of Europeans[4] and nearly a quarter of UK adults.[5] To make matters worse, degenerative diseases do not exist in isolation; in the US, about 40 percent of adults have multiple chronic conditions.[6]

Far from being "diseases of affluence," the WHO notes that conditions like heart disease and stroke are the leading causes of death in both developed and developing countries alike. Only in the lowest-income nations are infectious diseases still the leading causes of death; yet, even in these countries, heart disease and stroke rank third and fourth, respectively, as top causes of death.

The WHO also highlights that obesity, a major risk factor in the development of chronic disease, has nearly tripled globally since 1975, with more than one billion people affected. In the Organization for Economic Cooperation and Development (OECD) countries, it is estimated that more than one in two adults and nearly one in six children are now overweight or obese.[7] In the US, it is such a problem that a jaw-dropping 42 percent of adults and 18 percent of children are now clinically obese. Obesity is also becoming a serious problem in Asia, Latin America, the Pacific, the Middle East, the Caribbean, and parts of Africa, despite the widespread presence of undernutrition. In fact, nearly two-thirds of overweight people now live in the developing world. A recent report by the Potsdam Institute found that if current trends in eating habits continue, by 2050, almost half the global population will be overweight.[8] And with each surge in weight, there will be a corresponding spike in heart disease, stroke, diabetes, and cancer.

Children are also being progressively affected by chronic conditions. Rates of childhood autism, diabetes, asthma, allergies, and attention deficit hyperactivity disorder (ADHD) have skyrocketed in recent years. In the US, figures estimate that more than 40 percent of children under the age of eighteen are now affected by some kind of chronic health condition.[9]

Another marker for chronic health problems is a decreased sperm count, which has been linked to a higher risk of premature death.[10] A major study in 2022, which analyzed data from fifty-three countries on six continents, found that the average human sperm concentration has more than halved since 1973.[11] This nosedive amounts to a fertility crisis of epic proportions, threatening to crash the already declining number of new births in developed countries and causing enormous socioeconomic and political problems in countries with aging populations. While the exact reasons for the fertility crisis remain unclear, lifestyle factors and pollution seem to be a key part of the problem.

So, what on earth is going on? What is the prime culprit of all this crazy ill-health? Certainly, part of the answer lies in something we are all very familiar with—stress. Research estimates that up to 80 percent of all doctors' visits are stress related.[12] In fact, stress is a key factor in almost all the leading causes of death, including heart disease, stroke, cancer, and respiratory disorders.[13] According to the US Centers for Disease Control and Prevention (CDC), American employers spend an astonishing three hundred billion dollars every year on healthcare and lost workdays linked to stress—that's more than the gross domestic product (GDP) of Finland. Stress also affects mental health, with the WHO reporting that one in four people in the world are affected by mental or neurological disorders at some point in their lives. Burnout has become the "nom du jour," with stress being so ubiquitous that the WHO describes it as the "health epidemic of the 21st century."[14]

A BRIEF HISTORY OF DISEASE

So why has modern living become so stressful that we are literally dying in droves? A glimpse of history, from our hunter-gatherer origins to the present day, may help to put our pressure cooker lifestyles in perspective.

Hunter-Gatherer Era

Archaeological evidence suggests that hunting and foraging was the subsistence strategy of Homo erectus and Homo sapiens for around two million years. These early humans lived in small tribes, hunting and foraging in a constant nomadic search for food. This might be considered the golden age of human health because of the plentiful food and ample leisure time that hunter-gatherers were thought to enjoy.[15] Individuals were fit and active, and they also had a highly diverse and nutritious diet. As they did not live in long-lasting dwellings, there was no risk of attracting pests or insects that might carry disease. Instead, the biggest threat to human health was from predators and the occasional surprise attack from a warring tribe.

Agricultural Era

Thousands of years ago, our ancestors stopped roaming and started farming. They lived in settlements, growing crops and domesticating animals. Because they could rely on food growing abundantly year after year in the same place, populations quickly increased, with settlements becoming homesteads and villages, which became towns and cities as civilization flourished. By 3000 BC, the time of the Egyptian dynasty, the world population had reached one hundred million, and by the time of Christ, it had doubled to over two hundred million.

Yet agrarian society exacted a heavy toll on human health. Diets became monotonous, with a smaller range of food creating nutritional deficiencies and spelling disaster if harvests failed. More people packed into smaller areas led to environmental degradation and an accompanying rise in disease. Permanent dwellings attracted pests and insects that spread infectious illnesses, and crowded living conditions with poor sanitation allowed pathogens to thrive.

Living in close quarters with domesticated animals led to the unleashing of deadly diseases like smallpox and measles. Animal and human waste contaminated water supplies, while practices such as slash-and-burn land clearance and deforestation brought humans into closer contact with disease-carrying wild animals and insects. Agriculture disrupted the ecological balance to such an extent that the bubonic plague and malaria emerged from exploding populations of rodents and mosquitoes. Most of the infectious diseases that humans suffer from today arose during this time, including tuberculosis, cholera, typhoid fever, diphtheria, and influenza. Epidemics and pandemics became commonplace as people fouled up the environment, and populations were decimated.

Industrial Revolution (AD 1800–AD 1945)

The agricultural era ended at the close of the eighteenth century with the birth of the Industrial Revolution. With it came another rapid rise in population; in the year 1800, there were one billion people, and by the mid-twentieth century, the world had more than doubled to 2.5 billion. This spawned a huge migration from the countryside to industrial towns. Poor working and living conditions were a major cause of illness at that time. The mass production of machines created high levels of pollution, and many workers suffered from industrial diseases such as black, brown, and white lung from coal mining and asbestos and cotton textile manufacturing. Lack of health and safety standards made chemical poisoning and industrial accidents commonplace.

The housing of the poor in industrial towns was overcrowded and lacked basic sanitation; there was no clean running water, and families shared privies that overflowed into the street and into drinking wells. People rarely washed themselves or their clothes, so lice and flea infestations were rife. There was no refuse collection, so rubbish piled up, attracting vermin. Disease flourished in these squalid conditions, with lethal outbreaks of cholera, typhoid, typhus, smallpox, and tuberculosis. The diets of the working population were woefully inadequate, as most could not afford fresh food, leading to malnourishment and compromised immune systems.

Two developments changed the course of human health during this time: the rise of modern medicine and public health reform. Mid-nineteenth century popular health movements and sanitary crusades resulted in the building of sewage systems and clean water supplies, improved personal hygiene, and better nutrition, which greatly reduced the prevalence of disease. There was also a significant reduction in birth rates related to improved living conditions. At the same time, the rise of modern medicine in industrialized countries like Britain and the United States ensured life-threatening conditions were treated with effective medical intervention, and the revolutionary inventions of antibiotics and vaccines further reduced the burden of disease.

Modern Era (AD 1945–present)

After World War II, the world witnessed an epidemiological transition in industrialized countries as infectious diseases were replaced by a meteoric rise in chronic "diseases of civilization," brought about by lifestyle changes coupled with longer lifespans. In the past eighty years, we have seen the creation of mega chemical and manufacturing industries along with soaring consumption of mass-produced goods, as big business provided for all the material comforts of modern life. Mass markets for convenience junk food burgeoned, contributing to a dramatic rise in obesity and conditions such as heart disease, diabetes, and cancer. Sedentary lifestyles associated with the advent of cars, computers, and effort-saving machines compounded the problem, along with work-related stress to sustain the materialist, high-consumption lifestyles of modernity.

The epidemiological transition from infectious to chronic disease is now occurring in rapidly developing countries such as China and Mexico. It is also predicted to happen soon in countries such as India and Bangladesh. Many developing countries are in fact experiencing a double burden of disease, as chronic illnesses are increasingly experienced by the rich, but infectious diseases continue to be prevalent among the poor.

The modern era is also known as the period of the Great Acceleration. Population growth has occurred at a dizzying speed, more than tripling from 2.5 billion in 1950 to 8 billion in 2023. This explosion of people is affecting every aspect of health, from food supply and social relationships to world politics and the environment, with hardly any time to adapt. Population growth has caused devastating poverty in many countries, leading to a rapid rise in infectious diseases, which has increased child mortality. Impoverished living conditions, lack of sanitation, and malnutrition have created a vicious cycle, as parents have more children in the hope that some survive, driving population growth even further. Tragically, infectious diseases are combining with a rise in obesity and chronic diseases in poor communities, as rapid urbanization decreases physical activity, while the global food industry targets the mass markets of developing countries with cheap, processed food, sugary drinks, alcohol, and tobacco.

Population growth and unsustainable human activity have not only caused social problems but also grave ecological stress, which has driven lethal outbreaks of zoonotic diseases such as COVID-19, AIDS, Ebola, SARS, and MERS. Profound levels of ecological degradation have ensued since the Industrial Revolution, with fossil fuel–powered industries and transportation polluting the air, while chemical farming has contaminated the water and soil. The dramatic growth in environmental pollutants has resulted in a huge increase in the human toxic load, which has caused a further rise in disease. Anthropogenic climate change caused by exponential economic growth, fossil fuel usage, and deforestation has begun to fracture the web of life, triggering the sixth mass extinction and causing profound changes to the health of humans and all life on Earth.

THE FUTURE WE CHOOSE

We are indeed at a turning point in history—a make-or-break moment that will determine the future of all life on Earth. This is a stark realization, and understandably, many people would rather bury their heads in the sand. However, there is much reason to be hopeful. For the first time in modern history, population growth is slowing and is expected to flatten out in the coming decades before declining by the end of the century.[16]

Moreover, at the forefront of science, a paradigm change is afoot with a unifying vision for the world, a "systems view" giving rise to much-needed joined-up solutions to our global problems. Humanity is far from doomed—we have all the technology, capital, and know-how we need to create a healthy, sustainable society. What we do in the next few decades depends on the mindsets we cultivate right now, and a shift in consciousness is already underway. By thinking holistically about our own health and the well-being of the planet, we can seize the moment and birth a new world order that not only supports our health but also actively encourages the web of life to flourish. As Christina Figueres highlights in her bestselling book *The Future We Choose*,[17] "Today we have the unique chance to create a future where things not only stabilize but get better. We can have more efficient and cheaper transportation, resulting in less traffic; we can have cleaner air, supporting better health and enhancing the enjoyment of city life; and we can practice smarter use of natural resources, resulting in less pollution of land and water . . . we can, together, reimagine our place in this world. As human beings, we all have the outrageous fortune to be here on this planet at this moment of profound consequence."

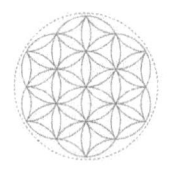

CHAPTER 2

THE CHALLENGES OF MODERN MEDICINE

Modern medicine, for all its advances, knows less than 10 percent of what your body knows instinctively.
—Deepak Chopra

Given the broad context of our modern-day health issues, it is perhaps not surprising that our healthcare systems are struggling under the scale of the momentous problems we face. Not only that, but conventional medicine does not have a great track record when it comes to curing the kinds of chronic conditions we face today. Arising in the late eighteenth century, the Western medical model was originally designed to treat acute infections and life-and-death emergencies that were prevalent during the Industrial Revolution, delivering lifesaving drugs and surgery to those in urgent need. It was not designed for the slow, degenerative diseases of today caused by poor diets, sedentary living, pollution, and the high levels of stress characteristic of modern life.

This chapter details the reasons why our healthcare systems are floundering. It highlights that Western medicine's reductionist approach has led to a tendency to treat the symptoms of our lifestyle illnesses rather than the underlying causes, and to view the mind and body as separate.

This has led to a quiet revolution at the grassroots level toward more holistic healing approaches and there is now an explosion of interest in complementary and alternative medicine and integrative medicine across the globe. Over the following chapters we discuss why there is hope of an emerging systems view of health, which sees our bodies as complex, interconnected networks nested within wider social and ecological systems that are all fundamental aspects of the web of life. In this holistic perspective, health is not just the absence of disease but a state of complete physical, mental, social, ecological, and spiritual well-being.

THE RISE AND FALL OF MODERN MEDICINE

The marvels of modern medicine are well-documented, saving the lives of countless people with such miracles as antibiotics, anesthetics and hi-tech procedures like open heart surgery and organ transplants. In his acclaimed book, *The Rise and Fall of Modern Medicine,* Dr. James Le Fanu[18] describes the medical achievements that have occurred since the Second World War as no less than a "therapeutic revolution," combating serious diseases such as polio, diphtheria, and tuberculosis; inventing intensive care and ventilators; creating minimally intrusive surgery techniques like keyhole surgery; and making great strides with diagnostic imaging technology such as x-rays, MRIs, and CT scanners. Latest advances include nanomedicine for diagnostics and stem cell regeneration, which has been used to repair everything from torn ligaments to brain injuries.

However, this so-called therapeutic revolution has greatly increased the cost of healthcare without contributing much in the way of lifestyle and preventive medicine, which has meant that the infectious illnesses of the past have been replaced by a new wave of chronic diseases that threaten to overwhelm healthcare systems.

MECHANISTIC MEDICINE

The pioneering systems thinker Fritjof Capra has written extensively on the benefits of holistic versus reductionist perspectives in Western scientific thought. In his acclaimed book, *The Turning Point,*[19] Capra explains the challenges of reductionist thinking for conventional medicine, detailing how the "Cartesian split" of mind and body that arose at the beginning of the scientific revolution has resulted in a dehumanizing and mechanistic approach to healing today.

Descartes was a seventeenth-century philosopher, mathematician, and scientist who is commonly regarded as the founding father of modern philosophy. He saw nature as consisting of two separate realms—mind and body, or spirit and matter, which existed independently of each other. Spirit was the realm of the church, while matter was the domain of science. Matter was thought to be made up of fundamental building blocks, which meant that nature could be reduced to its smallest components and analyzed to understand the workings of the whole. Under the trinity of Descartes, Francis Bacon, and Isaac Newton, the scientific method was born, and with it, a new era of invention and mechanization, which revolutionized the way we perceived the world. In the Age of Reason, the idea of nature as an organic system was replaced with the metaphor of a machine, and the human body was likened to a piece of clockwork. Descartes famously declared: "I consider the human body as a machine . . . My thought compares a sick man and an ill-made clock with my idea of a healthy man and a well-made clock."

This paradigm, which has dominated science for the past three hundred years, has given rise to what Capra calls "mechanistic medicine," which uses chemical drugs and hi-tech surgery to fix the machine. Diagnostic tests establish what is wrong, surgery repairs the affected body parts, and pharmaceuticals cure the symptoms.

Mechanistic medicine has some crucial shortcomings, the most obvious of which is that humans are not machines. Ironically, the healing process itself is not studied in medical research because it is a holistic process that's hard to understand within a mechanistic framework. Reductionism is the very basis of scientific analysis, yet it has one major flaw—it ignores the idea that the whole is more than the sum of its parts. When the parts of a system are isolated, the connections between the parts are lost, so it is no longer a living system. If the whole is more than the sum of its parts, then nature cannot be properly understood by simply dismantling it. This means we can never hope to fully explore complex systems such as the human body and how it heals through a purely reductionist lens.

DRAWBACKS OF CONVENTIONAL MEDICINE

Reductionist thinking in medicine has become the subject of much debate in recent years, particularly with the rise of alternative medicine. Proponents of complimentary and alternative medicine (CAM) highlight some key drawbacks of conventional medicine as possible reasons why our healthcare systems are struggling to cope with the global health crisis.

Ever-Increasing Levels of Specialization

Because reductionism is central to the scientific method, high levels of specialization have occurred within all fields of science, and nowhere is this more evident than in medicine. Medical research has split into ever narrower fields, and new technologies, drugs, and protocols have enabled control over ever more minuscule processes. However, this overspecialization has made it difficult to synthesize knowledge and forge new approaches to healthcare. This is compounded by a lack of funding for the kind of interdisciplinary or trans-disciplinary research and development that could drive more holistic clinical discoveries.

Reductionism has also led to medical specialists being favored (and therefore better paid) than family doctors, which critics argue has led to a declining ability to deal with the simple day-to-day health needs of the population. A generation ago, the ratio of specialists to general practitioners was fairly equal, but now, due to the higher esteem afforded to specialists, smaller numbers of doctors choose to practice general medicine, even though the vast majority of health complaints require a family doctor.[20] In the US, this overemphasis on specialization has led to a surplus of surgeons and, according to some, an overuse of surgical procedures to address health problems.

Mind-Body Dualism

The mind-body dualism of the Cartesian worldview has led to a split within medicine between doctors and psychiatrists. Doctors concern themselves with treating the body, psychiatrists and psychologists with healing the mind, and there is often little communication between the two. This has resulted in serious gaps in our understanding of disease that are only now beginning to be redressed. For instance, stress has only recently been acknowledged as a key cause of many diseases, and the role of mental-emotional factors in healing is still a gray area for many in the medical profession.

The limitations of this mind-body split are increasingly apparent with regard to the treatment of psychiatric illness. Research on mental disorders has historically been given less funding and attention, and psychiatrists are deemed somehow less important than physicians, even though they are medical doctors with formal training.[21] Psychiatrists have reacted by trying to understand mental illness in terms of biology and the functions of the brain. In framing mental issues in a physical way, psychiatrists have justified treating them with physical means, suppressing symptoms with medications which do little to heal the underlying emotional issues of the patient. Psychiatric facilities are often underfunded, resorting to medicating patients to cope with increasing numbers without offering them much in the way of therapy or counseling to address underlying causes. As such, mental hospitals have been criticized for being alienating, prison-like institutions that are anything but healing sanctuaries for the soul.

Western psychotherapy has filled the gap that psychiatry has left in healing mental illness, but psychotherapy is often underfunded by state healthcare systems, leaving the poor and marginalized in society to fend for themselves. Funding for physical treatments diverts resources from mental health services, leaving little budget to spend on the rising numbers of people suffering from mental health issues. Waiting lists for psychotherapy in public healthcare are untenably long, so people who can afford to, pay privately. Mental health services are systematically underfunded all over the world, leaving the burden of mental health issues to be borne by individuals, families, and communities—particularly disadvantaged social groups and ethnic minorities who often face the biggest challenges in terms of mental well-being.[22]

Treating Symptoms, Not Causes

One of the biggest criticisms of conventional medicine is that because of its reductionist underpinnings, it has tended to disregard the wider social and environmental context in which disease is found. In doing so, Western medicine has focused primarily on treating the symptoms of ill-health rather than its underlying systemic causes.[23] The emphasis is on the individual rather than the social systems they are embedded in; hence, the focus is on disease management rather than prevention. Instead of trying to understand why an illness occurs so that root causes can be addressed, doctors analyze the mechanisms of the disease so that it can be treated with drugs or surgery.

For instance, someone who experiences chronic stress may suffer from repeated infections. A doctor may attempt to treat these with antibiotics, but because the patient is not prescribed stress-management tools, he or she may inevitably develop a more chronic condition, either physical or mental, or even a "social disease" (as in the case of substance abuse, crime, and violent behavior). Critics argue that in ignoring underlying causes, modern medicine takes a "whack-a-mole" approach, which merely increases the chances of patients developing more serious illnesses down the line, resulting in skyrocketing costs within the healthcare system.

Time Pressures

This is not to blame doctors. Physicians have very short windows of time to see their patients—usually around fifteen minutes[24]—which is hardly enough for a full exploration of stress levels and lifestyle factors. Despite the best of intentions, time pressures inhibit doctors from being able to listen to their patients' issues in depth, and physicians are given few resources and training in preventive health measures such as nutrition, exercise, and self-care. For instance, over the five or six years students are in medical school, they are given, on average, ten to twenty-four hours of training on nutrition, despite the huge impact food has on our health.[25]

Disempowerment

Because drugs and surgery are the preferred treatments for modern medicine, there is arguably an ingrained belief in society that only doctors can understand why people are sick and that medication or surgery is the best way to become well. This fundamentally disempowering view has meant that patients may be disinclined to believe that their lifestyle, emotional state, or social relationships have a bearing on their illnesses, or that self-care has the power to prevent and, in some cases, even reverse disease. The dominant view of the body as a machine has led to a fear that it is in constant peril of breaking down and that only doctors and prescription medication can fix it. The idea that our bodies have inherent self-healing power, or that living habits and social and environmental factors play a major role in our health often gets overlooked.

Doctors are sometimes viewed as cure-alls, regardless of a person's lifestyle, and because only medical staff have the training to understand the results of clinical tests, patients often feel that they alone can diagnose and therefore "heal" them. This has been compounded by historically exaggerated views among the public about the power of genes in the making of bodies and minds, which has encouraged some patients to be rather reluctant to see their own life choices and mindsets as reasons for their illness.

Disempowering beliefs also exist with respect to infectious diseases, which has led to a victim mentality whereby bacteria and viruses are viewed pejoratively as "germs," and that only antibiotics and medication can provide a cure. Yet, bacteria and viruses have lived symbiotically in our bodies since the very beginning and are vital to our health and well-being.

Moreover, as the study of immunology shows, there are very few microorganisms that cause disease in virtually every host. Most are opportunistic pathogens that cause illness mostly in people with compromised immunity.[26] The reason why some of us get sick while others do not is that sometimes we are in a more receptive state when we are exposed to bacteria and viruses, depending on our levels of stress and fatigue, nutrition, sleep, living habits, and so on. The study of epidemiology has added to this model with the "epidemiological triad"[27] of host, agent and environment (including social and physical environment), as this has a huge impact on our health. However, the idea that germs and genes are the primary cause of disease is quite entrenched, leading many to have a dogmatic faith in "magic bullet" solutions to address health problems.

The Dominance of Big Pharma

The emphasis on drugs to manage health problems has resulted in a trillion-dollar pharmaceutical industry. In 2019, sales were nearly $1.3 trillion worldwide—roughly equivalent to the GDP of Mexico.[28] Nearly half of this total came from the US, even though it makes up under 5 percent of the world's population. Prescription pills are almost part of American culture; one in two adults are estimated to be taking some form of medication, while a third of older adults take five or more medications (known as "polypharmacy").

In noteworthy books such as *Pharma* by Gerald Posner,[29] *Overdosed America* by John Abramson,[30] *On the Take* by Dr. Jerome Kassir,[31] and *The Truth about Drug Companies* by Dr. Marcia Angell,[32] the pharmaceutical industry stands accused of co-opting any institution that stands in its way, from governments to regulatory bodies, academic medical centers, and the medical profession itself. There is much controversy around the industry's provision of potentially biased information to health professionals, highly prevalent advertising in journals and conferences, sponsorship of medical schools, funding of independent healthcare organizations, and the hiring of doctors as paid consultants on medical advisory boards. Pharmaceutical companies pay cash for speaking engagements and offer free meals, travel, gifts, and stocks to incentivize doctors to prescribe branded drugs over cheaper generic alternatives.[33] There is also ample evidence that the industry manipulates the findings from clinical trials to suggest their drugs are more effective than they really are.[34]

Pharmaceutical companies have also been accused of "disease mongering," whereby companies, in league with certain doctors and patient advocacy groups, attempt to maximize drug profits by convincing people that their usually mild ailments urgently need medication.[35] Risk factors such as high cholesterol and high blood pressure are declared diseases in their own right, and "normal" limits are redefined to expand drug markets. Pharmaceuticals approved for serious illnesses such as clinical depression are indicated for milder conditions such as shyness (rebranded as social phobia or social anxiety disorder), and other normal problems such as premenstrual tension and heartburn are medicalized as premenstrual dysphoric disorder and gastroesophageal reflux disease (GERD).

In the US, where direct-to-consumer advertising for medication is legal, viewers are bombarded with drug promotions that distort and exaggerate the prevalence of disease, changing perceptions of ailments and convincing otherwise healthy people that they are sick (the so-called worried well). In other countries where direct-to-consumer advertising is banned, disease awareness campaigns sponsored by pharmaceutical companies play a similar role in promoting the idea of a "pill for all ills."

The lobbying power of the pharmaceutical industry within the government has also come under much scrutiny, particularly in the US, where drug pricing debates have led to multi-million-dollar campaigns by Big Pharma to stave off possible pricing regulations.[36] The industry's enormous lobbying power, combined with significant campaign spending and the revolving door between government agencies and lobbying firms, has made it difficult for policymakers to implement reform on the problematically high expense of prescription drugs.

The High Cost of Healthcare

The cost of drugs and hi-tech health solutions, coupled with aging populations and the sheer number of people suffering from chronic conditions, has led to soaring healthcare costs that threaten to bankrupt governments. With around three-quarters of spending on chronic health issues, the United States healthcare budget has risen by nearly a trillion dollars over the last twenty years, to a staggering $4.1 trillion a year, or about $12,530 per person.[37] That is an incredible 19 percent of GDP, compared to just 5 percent in 1960.[38] To make matters worse, healthcare is expected to rise by *more than half* of total GDP by 2080. Similar rises are likely to be seen in all OECD countries, with most nations spending a fifth of GDP on healthcare by 2050 and catching up with the US figure of over 50 percent by 2100.[39] Unless the healthcare crisis is resolved quickly, governments around the world stand to become insolvent.

Side Effects

There is no doubt that while the body has a sophisticated immune system and astonishing self-healing capabilities, the use of medicines (both natural and synthetic) throughout human history has significantly helped the healing process. In terms of modern medicine, one only needs to think of antibiotics to see the remarkable impact this has had on combating infection. Yet while the use of drugs in critical situations is undoubtedly lifesaving, pharmaceuticals are arguably less effective at treating everyday health issues, and even more problematic when treating chronic ones. This is not only because drugs often treat symptoms rather than the causes of disease but also because they have side effects.

Although derived from plants, the chemicals used in pharmaceuticals are concentrated in potent doses that can be harmful without the modifying trace elements that occur alongside them in the natural plant extract. These trace elements were once considered unimportant, but in fact studies have found they play a critical role in limiting the potential "sledgehammer" effect of the active ingredient.[40] Where pharmaceuticals need to be prescribed in precise amounts because of their potency, herbal medicine can be prescribed in comparatively imprecise quantities without concern for side effects because of these modifying effects. Another difference is that herbal medicine has antibacterial properties that stop the bacteria from reproducing rather than killing them outright, which avoids the risk of mutation and antibiotic resistance. In contrast, the oftentimes indiscriminate use of antibiotics in conventional medicine has resulted in a crisis of antibiotic resistance, which stands to wipe out the upper hand humans have had against infectious diseases since the Industrial Revolution.

Until recently, drugs were considered to have only a minimal risk of side effects. However, the body is an immensely complex system that requires sophisticated regulation to function properly. Because pharmaceuticals are used to influence complicated and subtle biochemical processes that are still barely understood, adverse drug reactions (ADRs) have become commonplace, occurring in 10 to 20 percent of hospital inpatients.[41] In fact, ADRs result in around 128,000 deaths in the US each year—from taking medications as prescribed.[42] Not many people know it, but new prescription drugs have a one in five chance of causing ADRs, even after being approved.[43]

Medical Errors

The emphasis on drugs and surgery to address health problems has led critics to argue that modern medicine sometimes creates unintended consequences that lead to more rather than less pain and suffering. The use of hi-tech medical care and pharmaceuticals has meant that accidents occur more often in hospitals than in many other industries. A 2016 John Hopkins University study revealed that 250,000 to 400,000 people die every year in the US due to medical errors.[44] This puts medical errors as *the third leading cause of death*, surpassed only by heart disease and cancer.

The risk of malpractice has led to a litigious environment in the US, with doctors trying to protect themselves by practicing "defensive medicine" and ordering more diagnostic technologies that contribute to increasing medical costs. The WHO reports that in low- and middle-income countries, a staggering 2.6 million people die from medical errors every year, mostly related to misdiagnosis and administration of drugs.[45] Complications from unsafe surgical procedures occur in 25 percent of patients and result in one million deaths annually, while a hefty four out of ten patients are harmed during primary and ambulatory care, again mostly due to medication errors.

Understanding Pain

One of the most pervasive uses of pharmaceuticals is for the treatment of pain. Because of the separation of mind and body in the Western worldview, pain is, for the most part, a poorly understood phenomenon. Medical research has yet to find precisely what causes pain or how pain is communicated between body and mind. Because there is a major psychological component to pain, it is not easily captured in scientific analysis. Pain is a fundamentally personal experience; it requires an understanding of the patient's mental state, expectations, belief systems, emotional support, social relationships, and so on, which are often beyond the remit of medical professionals. Instead, doctors and pharmacists tend to focus on the chemical processes that produce pain in the body and the medications that can be used to suppress them. Because the useful role of pain in recovery and healing is often dismissed in modern society, there is great resistance to feeling any kind of pain, and "magic bullet" solutions are often readily taken by the public.

Yet advocates of alternative medicine argue that pain and discomfort are our body's way of calling us to pay attention to what needs to be healed in our lives. This suggests that by focusing on symptom suppression, the pharmaceutical approach to health may well stand in the way of our natural healing process and prevent us from facing what's really causing our health problems in the first place.

In the US, the overprescribing of painkillers has resulted in a well-documented opioid crisis, described as one of the biggest mistakes in modern medicine.[46] It began in the 1990s, with pharmaceutical companies promoting opioids for chronic pain conditions while greatly understating their addictiveness. Over the ensuing years, opioids became the default treatment for even relatively minor pain, while the increasingly high doses prescribed quickly built up tolerance and resulted in a tragic addiction epidemic that caused hundreds of thousands of deaths. The opioid epidemic fed a burgeoning market for cheap heroin and, more recently, fentanyl—the deadliest opioid in the world—which is up to one hundred times more potent than morphine and many times that of heroin.

Death Denying

Ultimately, the Western medical model reflects the preoccupation of modern society with the denial of old age and death. Far from being the fault of medical professionals, the fear of death is deeply ingrained in Western culture. The schism that occurred between science and religion during the Age of Reason heralded a modern era where spirituality is often eschewed as "woo-woo," and death is denied as a fundamental part of life. The whole subject of death is a societal taboo, and dying as a natural experience is completely removed from our lives. We exclude the aged and the sick by relegating them to nursing homes and residential care. Bodies are carried out of hospitals secretly in the dead of night, and the death of a patient is often viewed as a failure by the medical profession. Morticians and undertakers work hard to keep the messiness of death away from us by preparing the corpse to look alive with cosmetics. There is little room for spirituality in the dying process; death, like disease, is seen as a much-feared enemy.

This deep resistance to our own mortality ignores the fact that death is a natural part of life. A century ago, people died at home surrounded by loved ones, with perhaps the family doctor and clergyman there to lend support. The dying person was touched and comforted by relatives, with plenty of opportunity for truth and reconciliation as intimate last goodbyes were said. Today, we die in hospitals surrounded by intravenous drips and state-of-the-art machinery, touched only by sterile latex gloves. Patients miss the healing power of human touch and are confined to clinical wards that do little to alleviate feelings of helplessness and anxiety. Often, death is a drawn-out affair, with intensive care units and medical intervention allowing patients to live far longer than nature intended. The dying process occurs in foreign surroundings, often not witnessed directly by family members. The existential experience of our own mortality has become a medical transaction; there is almost nothing natural or dignified about it.

CONCLUSIONS

As we have seen from this discussion, the challenges faced by modern medicine are deeply rooted in the historical evolution of the Western medical model and its emphasis on reductionist thinking. The limitations of conventional medicine in addressing chronic lifestyle illnesses, including treating symptoms rather than underlying causes and mind-body dualism, has led to a growing interest in integrative, functional, and alternative medicine, signaling a shift toward a more comprehensive and interconnected approach to healthcare. However, the dominance of pharmaceuticals, the high cost of healthcare, medical errors, and the denial of death as a part of life in Western society present significant obstacles to achieving truly holistic and patient-centered care. As we navigate these challenges, it is essential to reevaluate our approach to health and healing, embracing a more integrative and compassionate model that considers the interconnectedness of physical, mental, social, ecological, and spiritual well-being.

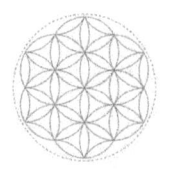

CHAPTER 3

REASON FOR HOPE? RECENT TRENDS IN HEALTHCARE

A physician is obligated to consider more than a diseased organ, more than even the whole man—he must view the man in the world.
—Harvey Cushing

Over the past few decades, there have been some major perceptual shifts that have changed the face of healthcare and give us reason to hope that we can find more holistic solutions to our global health challenges. First, there has been an explosion of interest in complementary and alternative medicine (CAM). The growing popularity of CAM has coincided with some seismic shifts in conventional medicine that are beginning to transform our approach to health and well-being, such as the rise of neuroscience and its revelations about neuroplasticity, mind-body interventions in psychology, and the discovery of epigenetics and the microbiome in the biological sciences. These shifts are explored here briefly with a view to painting a picture of what healthcare might look like in the future as more integrated forms of medicine, which include lifestyle and preventive approaches, come increasingly to the fore.

THE GROWTH OF ALTERNATIVE MEDICINE

The limitations of modern medicine have led to considerable dissatisfaction with traditional healthcare among the general populace, who are increasingly seeking more holistic approaches to address their health problems. While conventional, or allopathic, doctors are often skeptical of alternative medicine, there has been a growing revolution occurring at the grassroots level as people seek out complementary therapies that facilitate self-healing and empowerment. Because they are not constrained by the mind-body dualism of the biomedical approach, alternative medicine practitioners often explore the mental, emotional, and spiritual aspects of ill-health, taking time to understand the patient's life history and personal circumstances—which can be therapeutic in and of itself. Another key reason people seek out alternative therapies is because they believe they are less likely to suffer from side effects.

There is now a plethora of CAM on offer, with four main branches that cover a wide range of treatments and therapies. These branches are mind-body medicine (including meditation, mindfulness, yoga, breathwork, guided visualization, hypnosis, and biofeedback), manipulative and body-based practices (such as chiropractic and osteopathic manipulation, craniosacral therapy, massage, reflexology, Rolf therapy, and the Alexander technique), biologically based practices (including herbal remedies, homeopathy, and supplements) and energy medicine (such as Reiki, acupuncture, qigong, therapeutic touch, healing touch, sound healing, and light therapy).

In the US, around half of people have tried some form of alternative therapy.[47] This interest has resulted in a two-tiered healthcare system: the mainstream, insured, conventional approach, and the privately paid alternative medicine approach. Because of their increasing popularity, some insurance companies in the US pay for acupuncture, chiropractic sessions, and mindfulness programs. In Europe, there is also a high level of acceptance for CAM, with usage increasing exponentially in recent decades. The most common forms of treatment are massage, acupuncture, homeopathy, osteopathy, and herbal remedies, and in some European countries, these are covered by insurance. In countries like Australia, CAM is estimated to be used by as much as two-thirds of the population,[48] while in developing countries, traditional alternative approaches using plants, herbs, and spiritual therapies are often used in lieu of more expensive conventional medicine. In fact, the WHO reports that around 80 percent of countries in the world use traditional medicine.[49]

Pioneering hospitals around the globe are now responding to patient demand by offering CAM as part of their medical treatments. For instance, the top fifteen academic hospitals in the US (including Johns Hopkins, Yale, and Duke) now offer therapies such as Reiki, acupuncture, homeopathy, therapeutic touch, massage, Chinese herbal remedies, and mind-body medicines such as meditation, yoga, biofeedback, and guided imagery.[50] In Europe, alternative medicine is increasingly offered in conventional medical centers, and, particularly in Germany and Switzerland, CAM is often provided by general practitioners and reimbursed through health insurance.[51]

MIND-BODY MEDICINE

The growing interest in alternative medicine has coincided with an increasing interest in the mind-body connection within medical research, driven largely by a recognition of the important role of stress in the development of disease. New interdisciplinary fields have arisen, such as neuroscience and psychoneuroimmunology, which study how our mental-emotional states affect our physiology. There is now a plethora of research on the benefits of mind-body techniques such as meditation, yoga, and breathwork in producing positive health outcomes, and mind-body interventions are slowly being introduced into the curricula of medical schools. As it moves toward the mainstream, doctors are increasingly referring patients to mindfulness-based stress reduction (MBSR) programs in traditional medical settings such as hospitals and outpatient centers. (See Chapter 11).

NEUROPLASTICITY

New research into neuroplasticity has strengthened the case for mind-body medicine, with the finding that the neural networks of our brains are not hardwired at birth but continue to restructure and rewire themselves with life experiences to make new connections.[52] While we have the most neuroplasticity when we are young, our brain responds to information in a continually evolving and dynamic process that continues right throughout adulthood.

This means we have a much greater capacity than previously thought to train the brain into good habits with healthy lifestyle choices and to create new neural pathways with positive mental attitudes. Nurturing environments, rich learning experiences, and stress-reduction practices build stronger brains and restore good health. Neuroscience has found that our thoughts can literally change the structure and function of our brains, which gives credence to the "power of positive thinking" in health. Such research has also highlighted why brain training exercises like meditation and creative visualization have the potential to change lives (more on this in Chapters 9 and 10).

EPIGENETICS

Another major shift is the pioneering research on epigenetics. A decade ago, medicine was dominated by the genome; medical thinking was influenced by genetic determinism, which saw genes as the probable cause of most chronic diseases. This gave rise to the disempowering belief that our genes were our destiny, that we were dealt our hand at birth, and that there was little we could do to prevent chronic illness.

However, just as the Human Genome Project was ending in the early 2000s (having found only a small genetic basis for human disease), research on the epigenome discovered something that took the medical world by storm—that genes could be activated or deactivated by environmental influences.[53] The human genome was found to be surrounded by enzymes and proteins that change the way our cells read genetic instructions, turning predispositions up or down like a dimmer switch. This means that our genetic inheritance is not fixed at all but determined by the way we live, feel, and think. The risk of developing a hereditary disease can thus be decreased by things like a nutritious diet, supportive relationships, and emotional well-being, or increased by factors such as environmental toxins, poverty, and stress.

Just as neuroplasticity has found that our brains are not completely hardwired, epigenetics has discovered that our genes are not completely hard-written. The realization that we can switch genetic predispositions on and off according to life experience has led to a renewed interest in the social and environmental factors that contribute to disease. In the battle of nature versus nurture, nurture has a new recruit, as our lifestyles and environment begin to take center stage once more in our understanding of health and well-being.

THE MICROBIOME

Another major shift is the huge amount of research that has been conducted in the past two decades on the "microbiome," which has led to a significant change in the way we perceive microorganisms. Until recently, our relationship with microbes was largely one of warfare as we attempted to tackle the infectious diseases unleashed since the agricultural era. However, recent research has found that within our bodies are microbial ecosystems made up of up to one hundred trillion bacteria, fungi, and viruses that are essential to our health.[54] The majority live in our gut and play a crucial role in immunity, digestion, neurochemistry, the central nervous system, and a host of other bodily processes.

Studies have found that the microbiome transforms our health in ways we never imagined and is foundational in protecting us from disease (see Chapter 5). However, environmental factors such as poor diet, stress, sleep deprivation, and chemical toxins have done untold damage to our "good bacteria," increasing inflammation, lowering immunity, and causing illness. Antibiotics, while controlling infectious disease, have decimated our microbiomes, contributing to a whole new set of illnesses such as inflammatory bowel disease, autoimmune diseases, obesity, diabetes, cancer, and neurological issues such as depression and autism. The microbiome lives not just in our gut but pervades all of life, playing a crucial role in the health of soil, water, and the air; in short, these microbial ecosystems are essential to the survival of all living organisms on the planet. This realization has led to a shift away from the idea that germs are our enemies to an understanding that bacteria and viruses are integral to life—and vital to human health.

THE RISE OF INTEGRATIVE MEDICINE

The scientific breakthroughs of the microbiome, epigenetics, neuroplasticity, and mind-body medicine have allowed us to move away from deterministic beliefs about germs and genes to a more empowering view in which our lifestyles and mindsets have a very real effect on our physical and mental well-being. The idea that you can change your habits, your mind, and therefore your health, has coupled with the burgeoning interest in holistic well-being to result in the emergence of "functional" and "integrative" medicine, which incorporates conventional medical approaches with lifestyle medicine and CAM to help people heal in a more comprehensive way. There are now national medical bodies for these pioneering approaches popping up all over the world, such as the US National Center for Complementary and Integrative Health, the European and British Society for Integrative Medicine, and the Australasian Integrative Medicine Association, among many others.

Due to patient demand, some pioneering hospitals have incorporated restorative spa-like facilities conducive to CAM, spurred on by the growing body of evidence that integrating conventional medicine with alternative therapies is indeed beneficial. For instance, a very large study of integrative medicine in 2014, which followed over 6,500 patients in a US hospital over three years, found that those who had received one or more complementary therapies had an impressive 47 percent reduction in pain and a 55 percent reduction in anxiety compared to those who did not.[55] A 2019 meta-analysis of thirty-four studies researching the effectiveness of integrative medicine for cancer patients found that incorporating alternative therapies such as qigong, mindfulness, Chinese herbal medicine, yoga, and acupuncture significantly improved the health-related quality of life for those patients.[56]

Doctor Andrew Weil, the so-called father of integrative medicine, discusses the philosophy behind the approach in his renowned book *Health and Healing*.[57] He explains that it takes a multidisciplinary approach where the best of conventional testing and diagnosis is combined with the best evidence-based holistic therapies, with the aim of restoring equilibrium in the patient. As an example, an integrative medical team might include physicians, nutritionists, acupuncturists, chiropractors, herbalists, massage therapists, and psychotherapists. There is a major emphasis on the key pillars of health—nutrition, sleep, exercise, relaxation, and social connection, based on the recognition that people have the power and responsibility to keep their minds and bodies in balance with good lifestyle habits and choices. Patients are seen as physical, mental, emotional, and spiritual beings connected to communities, cultures, and ecosystems, all of which are relevant to their health and well-being. By looking at the whole person, integrative medicine attempts to address underlying causes by recognizing interdependent systems, thus avoiding a purely symptomatic approach to health.

In the integrative model, health professionals are viewed as facilitators rather than instigators of health, encouraging the patient to take responsibility for their own healing. The doctor-patient relationship is one of empathetic listening and assistance, so that the patient feels understood and empowered to make decisions themselves. The root causes of disease are researched using extensive history-taking, examinations, and laboratory testing, and evidence-based treatments are found that incorporate appropriate lifestyle changes and supplementation with alternative therapies. Programs emphasize the multifaceted nature of ill-health and the inherent healing capacity of the patient. The interaction between mind and body is emphasized, and patients are encouraged to contemplate the underlying causes of their illness, seeing it as an opportunity to make significant changes in their lifestyle, personal relationships, and mindsets.

As stress is so often a major factor in disease, healthy ways to release stress are suggested, and guidance is given on disease prevention as well as treatment, enhancing the patient's capacity for self-care.

A RETURN TO MEDICINE'S HIPPOCRATIC ORIGINS

Integrative medicine is, in many ways, an attempt to reconcile with the Hippocratic underpinnings of Western medical science. The writings of Hippocrates, who lived in ancient Greece around 400 BC, have had a lasting influence on modern medicine, with its seminal statement on the ethics of medical practice, the Hippocratic Oath. At the core of the Hippocratic writings is the idea that disease is caused by environmental factors, diet, and living habits rather than demons or supernatural forces, as was commonly held at the time.

Medicine was espoused as a scientific discipline that included prevention as well as treatment of disease. The environmental factors influencing health were discussed in detail, including food, water, air quality, the surrounding ecology, and general living habits. The connection between humans and nature was integral, with health considered to be the result of balanced minds, bodies, lifestyles, and the maintenance of equilibrium with the environment. The physician's role was to facilitate "nature's healing power" and to assist patients in healing themselves. The main themes of Hippocratic medicine—health as a state of balance, the healing power of nature, the mind-body connection, the empowerment of patients, and the importance of environmental influences—are all key aspects of integrative medicine.

A SYSTEMS VIEW OF HEALTH

We can see from this discussion that while reductionism tends to treat symptoms, integrative health approaches treat "systems." Connections and relationships take primacy, which means that the patient is seen as a whole person and much more than the sum of his or her parts. This emphasis on holistic health is indicative of a wider move away from the Cartesian view of the world as a machine toward the world as a network. This paradigm shift is outlined in detail in Fritjof Capra's latest book, *The Systems View of Life*, coauthored with Pier Luigi Luisi, professor at the University of Rome.[58] In this seminal work, the authors outline how, in the past three decades, "systems thinking" has overtaken reductionism at the cutting edge of science. While for hundreds of years, scientists were obsessed with taking things apart, the emerging model attempts to understand things as an integrated, dynamic whole. Capra and Luisi Luigi assert that the network is thus replacing the machine as the central metaphor for nature in science. The focus of pioneering studies is no longer to isolate and analyze fundamental building blocks, but rather to understand life as an interconnected web of relationships, where parts are really patterns, and everything is an interaction.

In the systems view of life, nature's networks are seen as inherently regenerative, creative and intelligent. The health of an organism is based on its ability to adapt to its environment and to reestablish balance when it has been disturbed through a natural process of self-healing. Stages of crisis and transformation may be involved in the healing process, resulting in a new state of harmony—a creative phenomenon called "emergence."

Capra and Luigi Luisi explain how systems thinking emerged in the 1920s and 1930s from a series of interdisciplinary dialogues between biologists, ecologists, and psychologists. Biology in the 1920s emphasized organisms as systems nested within other systems so that, in the case of the human body, cells form tissues, tissues form organs, and organs form organisms, which are themselves nested in wider social systems and ecosystems that are all intertwined. Systems thus have a dual role as parts and wholes, requiring the balance of both integrative and self-assertive tendencies.[59]

Organismic biology gave birth to the science of ecology, which studied organisms in terms of their relationship with the environment. Ecology first introduced the concept of "networks," describing them as patterns of feeding relationships (the food web) and ecological communities (ecosystems).

This new way of thinking in science was supported by the revolutionary discoveries in quantum physics in the 1920s, which led physicists to see the universe as an interconnected web of subatomic relationships that form an indivisible whole. Particles were no longer discreet "things" per se but wave-like patterns of probability, a complex and inseparable network of connections that belied the fundamental unity of the universe. Even the consciousness of the observer could not be separated from this unified field, thus shattering the illusion of mind-body dualism at the heart of the Cartesian worldview.

Using this model, a systems view of health involves a multitiered approach that sees individual well-being as intimately connected to the health of society and the planet. Systemic solutions to the global health crisis therefore entail a combination of conventional and alternative medicine at the individual level, public health reforms at the societal level, and a concerted attempt to heal the environment and rekindle our spiritual bond with nature at the global level.

Because individual health cannot be separated from planetary health, individual responsibility and lifestyle changes can only go so far before we hit the deeper structural barriers to health that are determined by politics and society. Integrative healthcare thus requires a focus on both internal and external issues. For Capra and Luigi Luisi, social healthcare involves health education, corporate responsibility regarding health hazards, and public health policies that provide for people's basic needs, minimize social stress, and encourage healthy, ecologically balanced ways of living.

CONCLUSIONS

As we have seen from this discussion, to have any hope of combating the current tsunami of chronic diseases we are facing, we must change not only the way we treat our illnesses but also the way we live and think. While this may seem like a tall order, a paradigm shift is already underway to help us navigate the choppy waters ahead. Rising up through the froth is a more holistic approach to health, one that sees our bodies as complex, interconnected networks nested within wider social and ecological systems that are all fundamental aspects of the web of life. In this emerging view, health is not just the absence of disease but, according to the constitution of the World Health Organization, "a state of complete physical, mental, and social well-being."[60] Reflecting the wisdom of Hippocrates, we add ecological and spiritual well-being to this description, making it a truly systemic model of well-being.

Like Hippocrates, a holistic view highlights an organism's ability to self-heal and to reestablish balance in the face of stress and change. This may involve stages, from healing crises to transformation, culminating in a new state of balance ("emergence"), which may in fact create a more transcendent state of health. Balance is about being in sync with oneself and the surrounding world. When we stress our bodies by treating any one area poorly—through, for instance, poor nutrition, inadequate rest, or lack of exercise—problems emerge in other parts of it, which can culminate in disease. Similarly, neglecting the broader systems within which we are embedded reverberates back to us in the form of increased social and ecological stress, which has a major impact on our well-being. We must address imbalances at both the micro and macro levels, which requires joined-up thinking that unites many areas of expertise. What we need is a systems view of health if we are to survive the stormy seas ahead.

The next part of this book discusses wellness at the individual level as a lifestyle balance between the key pillars of health: nutrition, sleep, exercise, and relaxation. Due to its scope and far-reaching implications, the fifth pillar, connection, is discussed in part three, including not only social connection but mind-body, environmental, and spiritual connection, which are all fundamental to the health of humanity and the planet.

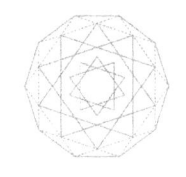

PART 2

THE FOUR PILLARS OF HEALTH

In balance there is stillness and beauty in the midst of chaos . . . this stillness and beauty at the heart of change is the magic of the hurricane's eye.
—Dr Andrew Weil

In a systems view of health the well-being of a living organism is seen in terms of the totality of all its connections. Even the smallest change in these relationships can cause a chain reaction that ripples out across the nested systems it inhabits, affecting everything in its wake. This is aptly described in chaos theory by the "butterfly effect," where the flapping of a butterfly's wings in Brazil can cause a typhoon in Thailand. This effect is real in the sense that even the tiniest disturbance can transform larger systems. However, the weather doesn't spin out of control because of a butterfly; systems have inherent stability because they are flexible and allow for change. Flexibility is maintained because of multiple feedback loops within the system, which form a virtuous circle to bring it back into balance.

Systems adapt to change continuously. They have to, for as the Greek philosopher Heraclitus highlighted, "the only constant in life is change." The balancing process is dynamic, fashioned from moment to moment in response to a multitude of constantly transforming conditions. Living organisms can maintain dynamic balance because they have evolved to be inherently adaptable and resilient. Considering that the web of life is always in flux, dancing in perpetual motion from the complexity of all the infinite variables that occur within nature, it is a miracle that equilibrium can occur even for an instant. Yet dynamic balance is our natural state of health. When something disturbs us so much that we lose our flexibility, this manifests as increased stress. The more that stress continues, the closer we come to our threshold of tolerance and the more rigid we become. As Capra and Luigi Luisi highlight, a loss of flexibility always means a loss of health.[61]

We all have self-healing capacity, the ability to re-establish dynamic balance and regain our well-being. The view of health as a fundamental state of balance is not new; it is acknowledged in many traditional healing practices and, as previously discussed, is a central theme of Hippocratic medicine. The idea is also present in conventional medicine. Claude Bernard, a 19th-century French physiologist, famously coined the phrase *milieu interieur*, to refer to the constancy of a healthy body's internal environment, even when the external environment fluctuates. The neurologist Walter Canon expanded on Bernard's views and used the term "homeostasis" to refer to the tendency of living organisms to maintain internal balance as a precondition of health.

If health is a state of dynamic balance or homeostasis, then ill-health can be considered a consequence of imbalance or disharmony, which causes stress to build up to such an extent that we reach a tipping point and become unwell. We all have our limits. Temporary stress is a normal part of life, but chronic stress is potentially very harmful and plays a significant role in most illnesses because it adversely affects the body's immune system. Relaxation is thus critical to health because it allows for a release of stress.

Integrative, functional, and preventative medicine sees relaxation as a key pillar of health, along with nutrition, sleep, and exercise. These pillars are fundamental to our well-being; therefore, finding balance within and between each pillar is central to disease prevention. The next chapters discuss each of these pillars in turn and how they interact with each other systemically to create health and well-being.

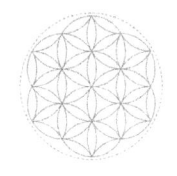

CHAPTER 4

RELAXATION

Relax! Life is Beautiful.
—David L. Wolper

As life, by its very nature, involves change, it naturally entails varying degrees of stress. Our busy lives can make us feel overworked and overwhelmed, and so we might come down with the occasional cold or flu that forces us to slow down and take a breather. These transitory phases of imbalance are not only normal, they can actually be helpful if we get some much need rest. Plus, minor infections make our immune systems stronger and more resilient over time. However, if stress becomes prolonged, we can be pushed to our limits, and a chronic condition may result. This is because the human body has not evolved to deal with the kind of relentless strain that is seemingly woven into the fabric of modern living.

In the first part of this chapter, we look at the stress response from a biological perspective and the extraordinary effect it has on us at both an individual and collective level. A brief history of stress is elucidated to put our modern-day triggers in context before the difference between "good stress" and maladaptive stress is discussed. The second part of the chapter is devoted to the importance of relaxation as a central pillar of health. The benefits of meditation, mindfulness, and creative activities are explored, along with the healing power of nature to calm our overstimulated nervous systems.

THE STRESS RESPONSE

In the famed book *Why Zebras Don't Get Ulcers*,[62] Robert Sapolsky explains how, in our hunter-gatherer days, stress usually came in the form of a life-threatening predator such as a lion or saber-toothed tiger, so we developed a highly effective way of dealing with such emergencies called the "fight-or-flight" response. Natural selection meant that those with the most heightened fight-or-flight reaction were the ones who survived, and so humans evolved to be masters of the stress response.

Fast-forward to today, and the same stress reaction that our ancestors used to survive an attack from a pack of hungry hyenas can happen every time we can't find our car keys or are late for work. It is sometimes activated just by thinking about work or our endless to-do lists. Each stressor elicits the same response from our nervous system as if we were facing the jaws of death. Modernity has hit us at lightning speed, yet our anatomy is still prehistoric. Having evolved over millions of years, our body has no dimmer switch to regulate our responses to the myriad of microstresses that the twenty-first century brings. So, as we hurry to catch the train because we are late for a meeting, the fight-or-flight response triggers a chain reaction that affects every system in our body, from our digestion to our brain functioning, to our ability to feel empathy for our fellow human beings.

First, the amygdala is activated, the primitive reptilian part of our brain that is geared solely toward our survival and primes us for fear and aggression. Stress hormones such as adrenaline and cortisol are released, making us feel tense and twitchy as alarm signals are sent throughout the body to prepare us to flee or fight to the death. We start to breathe quickly, hyperventilating to get enough oxygen to the muscles, and our heart pounds as blood pressure increases to enable blood to travel faster around our body. As the blood flow is redirected to major muscle groups, we start to feel clammy and our face flushes. Our blood fills with clotting agents to prepare for possible wounds, and the immune system floods us with antibodies to deal with potential germs. Our pupils dilate to take in more light, our senses become heightened, and we are hypervigilant about any sights and sounds that might be dangerous. Anything that isn't needed for survival is shut down to conserve energy, including our digestive and hormonal systems.

Various parts of the brain are inhibited, too, such as memory and sensory perception—other than tunnel vision for the challenge ahead. The most evolved part of our brain, the prefrontal cortex (responsible for reasoning and emotional regulation), shuts down. The calamitous result is that our capacity for clear thinking evaporates, and we lose touch with any feelings of empathy, love, and compassion as instinctive fear and aggression engulf us. "Keep Calm and Carry On" was the motto of the British in wartime for a very good reason—because stress and panic is the very antithesis of astute decision-making, cooperative behavior, and inspired action.

Another fascinating effect of amygdala activation is that when our stress levels are raised, a cloud of "alarm pheromones" is emitted through the pores of our skin. Research has found that people around us can detect these pheromones, and subconsciously react with stress hormones of their own.[63] This can cause a vicious circle as one person's stress is passed on to those around them, resulting in a bunch of strangers on edge for no apparent reason. Science shows that we really can smell fear, causing an emotional contagion of second-hand stress that ripples out into the collective. [64]

Researchers have also discovered that we are all empaths. We have "mirror neurons" in our brain which are tiny cells that allow us to tap into what others are feeling. This helps us to empathize and feel more socially connected, however it also means we can pick up on other people's anxiety and moods just by being around them. The cues can be subtle, yet they have a big impact on our own mental and physical well-being.

So, what happens to our bodies when we de-stress? Our sympathetic nervous system (which is responsible for fight-or-flight) is deactivated, and our parasympathetic nervous system takes over, eliciting the "rest-and-digest" response. The parasympathetic branch works at a much slower rate than the sympathetic one, easing our heart rate, relaxing our muscles, activating saliva production and digestive enzymes so we can nourish ourselves and recover. Our parasympathetic nervous system is responsible for maintaining homeostasis, ensuring that our biological housekeeping—everything from body temperature and metabolism to tissue repair—is in good working order. It enables us to relax and heal so that we can function normally again.

Our bodies are a delicate balancing act between these two branches of our anatomy. If they are not in harmony, we find ourselves constantly reacting to everyday stress with exaggerated responses. The slightest trigger can stop us from being able to problem-solve, learn, digest, procreate, or feel love for others. We overreact to our child not cleaning their room, the lid not being put on the milk bottle properly, or a minor traffic jam that makes us late for work.

It takes twenty to thirty minutes for our systems to calm down from each stress trigger. During that time, we may often encounter another stress, perhaps as we just manage to catch that train but realize we've forgotten our presentation, or we open our emails to discover a problem at work. This fleeting moment of adrenaline rush causes the fight-or-flight response to start all over again, from which we need another half an hour to recover. And so it goes on throughout the day until we arrive home utterly exhausted and wonder why we are so wired that we cannot hold a civil conversation with our family or get to sleep that night.

Living in a prolonged state of high alert when there is no good reason for it becomes extremely detrimental to our health. Chronic stress leads to digestive issues, which can cause us to gain weight, as excess cortisol increases sugar cravings and slows down our metabolism. Stress can also increase the likelihood of emotional eating, skipping meals, and exercise routines that go out the window. Stress disrupts our sleep, resulting in a vicious circle as we are less well-rested to deal with the challenges of the next day. Being on constant red alert affects reproduction, one of the many possible reasons for falling sperm counts and increasing rates of infertility in the West.[65] Most importantly, stress exhausts our immune system, suppressing germ-destroying T-cells and causing inflammation, which is the root cause of most chronic diseases.[66]

Stress also exhausts the cardiovascular system, causing our arteries to harden, which leads to heart attacks and strokes. It sends our immune system into overdrive and can increase our chances of developing an autoimmune condition. Stress can even lead to premature aging (as cortisol breaks down collagen in our skin) and weak bones (as cortisol blocks calcium absorption required for bone density). Stress doesn't just affect the body, it affects the brain, causing changes in its structure and function so that we are more susceptible to mental illness, memory loss, brain shrinkage, and brain cell loss.[67]

A BRIEF HISTORY OF STRESS

Modern living is so demanding that challenge seems built in to virtually every waking moment. How did it all get to be so stressful? Will Williams, founder of Beeja Meditation and author of *The Effortless Mind*,[68] asserts that the seeds of twenty-first-century stress arose when we made the most significant discovery in human history after fire: farming. Prior to this, we were nomadic hunter-gatherers living in small tribes, with nervous systems specialized for our roaming lifestyle. We had evolved slowly and gradually over millennia, with our ancient anatomy equipped for a life that involved searching for food a few hours a day, interspersed with plenty of time for rest and play. With the advent of the agricultural era, all that changed, and the effects were felt at every level of our existence.

Agriculture made life much harder for individuals by creating more work, less leisure, and a ballooning population to worry about. We toiled from dawn till dusk in the fields growing crops. Our bodies got stressed in new ways, with our spines and joints paying the price as we stooped over crops and crouched for lengthy periods to grind grains.

While for the first time in history, we felt in control of our food source and, therefore, masters of our own destiny, our sense of security was undermined by two important factors: the unleashing of infectious diseases as we started fouling up the environment, and inclement weather which could destroy crops and raise the specter of famine. Because we no longer had the flexibility of responding to disease and droughts by picking up sticks and moving on, the stress of trying to anticipate and control nature emerged for the first time, which must have been deeply draining psychologically. As we became less able to adapt to our changing environment, a certain rigidity and austerity crept into our lives.

Social relationships changed with agriculture too. Populations exploded because of the increased availability of food, causing pressure to feed so many new mouths. Williams calls this the moment when we "officially stepped onto the treadmill of incessant workloads and a never-ending trajectory of growth . . . as we needed to keep growing just to stand still." Once land and animals were kept in enclosures, we were no longer nomads living in cooperative tribes but farmers with private property, so we became protective, competitive, and less open to sharing. Social dynamics changed as we moved from settlements and villages to towns and cities, with increasingly complex hierarchies, bureaucracy, and politics. As populations expanded, we lost track of social connections; where once we knew our entire tribe by name, we began to barely know our neighbors.

As the agricultural era gave way to the Industrial Revolution, social relationships became increasingly complicated and stressful. Social cohesion declined as market specialization made the division of labor more pronounced, sharpening the divide between social classes. As we shifted to ever more urban surrounds, we felt increasingly disconnected from nature.

By the mid-twentieth century, we were polluting the earth and our bodies so badly as we chased the dragon of consumerism and unlimited economic growth that our health began to collapse. The phrases "rat race" and "daily grind" became common terms to describe our experiences of life. As Gabor Mate highlights in his bestselling book *When the Body Says No*,[69] we now work so hard that the world's biggest killer, heart disease, is mostly caused not by smoking but by job strain. Technology that was meant to make our lives easier has created different challenges as we grapple with new ways of organizing information and society. With the birth of the internet, we've retreated into digital worlds, living virtual lives in constant communication with each other. We have around-the-clock media, smartphones, artificial lights, and cities that never sleep. In the

Information Age, our nervous systems are completely overloaded. In *The Organized Mind*,[70] Daniel Levitin highlights that the average American takes in around five times more information every day than they would have thirty or forty years ago. Our world simply never rests; we have sped up to such an extent that our bodies' fight-or-flight responses are no longer fit for purpose, so we are set off by the slightest trigger.

BURNING OUT

The sheer amount of stimuli associated with modern life has pushed us past our collective tolerance levels of stress—and unsurprisingly, skyrocketing levels of chronic disease have resulted. This is the so-called burnout phenomenon, a term first coined in the 1970s by American psychologist Herbert Freudenberger, which has since received considerable research attention.

A recent study using data from the 2015 European Working Conditions Survey found that 10 percent of the European workforce and 17 percent of workers in non-European countries were experiencing burnout, while another large study reported burnout in 28 percent of American Millennials.[71] During the COVID pandemic, a 2020 survey of 1500 people by Indeed, the giant job aggregator site, found that around 43 percent had experienced burnout, while in 2021, the figure was up to 52 percent.[72]

When we come down with a mild illness and take a well-earned rest, our bodies recover quickly as we take a change of pace. Illness like this has a function; it is telling us to "go back to our cave" as our ancestors did, to rest and release all that accumulated stress. However, with growing work and family commitments, not to mention office cultures that frown upon taking too much time off, many of us soldier on despite feeling under the weather, and so we gradually stop listening to our bodies.

Over the years, these incremental abuses add up, and as we continue to shoulder all that background stress without creating space to truly relax, we can develop something more chronic. In this prolonged red alert state, biochemical changes occur, meaning our bodies overdose on cortisol and literally stew in our own stress juices. Stress makes the immune system respond with inflammation, and over time, chronic inflammation manifests as disease.[73]

Another effect of chronic stress is the loss of "adaptation energy," a term coined by Professor Hans Selye, who was the first scientist to identify stress as a cause of illness in the 1930s.[74] Adaptation energy refers to the idea that energy expended coping with one stress, such as staying up late, will leave us with less energy to cope with another, such as a deadline at work the next day. The more stressed we are, the less we can adapt to the changing demands of our environment. When we have low adaptation energy, a vicious circle ensues as our threshold for the fight-or-flight response is reduced so that every little microstress becomes a trigger that lowers our adaptation energy further until, eventually, we experience burnout. Low adaptation energy means loss of flexibility, and inflexibility leads to loss of health.

FINDING BALANCE

Stress and relaxation are essential aspects of evolution; both are required to learn and grow. Dr. Andrew Huberman,[75] a well-known neuroscientist and podcaster, explains that learning and creativity require two vital inputs: urgency and focus, and relaxation and sleep. Urgency creates the low-level stress that we need to focus on a problem, while relaxation and sleep create the space we need to integrate what we've learned and be more creative. Both inputs are required for learning and growth, with the most powerful brain changes happening when we focus and have enough of an internal sense of urgency to be motivated, combined with plenty of rest to allow neuroplasticity to occur.

Acclaimed books such as *Cure* by Jo Marchant[76] and *The Upside of Stress* by Kelly McGonigal[77] highlight that the impact of stress depends largely on our mindset. If we catastrophize about our problems and see them as unsolvable, we will probably go into full panic mode and find it more difficult to make good judgment calls. In this state, even once the problem is over, some people still cannot switch off, handwringing instead and experiencing anxiety about imagined future emergencies. However, if we reframe our problems as challenges rather than threats, we get a low-level stress response where our heart pumps more efficiently and supplies our body with oxygenated blood, which helps to boost our performance and focus. This kind of stress has an upside, as we can use it to improve and become better versions of ourselves.

"Good stress" helps us rise to a challenge, rewiring the brain in a positive way by building strong connections and resilience. Crucially, though, this only works if we also know how to relax. The key is finding a way to manage the seesaw between stress and relaxation so that we achieve balance. This means being able to switch easily between the two states, just as cats do when they fall asleep in the sun two minutes after being chased by a dog.

Clearly, we need to find more evolved ways to relax than television, TikTok, and tequila. We can distract or numb ourselves, but this is a maladaptive response to stress that works only for a short time; it does not solve chronic problems and will very likely make things worse in the long run. Dr. Rangan Chatterjee, bestselling author of *The Four Pillar Plan*[78] and *How to Make Disease Disappear*,[79] claims that of all the pillars of health, relaxation is often the hardest one for his patients to master because they find it difficult to carve out time for themselves and prioritize "me-time"—even if this is just fifteen minutes a day. When they do make the time, people often don't know what to do with themselves because they have so much nervous tension that relaxation eludes them. The cultural conditioning to strive and push ourselves is so strong that our "work hard, play hard" mentality means we simply don't know how to switch off.

THE FINE ART OF R&R

Relaxing hobbies are as diverse as the people that engage in them, ranging from the physical (such as exercises like cycling or dancing, covered in Chapter 8) to the spiritual (such as meditation, mindfulness, and yoga, covered in Chapter 9).

Creative activities are also very helpful for stress management. A plethora of research shows that creativity reduces cortisol levels while increasing "feel-good" hormones such as dopamine and serotonin, helping to lower stress, anxiety, and depression.[80] This is a major reason why so-called creative interventions like music and art therapy are increasingly used by psychotherapists. Even simple things like knitting or crafting can be relaxing, releasing the pleasure hormone dopamine, which is a natural antidepressant.[81]

When you are immersed in a creative endeavor, your mind slows down as you get in "the zone" and focus on the task at hand. Creative activities are like a mindfulness practice because they stop our minds from wandering and help us to be more present. However, they cease to be relaxing the moment we become perfectionists and stress about how our work will be judged or perceived by others. Learning how to switch our analytical left brains off and trust our creative right brain is an art in itself.

Interestingly, neuroscience shows us that creativity not only alters our brain chemistry but also triggers the parts of our brain that processes thoughts and feelings, helping us to find catharsis.[82] Artistic endeavors like painting, playing a musical instrument, performing or writing are all great stress relievers because they allow us to cope with challenging situations through expression rather than bottling emotions up.

Creativity also relaxes us whether we are actively participating in an activity or simply observing a sublime work of art by someone else. In fact, scientific studies have found that contemplating a beautiful painting stimulates the pleasure centers in the brain and increases blood flow by up to 10 percent—the equivalent of looking at a loved one.[83] Thanks to those mirror neurons in the brain, when we appreciate a work of art, we could potentially be firing the same neural pathways as the artist did when they created it. This sense of being drawn into an art form is called "embodied simulation,"[84] engendering a shared sense of inspiration.

Singing is another good way to relax, as it activates the vagus nerve, one of the cranial nerves that connect your brain to your gut. The vagus nerve is part of the parasympathetic nervous system, so when it gets stimulated, it plays a key role in relieving stress.[85] We don't have to be good singers to get the benefits; because it is connected to our vocal cords, even humming creates "vagal tone,"[86] which cultivates emotional regulation, greater connection, and physical health. Singing in the shower or humming a tune while you get dressed is actually good for you.

Deep relaxation techniques like meditation are different from exercise and creative activities in that they are mind-body experiences that turn our awareness inward and cultivate stillness. As such, they are a skill to be mastered, like any other. Meditation can lead to mental and emotional well-being as well as elevated states of consciousness because it allows the nervous system to release deeper layers of stress that have accumulated over time. The science behind practices such as meditation, mindfulness, yoga, and breathwork are covered in Chapter 10, but they all give similar relaxation benefits. Because the brain is given the space to process and release stress and trauma, its computing power is freed up to be more productive and creative. Slowing down, tuning in to the body, noticing the breath—these are all ways to activate the neural pathways that stop our minds spinning from all that background stress so that we can develop greater self-awareness and get in touch with how we really feel inside. This creates the bandwidth to connect with deeply held emotions and release negative patterns and beliefs, promoting mental and physical well-being. The deep relaxation that results is very liberating, triggering the kind of inner growth and wisdom that leaves us in a more transcendent state of health. The increasing speed and complexity of living make these techniques not only invaluable but essential for evolving more adaptive ways to cope with the stress of our busy modern lives.

THE HEALING POWER OF NATURE

Another important component of stress management is being out in nature. Research shows that the relaxing effect of being in the great outdoors creates many beneficial changes in our bodies, from reduced blood pressure and heart disease, promotion of cancer-fighting cells, and reduced symptoms of ADHD to improved concentration, memory, and sleep.[87] Spending just ten to fifteen minutes in nature slows down our brain waves, heart rate, and breathing and allows blood pressure to drop as the stress hormones cortisol and adrenaline are reduced. A weekly half-hour walk in a park can help people get their hypertension under control, and a walk in nature for ninety minutes has been found to dramatically reduce anxiety and depression.

People who spend just two hours in nature a week are reported to have much better mental and physical health than those who do not. Evidence suggests that regular access to greenery lowers the risk of mood disorders, neuroses, and stress-related issues and that more exposure to nature during childhood reduces the risk of mental health issues in later years.[88]

Being near the water has particularly calming effects, with "blue spaces" such as the sea, rivers, lakes, and waterfalls being extremely beneficial to health. The book *Blue Mind*[89] by marine biologist Wallace J. Nichols highlights studies showing that people who live near water are significantly happier overall, with lower levels of stress and anxiety, as well as lower heart and breathing rates. A key reason is that the negative ions from moving water have amazing therapeutic benefits, including elevating our mood by increasing serotonin (the happy hormone), improving energy levels by giving us a boost of oxygen, purifying our blood, balancing the autonomic nervous system, promoting deep sleep and healthy digestion, as well as enhancing our immune function and clearing the air of allergens and pollution. The power of water is so amazing that aquatic therapists use it to help post-traumatic stress disorder (PTSD), anxiety disorders, addiction, autism, and more. Neuroscientists advocate spending time in nature as an important ingredient for brain health because it boosts cognitive function and creativity.[90] The health benefits of nature are irrefutable—our nervous systems are simply designed to be in the natural world.

Spending time in nature can also lower social stress by reducing hostility and increasing our inclination to be more generous and helpful toward others. A study by the University of California found that people who spend just one minute staring up at a tall grove of trees reported feelings of awe and wonder, after which they were more likely to help a stranger than people who looked at buildings.[91] The study concluded that when we are tuning in to something larger than ourselves, people feel less selfish and entitled and are consequently more heartfelt and generous.

Experiencing moments of appreciation for the natural world has also been shown to reduce inflammation in the body and lower the risk of chronic disease. Urban planners are now being encouraged to pay more attention to green spaces as a way of increasing quality of life for city dwellers, with studies finding that the greener the city, the healthier and happier its citizens.[92]

Forest Bathing

Forest bathing or *shinrin-yoku*, a Japanese term for taking an immersive stroll in the woods, has become increasingly popular as a way of benefiting from the healing effects of nature. Encouraged by the Japanese government in the 1980s as a way of preventing lifestyle diseases and encouraging forest conservation, there is now a plethora of research on its benefits.[93] These include renewed vitality, strengthened immunity, weight loss, longevity, and greater levels of peace and happiness. The evidence is now so overwhelming that many countries are following suit and encouraging doctors to prescribe forest bathing as a preventive medicine to cut healthcare costs.

So, what exactly is behind the secret power of trees to make us feel so much healthier and happier? One answer is "phytoncides." Trees give off scents from the essential oils they produce to protect them from bacteria, insects, and fungi. When we take a walk in the woods, the fragrance of the forest does all sorts of wonderful things to our bodies. First, inhaling phytoncides calms us down by activating the vagus nerve.[94] Second, it boosts the immune system and increases cancer-fighting natural killer (NK) cells. In fact, studies have found that NK cells are higher for weeks after just a couple of walks in the woods.[95] Other research has found that even the simple act of infusing a room with essential oils such as sandalwood or eucalyptus has a similar effect as being in a forest.[96] There is real science behind these benefits and a chemical basis for the calming effects of nature.

In tandem with these health benefits, there is a spiritual element to shinrin-yoku, as forest bathers become more mindful of the subtleties of nature. The idea of forest bathing is to take in the serene atmosphere and use all five senses to perceive the marvels around you—the virbant colors of the leaves, the calming sounds of birdsong, the refreshing touch of the grass on your feet, the sweet fragrance in the air, the delicious flavors of forest fruits. This kind of present-moment awareness is a way of slowing your mind down, leading to greater calmness, mental clarity, and a sense of connectedness. These kinds of nature experiences have been encouraged by spiritual teachers for millennia. Today, alternative healers, mindfulness practitioners, nature-based therapists, and alternative healers encourage people to feel more connected to nature and to themselves by perceiving their environment in a more immersive, spiritually uplifting way, thus fostering an awareness of the sacredness of life.

Grounding

Being in nature has another vital benefit: it grounds us. Every cell in our body becomes immediately grounded when we touch the earth directly—whether that's walking barefoot on the grass or getting our hands dirty in the garden. This is because the planet has its own vibration, called the Schumann resonance, which our nervous systems are naturally attuned to.[97] At 7.8 hertz, it is called the Earth's heartbeat, and studies have found it to be deeply soothing to the human body. Our circadian rhythms use not only light and dark but also the Schumann resonance to sync our internal body clocks to the rhythms of nature. When our internal timing is off, so are the myriad of biochemical reactions in our body, resulting in poor health. Our sleep is particularly impacted by the Schumann resonance because our bodies use it as a baseline to reset our melatonin-serotonin balance, impacting our wake-sleep cycle.

The enormous changes in our lifestyle in the past century, including the myriad of man-made electromagnetic frequencies (EMFs) we are exposed to each day, have created an electrical disconnect with the harmonizing rhythms of the Earth, which has affected our biological clock. Reconnecting to the Schumann resonance ensures that we share the same electrical potential as the Earth, so as we attune to the planet's heartbeat, we are better able to maintain our own healthy rhythms. While further research needs to be done on its effects, studies suggest that walking barefoot on the grass or on the sand, taking a swim in the sea, or—as the old hippies used to advocate—hugging a tree is extremely healing and revitalizing, doing everything from easing pain and inflammation to maintaining a healthy pulse, reducing cardiovascular risks and improving the restfulness of sleep.[98] There is even evidence to suggest that such activities can have benefits for the endocrine system of people with diabetes and thyroid disorders.[99]

Along with balancing our circadian rhythms, another benefit of the Schumann resonance is that it puts us into an alpha brainwave state, which is one of the key reasons why we find nature so relaxing. These slower alpha waves help us to feel calmer and less anxious, improving mental clarity, creativity, and emotional well-being. When we are connected to the energy of Mother Earth, everything from our brains to our heartbeat and muscles relaxes, healing us at every level.

CONCLUSIONS

In this chapter, we have looked at the pervasiveness of chronic stress in society and how incredibly damaging it is at a physical, mental, and emotional level. Yet there are ways to deal with stress that don't involve numbing ourselves with intoxicants or using distraction and avoidance tactics that only make things worse. We can use the power of our minds to reframe stress from a threat to a challenge and turn difficult situations to our advantage by learning and growing from them. However, this only works if we also know how to use our downtime to relax. Exercise, creative arts, and getting out in nature are all great ways to switch our busy minds off and de-stress.

Even better are mind-body-spirit practices such as meditation and mindfulness, which have a profound impact on our nervous system, releasing accumulated stress from the past and helping us to perform at our peak in the present. Stress management is an essential life skill, and educating both adults and children on how to relax at a deep cellular level is fast becoming an imperative in our hyperdemanding world.

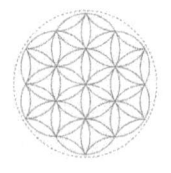

CHAPTER 5

NUTRITION

Man is what he eats.
—Lucretius

The importance of good nutrition for health cannot be understated. Our diets have a huge impact, not only on our own well-being but also on the well-being of the whole planet. With the right food choices, we have the power to heal body and mind, creating a giant ripple effect that can quite literally save the world. Because nutrition has both human and environmental impacts, a single chapter does not do it justice, so this pillar is split in two. This chapter focuses on the effect our diets have on our individual health, while the next chapter focuses on the impact our food choices have on the planet.

NUTRITION AND INDIVIDUAL HEALTH

As outlined in the previous pages, the stress of modern life is quite literally killing us, exhausting our immune systems and causing inflammation, which over time manifests as chronic disease. Our nutrition plays a critical role in our health, either feeding the stress cycle or breaking it, depending on our choices. We are what we eat, so food can be our medicine or our poison.

It is well-known that the typical Western diet is pretty unhealthy. Here's why in five easy-to-remember facts:

1. The Western diet is overly processed and, therefore, highly inflammatory.
2. We have monotonous diets lacking in diversity, which is bad for both our gut health and the biodiversity of the planet.
3. The Western diet is overly meat-heavy, which causes inflammation in our bodies and ecological degradation in the world at large.
4. We lack omega-3 fat in our diet, which is essential for brain health, as well as being anti-inflammatory.
5. We have lost the art of eating mindfully, so we are less aware of what and how we eat, leading to unhealthy, unsustainable food choices and habits.

This is why our diets are one of the biggest causes of ill-health and early death in the world. In the following sections, each of these five factors is discussed in a historical context, exploring the micro and macro impacts of the Western diet (which is also tellingly called the Standard American Diet, or SAD). While there is certainly plenty to be sad about, there are also reasons to be positive, and each section ends with "the good news," outlining healthy, sustainable nutritional choices that can transform both body and mind.

THE PROCESSED WESTERN DIET

Before the modern era, people's diets were constrained by where they lived, and so they ate simply, consuming locally grown, seasonal, organic produce. With the rise of technology, our food systems underwent enormous change. The mechanization of agriculture in the twentieth century led to sweeping transformations, as farm machines helped us to produce more food. Industrial agriculture began after World War II when weapons such as Agent Orange and DDT were commercialized to become pesticides.[100] A new chemical age of farming began, with the widespread use of insecticides and synthetic fertilizers creating higher yields and increasing crop production by threefold.

As we kissed our homegrown organic diets goodbye, we welcomed in a new era of processed food, with the canned goods and instant meals made for troops on the battlefield becoming staples in the civilian world. Wartime food shortages had primed the population to value quantity over quality, and mass production of factory-made products was optimized for mass appeal, convenience, and shelf-life rather than health or nutritional benefits. The manufacturing technology of wartime was innovated for the postwar world, and the production of cheap, processed food was marketed with slick advertising campaigns, highlighting its ease and convenience for busy, modern workers.

Women, who had taken over many of the jobs of men in wartime, entered the workforce in increasing numbers and swelled the demand for ready-made meals. Home refrigerators became more affordable, and convenience food became easier to store. Mass markets burgeoned, and the food system became increasingly globalized as preservatives, freezers, ships, and airplanes made it possible to store produce for months and transport it quickly around the world. As consumers were no longer restricted to locally grown produce, the Western diet spread like wildfire around the world, and our palates—as well as our health—underwent a radical change.

The original "fast-food nation" is of course the United States of America, where the popularity of hot dog and burger stands in 1950s California gave birth to a global phenomenon. Brands like McDonalds and Coca cola swept the world from Paris to Peru, soon addicting us to high-calorie meals loaded with refined carbohydrates, sugar, salt, and additives but critically low in fiber and essential nutrients.

Convenience food now accounts for a large proportion of our nutrition. A staggering 70 percent of packaged food in the US is classified as "ultraprocessed" (meaning the food is so altered that the underlying ingredients can hardly be recognized), representing around two thirds of all calories consumed by Americans.[101] Elsewhere, ultraprocessed food accounts for approximately half of all calories in the UK, Canada, and Australia, while in France, a nation known for its love of good quality produce, the figure is still over a third.[102] China is rapidly following on the tails of the West, with processed food consumption currently less than a third of food purchases but growing at a rate of 50 percent each year.[103]

According to recent research, the sale of processed food is growing at its fastest rate in developing countries, where globalization has resulted in unhealthy food becoming cheaper and easier to buy, while the price of fruit and vegetables has steadily gone up.[104] A recent UNICEF report found that half the world's children under five suffer from "hidden hunger" caused by eating cheap, processed food.[105] Children raised on ultraprocessed diets are so malnourished that their cognitive development becomes damaged, which leads to poor school performance. This cascades into social problems such as increased poverty and crime, creating a vicious circle.

Paradoxically, hunger and obesity often go together. Those on lower incomes are more likely to eat cheap food high in calories but lacking in essential nutrients, resulting in a double whammy of malnutrition and weight gain. The consumption of "empty calories" is also happening in the higher-income groups of different cultures following the introduction of Western dietary habits. Combined with the increasingly sedentary lifestyle of the modern world, "energy in" is often more than "energy out," with weight gain the obvious result. The shift to processed fast foods is a major reason for the epidemic of obesity and chronic disease occurring around the globe. If current trends continue, we will have billions more people overweight in the next few decades, the vast majority being in low-and-middle-income countries. In China, for example, around two-thirds of adults are projected to be overweight or obese by 2030.[106]

So, why exactly is processed food so bad for us? Chemical additives, for one. Food manufacturers use additives to increase shelf-life and improve taste, texture, and appearance. However, they are also associated with everything from digestive problems, hyperactivity, insomnia, irritability, headaches and respiratory problems, as well as more serious issues like heart disease, cancer, and early death.[107] Processed food contains high amounts of added salt, which increases water retention, taxes the kidneys, and can lead to high blood pressure, cardiovascular disease, and stroke.[108] Sodium nitrate, a common ingredient in processed meats, has been linked to several types of cancer. Emulsifiers (also called thickeners) are commonly used in convenience foods and affect the gut microbiome, increasing the risk of inflammatory bowel disease. Preservatives in carbonated drinks have been linked to ADHD and cancer development. Trans fat raises cholesterol and contributes to diabetes and heart disease. Artificial flavoring is toxic to bone marrow cells; artificial sweeteners can be cancerous.[109] The list goes on.

Processed food also contains high levels of refined carbohydrates, which not only increases the risk of obesity, high blood pressure and cardiovascular problems but also hyperactivity, anxiety, depression, and even higher rates of suicide.[110] In contrast to whole grains (which are rich in fiber, vitamins, and minerals), refined grains are basically "empty calories," having been stripped of all their fibrous goodness. The refined carbs found in white bread, pasta, rice, pastries, breakfast cereals, and snacks are energy-dense, easy to digest, and turn into sugar very quickly, causing blood sugar levels to skyrocket. These sugar spikes give us a quick burst of energy, followed by a sugar low (mimicking diabetes), which makes us feel tired and stressed—and paradoxically hungry again, no matter how many calories we've just eaten. Chinese takeaways are famed for filling us up and then leaving us feeling hungry a couple of hours later for this very reason. Big spikes in blood sugar also trigger hormonal responses, which can result in mood changes such as anxiety and irritability.

In the long term, the empty calories of refined carbs convert into visceral fat, which builds up inside our abdomen and wraps around our internal organs, creating a "potbelly" effect. Visceral fat is particularly dangerous because it produces the chronic inflammation that is at the core of so many diseases—research shows that it is linked with heart disease, type 2 diabetes, cancer, stroke, and Alzheimer's.[111]

Processed food also tends to be high in added sugar, which is included in everything from drinks and sauces to soups and sandwiches, ostensibly to make things taste better. Sugar causes insulin resistance and is implicated in a variety of chronic diseases, including obesity, diabetes, heart disease, and cancer. Not many people know that sugar is also bad for the brain, leading to cognitive decline and even dementia in old age. One of the most insidious aspects of sugar is its addictiveness, releasing opioids and dopamine that induce reward and pleasure so that the more we eat, the more we crave. Sugar is sneaked into so many foods (including many that we do not suspect) that our palettes have adapted, making healthier foods taste bland in comparison.

This kind of food addiction only adds to the daily stress of modern life. Processed food in fact creates a vicious cycle. When we feel burned out, we crave sugary, starchy, or fatty meals high in calories that give us quick energy. Because our sugar high is soon followed by a plummeting low, we are left feeling worse than before, and so the cycle repeats. This is amplified by the fact that when we are feeling anxious, the communication pathways in our body stop functioning properly, and the signals in our nervous system become scrambled on their way to the brain. So, we might find ourselves grabbing a bagel when our bodies are really asking for broccoli—the request for specific nutrients gets heard as a blunt order for food, and we miss our body's subtler cues.

Drinking alcohol is another way we feed the stress cycle. While it may feel relaxing at the time, our body goes into quite a serious state of fight-or-flight as it tries to process the poisonous effects of ethanol, which is why we get hangovers the next day. Alcohol is another refined carb that causes visceral fat—hence the well-known "beer belly" effect.

The stress cycle is intimately connected with visceral fat, weight gain, and obesity. Hormonal regulation changes dramatically in response to stress, causing the hunger hormone ghrelin to be activated so that we feel famished and then want to "stress eat"—causing "stress fat" that makes a beeline for our middle. However, the urge to eat is not because we need more calories but because our brain is preparing our body for a potentially dangerous situation, like a run-in with a predator that would have required all our ancestors' energy to handle. The stress cycle also causes all sorts of digestive issues because it impacts our microbiome, leading to bloating, gas, acid reflux, irritable bowel syndrome (IBS), and ulcers. Because metabolic imbalances mean that our food does not get digested well, we get nutrient deficiencies, which can cause a whole host of other problems.

A key reason that processed foods are linked with so many degenerative diseases is that they are a major cause of inflammation. This occurs because of a three-way interaction between our gut, our brain, and our immune system. Our gut is connected to our brain via an information highway called the "gut-brain axis." Processed food is very detrimental to our gut flora; when we eat bad food, it sends a signal to our brain that we are under attack. This activates the fight-or-flight response, and our immune system reacts with inflammation—just as if we had food poisoning. Processed food can also damage our gut lining, leading to a "leaky gut," which inflames our immune system by allowing harmful substances to enter the bloodstream. A leaky gut can even lead to a "leaky brain," causing cognitive problems and brain disorders. Digestive health issues like these can even be passed on to later generations with epigenetic changes—highlighting just how impactful our diet is on both present and future generations.[112]

The gut-brain axis means that the food we eat also has a very real effect on our mental health. We can literally "eat ourselves happy"—or unhappy, depending on our food choices. The trillions of bacteria, viruses, and fungi found in our gut are like a miniuniverse that is foundational for life, health and, most interestingly, human cognition (see Box 1). If we treat our microbiome poorly, we can feel anxious or depressed. If we treat it well, it can lighten our mood. Bad food leads to bad bacteria and poor gut health, which increases our reactivity to stress, feeding the stress cycle.[113]

A balanced diet that nourishes our good bacteria with plenty of colorful, plant-based whole foods lowers stress and sends signals to the brain that life is good, inducing feelings of well-being. Scientists call the microbiome "the brain's peacekeeper" because around 95 percent of the body's serotonin (our happy hormone) is made in the gut. The gut also produces dopamine (the pleasure hormone), GABA (the calming hormone) and oxytocin (the love hormone). If we keep our microbiome happy with nutritious food, those little gut bugs return the favor.

In turn, the brain can alter our microbiome, with even mild stress changing the microbial balance in our gut, which makes us more vulnerable to anxiety, depression, and disease. The interrelationship is so profound that studies have found that probiotics can improve the symptoms of psychiatric disorders, including mood disorders, autism and obsessive-compulsive disorder (OCD).[114] The benefits of probiotics are so great that they not only lower the stress hormone cortisol but can even improve memory and cognition.[115]

Our microbiome is the lynchpin to our well-being. Good nutrition is central to its upkeep, helping to break the stress cycle, calm the mind, and tell our immune system we are safe and sound. In fact, 70–80 percent of our immune system is found in the gut.[116] An imbalanced microbiome is called "gut dysbiosis" when too many harmful bacteria are present. Gut dysbiosis, along with a lack of diversity in the gut, is associated with a multitude of health problems, from digestive issues, obesity, diabetes, and depression to autism, allergies, asthma, bowel disease, rheumatoid arthritis, Parkinsons, and cancer. Gut dysbiosis can even affect whether cancer drugs work effectively, and there is growing evidence to suggest that repairing a person's microbiome can lead to cancer remission.[117]

The Good News

The microbial universe within us is a major determinant of whether we enjoy a long and healthy life. This means we can look after our body and mind by looking after our gut. The kind of nutrition that is good for our microbiome is rich in fiber and full of a wide variety of vegetables, fruits, whole grains, legumes, nuts, seeds, fish, and healthy fats such as olive and avocado oil.[118]

Inspired by the eating habits of France, Spain, Italy, and Greece in the 1960s, the much-studied Mediterranean diet (MedDiet) is lauded because it is full of these foods. Plant-based whole foods contain prebiotic fibers that feed our microbiome and reduce stress hormones. Fiber-rich food also digests slowly, avoiding blood sugar swings and allowing us to feel fuller for longer, which helps to maintain a healthy weight. Dietary fibers are what the microbiome uses to make short-chain fatty acids, which are vital for gut and brain health.

The MedDiet is also high in anti-inflammatory antioxidants, vitamins, minerals, and polyphenols. Fermented food, such as yogurt, cheese, and olives, are rich in gut-loving probiotics. Red meat is minimized (and processed meat avoided altogether), with poultry, dairy, seafood, and fish eaten in moderation. There is an emphasis on oily fish such as salmon, mackerel, and trout, which are rich in anti-inflammatory omega-3 fats.

The MedDiet has been called "the gold standard" of all diets for two reasons. First, it has a long list of health benefits, from digestive health and reduced rates of obesity and chronic disease to a longer life expectancy. Meta studies show that it reduces cancer by up to an astounding 61 percent, diabetes by 69 percent, heart disease and stroke by 29 percent, cognitive decline by 36 percent, and early death by 31 percent.[119] It also eases depression and helps with weight loss as well as weight maintenance.[120] As it is mainly plant-based, the MedDiet has a smaller carbon footprint, is less resource intensive and has a lower impact on ecosystems and biodiversity.[121] Another heartening benefit is that surveys have found the MedDiet to be the number one easiest diet in the world to follow.[122] There is hope at hand to turn our "sad" diet into a happy one simply by choosing the right foods.

BOX: THE MICROBIOME

Humans have evolved to live with microbes for millions of years. In turn, microbes have coevolved and adapted to play a central role in our health—so much so that we cannot survive without them. Our microbiome is a perfect example of a nested system, a microscopic community living symbiotically within us, forming an inseparable web of interconnections within our bodies.

The bestselling book *Gut* by Giulia Enders[123] explains just how incredible our microbiome is. Our gut flora is made up of a complex universe of one hundred trillion bacteria, viruses and fungi. The cells of our body number just ten trillion, so they exceed us ten to one. With 90 percent of the cells in our body being nonhuman, the line really does blur between where microbes and humans begin. There are many thousands of species living in our gut, and each of them plays a different role in our body. No two people have the same composition—not even twins. Bacteria are on just in our gut but on all our body surfaces, mucous membranes, mouth, and skin, each hosting their own unique microbiomes vital for our well-being.

We are first exposed to microbes as we pass through our mother's birth canal. As we grow, our gut flora begins to diversify, and the greater the diversity, the stronger and more resilient our microbiome becomes. The health of our gut is directly proportional to the variety in our diet because different foods provide different nutrients that promote the growth of various types of bacteria. Our good gut bugs love colorful plant-based whole foods full of fiber and nutrients, while their anathema is a homogenous, processed diet lacking in prebiotic nutrition and full of sugar or additives. Lifestyle factors such as too much stress, not enough sleep, and lack of exercise also have a negative effect on our gut flora, as does alcohol, cigarette smoking, pesticides, and pollution.

Another killer is antibiotics. In the acclaimed book, *Missing Microbes: How Killing Bacteria Creates Modern Plagues*,[124] the microbiologist Dr. Martin Blaser explains how we are assaulting the "invisible Eden" in our bodies with our overreliance on these medicines, which are causing severe health consequences that go far beyond antibiotic resistance. It takes a few weeks for our microbiome to return to normal after a course of antibiotics, but it can take upward of six months to fully recover. Antibiotics can thus contribute to a whole new set of physical illnesses and secondary infections. They can also affect mental health, with studies finding that a single course of antibiotics can cause a significant increase in the risk of depression.[125]

Our gut microbes affect our biology throughout life by regulating our digestion, immune system, and brain health. These tiny creatures protect against disease and manufacture vital vitamins and neurochemicals, transforming our health in ways we never thought possible until very recently.

The fascinating thing about microbiomes is that they are not just limited to humans. There are microbiomes in all ecosystems, from the soil, the ocean, and rivers to the air itself. There is in fact a microbial web that reaches across the entire planet, sustaining all life. There are a trillion species in this planetary microbiome and five million trillion

trillion bacteria. That's five with thirty zeros after it—more than there are stars in the universe! To view bacteria and viruses as invisible enemies that threaten our health is to misunderstand the essential, life-giving role of these critical creatures, which uphold the very fabric of our existence.

Crucially, the microbiome plays a starring role in protecting our planet from climate change. The plethora of bacteria in the soil and oceans remove carbon dioxide from the air as part of nature's carbon cycle. These microbial ecosystems are now under attack, causing catastrophic reactions throughout the food web. This assault on the bacterial foundations of life is the root cause of the sixth mass extinction. Just as we are poisoning our own bodies, so we are poisoning the web of life. Nature is reciprocal; the actions we take in the coming years to nurture both our personal and planetary microbiome will determine the future of all life on Earth.

DIVERSITY IS KEY

Augmenting the problem of our overly processed Western diet is that modern tastes are surprisingly monotonous. Studies of relatively untouched hunter-gatherers have found that these communities typically eat around two thousand plant varieties over the course of a lifetime. This equates to a staggering one hundred grams of fiber a day (equivalent to twenty bowls of cereal).[126] In contrast, modern agriculture has reduced our nutritional diversity to such an extent that we now get around 75 percent of our calories from just twelve crops and five animals. Within those twelve crops are three staples: wheat, rice, and corn, which account for two-thirds of global food consumption. Not surprisingly, the uniformity of our diets has reduced the diversity of our gut bacteria by half compared to hunter-gatherer societies, with our fiber intake decreasing by a factor of ten.

Depending on so few foods poses problems for our health, our food supply, and the farmers who grow them. Skeletal remains of early agriculturalists show that the lack of diversity in their diets led them to suffer from grave vitamin and mineral deficiencies that stunted their growth and caused tooth decay. In fact, in the seminal book *Sapiens*, Yuval Noah Harare argues that one of the biggest downsides of farming was the lowered nutritional value that arose from being overly reliant on cereal grains like wheat, which is both hard to digest and lacking in essential nutrients and vitamins.[127] Compare this to the variety of seasonal vegetables, fruits, nuts, seeds, and roots that we used to enjoy as hunter-gatherers, and it is easy to see why agrarian life soon led to a major decline in health.

While human stature has returned to preagricultural levels, our repetitive diet has meant that nutritional deficiencies continue to be a major health problem. Research shows that the typical Western diet is low in several important nutrients.[128] Iron deficiency, which causes anemia, is very common, affecting more than 25 percent of people globally. This number rises to 40 percent of pregnant women and 42 percent of children under five years old, which is why iron-fortified children's food has become so popular.[129] Vitamin D deficiency is another major problem, affecting an estimated one billion people around the world in both developed and developing countries, causing rickets and soft bones. Iodine deficiency affects nearly a third of the world's population, causing enlargement of the thyroid gland and weight gain. Magnesium deficiency affects a large proportion of adults (especially older ones) and is associated with a variety of conditions, including type 2 diabetes, heart disease, and osteoporosis. Calcium deficiency is common, especially among older people, which, with reduced weight-bearing, causes osteoporosis. Other common deficiencies include vitamin B12 (causing blood disorders and impaired brain function) and vitamin A, which is common in developing countries (causing blindness and suppressed immune systems).[130]

The Good News

Eating a variety of wholesome organic food nurtures our microbiome—particularly "eating the rainbow," which involves fruit and vegetables of assorted colors with different phytonutrient benefits to ensure our gut flora flourishes. The impact we can have by adding just a little more variety to our diets is enormous—even if that's simply swapping in a new vegetable each week into our shopping baskets. Buying an organic veggie box from a local farm is a wonderful way to broaden palettes and try new recipes, at the same time as eating seasonally and supporting local communities. There are all sorts of new businesses popping up to support diversifying our diets, such as Oddbox's "wonky veg box" in the UK, which gives you a surprise selection of local fruit and vegetables, including ones that supermarkets won't buy because they're the wrong shape or color.

EATING ORGANIC FOOD

A key reason why our nutrition is causing an exponential rise in chronic disease is due to the ingestion of environmental toxins. The food we eat contains not only pesticides and herbicides but also industrial chemicals (like dioxins), heavy metals (like mercury and cadmium), and BPA (a chemical compound that leaches into food and drinks from plastic containers). The pesticides and herbicides sprayed onto crops to increase yields are augmented by chemicals dispersed into the air by industrial processes and traffic, falling onto crops and binding to the soil. Pesticides like glyphosate (commonly known as Roundup, one of the most commonly used herbicides in the world) are highly water-soluble and run off into ditches, streams, and rivers, contaminating groundwater and freshwater supplies. Having entered the water cycle, it rains down on soils, plants, and water sources, contaminating the food that we eat and the water we drink. Tap water contains not just pesticides but heavy metals such as lead, mercury, copper, aluminum, uranium, and other toxins like arsenic and ammonia. It also contains estrogen from birth control pills and livestock waste.

While pesticides are regulated so that they occur in our food in trace amounts, the concern is that those that are oil-based build up in our bodies over time. Research has shown that humans are now universally affected by man-made toxins no matter whether they live in the Himalayas or Hawaii.[131] Oil-based chemicals cannot be degraded or excreted, so they become increasingly concentrated as they move up the food chain, accumulating in animal fats until they reach the apex where humans reside. The human toxic load is now so high that our adipose (fatty) tissue contains hundreds, if not thousands, of synthetic chemicals. In the annual "National Human

Adipose Tissue Survey" conducted by the US Environmental Protection Agency between 1970–1989, it was found that 100 percent of the sample had nine of the top fifty-four chemicals classed as dangerous.[132]

The chemicals we ingest cause many chronic health problems, with the areas most affected being the digestive, immune, endocrine, and nervous systems. Common problems include:

Pesticides: associated with gut issues (such as leaky gut, inflammatory bowel disease, and celiac disease), respiratory disorders, mood disorders, ADHD, brain tumors, Parkinson's disease, and cancer.[133] They can also lead to congenital defects and learning disorders and lower IQ in children exposed in utero.[134]

Dioxins and PCBs: causing hormonal problems, diabetes, heart disease, developmental issues, and cancer.[135]

Antiandrogens (endocrine-disrupting industrial chemicals): linked with feminization of fish and human infertility.[136]

BPA: mimics estrogen and thus increases the risk of infertility and reproductive problems (as well as type 2 diabetes and obesity).[137]

Mercury (found particularly in oily fish): a neurotoxin that damages the brain and nerves.[138] It is particularly dangerous for pregnant women since it can affect the developing nervous systems of unborn babies.

The Good News

Nurturing your gut microbiome protects against the ill effects of pesticides by promoting digestive health, detoxification, and a strong immune system. Pre-and pro-biotics also feed the microbiome, and there is now a growing interest in cleansing superfoods such as turmeric, chia seeds, goji berries, and wheatgrass, as well as intermittent fasting as a way of detoxifying the body of unwanted chemicals.

Eating organic food is clearly one of the most impactful things you can do to protect your gut. Organics have many benefits, not only because they have fewer chemical residues, but because they are often naturally tastier, with a higher nutritional value compared with conventionally farmed food. Reviews of many different studies have found that organic food provides higher levels of antioxidants, which protect against free radicals, the unstable atoms that damage cells and cause aging as well as a host of illnesses.[139]

Because organic food tends to be more expensive than conventionally farmed food, public policy is sorely needed to encourage more people to buy it. A recent report by IFOAM (a worldwide umbrella organization for the organic movement) suggests all the different ways that policymakers can make organic food more accessible.[140] Their recommendations include providing price incentives for consumers (such as tax breaks and exemptions on import and export tariffs for organic goods), as well as public procurement, support for environmental stewardship, and investment to make organics more profitable for farmers. Food labels are often confusing, and governments need to get behind organic certification standards and nationalized logos to make it easier for consumers to choose organic products. There is also a role for policymakers to provide education about the health benefits of organic food, supporting ecoliteracy and the link between healthy nutrition and ecosystems in schools.

REDUCING MEAT CONSUMPTION

Perhaps the most controversial aspect of Western nutrition is that people tend to eat a lot of animal products. The relative merits of different diets have been hotly debated over the years, with vegans condemning meat-eating and carnivores, in turn, lambasting plant-based diets. Each group is passionate about the eating habits that have helped their health, weight, or how they feel. However, such acrimony overlooks the fact that our bodies are unique; what works for one person may not work for others, and so diets need to be as diverse as the people who eat them.

What cannot be denied, though, is that too much of a good thing can be bad for us, which is why the meat-heavy Western diet has become a serious problem. Meat consumption provides us with essential nutrients, including iron, zinc, magnesium, B vitamins, and of course, protein. However, we eat so much of it that the United Nations Environment Program (UNEP) estimates that meat production has increased by a staggering 260 percent in just fifty years, with over seventy billion livestock slaughtered each year for food.[141] The average American now eats double the amount of meat nutritionists recommend, with serious consequences for health.[142]

The key issue is that large quantities of both red and processed meat increase inflammation. Red meat has a sugar called Neu5G, which the immune system sees as a foreign invader and attacks.[143] If you eat too much red meat and the inflammatory response becomes prolonged, it can lead to chronic diseases such as cancer, heart disease, and type 2 diabetes. Neu5G is abundant in beef, lamb, and pork and in dairy products like cheese. Red meat also contains a nutrient called L-carnitine, which when consumed in excess can lead to hardened arteries.[144] Everything in moderation is clearly the lesson here.

Processed meat is much more hazardous to health. A 2014 meta-analysis of over eight hundred studies by the WHO found that there is a substantial link between processed meat and cancer because it contains high amounts of salt, sugar, and preservatives.[145] Smoked meats and meats grilled over high heat have also been shown to increase the disease. In 2015, the WHO classified processed meat as "carcinogenic to humans" (putting it in the same category as tobacco), while red meat was classified as "probably carcinogenic." The WHO noted epidemiological evidence highlighting that the risk of getting bowel cancer increased by 18 percent for every 50 grams of processed meat and 17 percent for every 100 grams of red meat eaten daily.[146]

The Good News

A modest amount of meat is permitted on a MedDiet—if it is of high quality and sustainably sourced (covered in the next chapter). The important thing at mealtimes is to make meat a side dish, not the starring act. Dietitians recommend no more than three-ounce portions and to choose white more than dark meat—preferably baked or grilled.[147] It is also important to only consume animals that have been well raised and fed a natural and healthy diet—for instance, cows that have been grass-fed rather than forced to eat unnatural diets from corn and soy.[148]

THE ALPHA AND OMEGA OF A HEALTHY DIET

Another reason why our nutrition is causing so much chronic disease in the world is because the Western diet does not contain enough omega-3 fatty acids. In *Sapiens*,[149] Yuval Harari describes how around seventy thousand years ago, Homo sapiens underwent a "cognitive revolution," where an increase in brain capacity allowed us to jump to the top of the food chain and communicate at a level never seen before. Our superior brain power enabled us to overwhelm the Neanderthals, using language and toolmaking to survive and flourish. Some fascinating theories have traced this brain development to early humans who lived by the water and ate more fish and seafood, which are rich sources of omega-3 fats. Some scientists hypothesize that it was this addition to our diets that supported the growth of a larger brain and ultimately led to the birth of language, technology and civilization.

While the idea that fish oils are what propelled human evolution forward is a topic of much debate, it gives us a clue as to the incredible properties of omega-3 and its importance in brain health. Omega-3 can help to prevent anxiety and depression because it raises serotonin and dopamine levels, as well as helping to prevent age-related mental decline and dementia.[150] It is particularly crucial for brain growth and development in infants. Getting a decent amount of omega-3 in pregnancy has numerous benefits for child development, including higher intelligence, better communication and social skills, fewer behavioral problems, and decreased risk of developmental delay and autism.

Another key attribute of omega-3 is that it is anti-inflammatory. Fish-eating communities in places like Japan have been found to have exceptionally low rates of heart disease and stroke because omega-3 reduces blood pressure, blood clots, and clogged arteries, as well as reducing insulin resistance, obesity, and diabetes.[151] Cancer is significantly reduced too. A major US study analyzing the health records of 170,000 people over ten years found that the risk of bowel cancer was reduced by 70 percent among those who regularly ate oily fish like salmon, sardines, and trout.[152] It has also been associated with lower risks of prostate and breast cancer.

Omega-3 can also fight autoimmune diseases, reduce asthma, increase bone and joint health, improve vision, skin, hair, and nails, and even support quality sleep by increasing melatonin production.[153]

The issue with omega-3 is that our bodies cannot produce it—we must get it from our diets. Unfortunately, the typical Western diet is low in the foods that contain it, including oily fish, nuts, and seeds. And there's another problem: Omega-3s need to be balanced with the omega-6 fats found in meat, dairy, and vegetable oils. The ratio should ideally be one to one, but the Western diet is more like twenty to one—a marked difference from the diet on which humans evolved and established their genetic predispositions. This imbalance has had devastating effects on our health, increasing the risk of heart disease, obesity, cancer, brain disorders, and autoimmune diseases.

One of the reasons why Omega-6 is so damaging is that refined vegetable oils that are high in it (like corn, soybean, canola, safflower, and sunflower oil) are added to many processed foods. Not only are people eating very little omega-3 and too much omega-6, but the development of trans fat has pushed omega-3 further from our diets. Trans fats like those found in baked goods and deep-fried foods are unsaturated fats that have been chemically altered so that they taste like saturated fats. The food industry uses them widely to improve taste while enabling "low saturated fat content" to be advertised on food labels. However, trans fats are extremely harmful to health and have been associated with heart disease and type 2 diabetes.[154] Ironically, recent studies have found that saturated fats, once demonized as a potential cause of hardened arteries, show no harmful effects on the heart or on total mortality.[155]

The Good News

Most people would benefit enormously from getting more omega-3 in their diet, from birth right through to old age. Sustainably sourced oily fish is an important part of a MedDiet, such as eating salmon, mackerel, trout, sardines, herring, pilchards, and sprats. Due to the problem of overfishing (covered in the next chapter), another way to ensure you have enough omega-3 in your daily diet is to take a high-grade, sustainably sourced omega-3 supplement. It is important to do your research, however, as some supplements are of inferior quality and may contain high levels of mercury, particularly if sourced from farmed fish. Fortunately, there are also plant-based omega-3 supplements available, such as seaweed, spirulina, chlorella, and marine algae (where omega-3 in fish originate, as they are eaten by smaller fish and move up the food chain). Other foods rich in omega-3 include flax, chia, and hemp seeds, as well as walnuts. There are also small doses in edamame, kidney beans, tofu, brussels sprouts, and avocado.

MINDFUL EATING

Food is our medicine or our poison. It can make us feel happy or sad, calm or anxious. It feeds our stress or it transmutes it. We can no longer overlook the fact that it is not just our body that is intimately connected to our diet but our consciousness. And yet, we are often very unconscious when it comes to food, not only in terms of what we eat but how we eat it. We make thoughtless food choices and eat mindlessly, snacking on the hoof, stress eating and comfort eating. We eat in front of the TV, not paying much attention to what we are consuming or what it tastes like. Food is simply fuel, a way to fill up an empty stomach. We are not mindful of how much we are eating or the way our bodies are reacting to our food. We multitask while we eat, wolfing down lunch at our desks or reading social media at the table. We are distracted and overstimulated, inhibiting digestion and feeding the stress cycle, which causes overeating, obesity, and illness. We have forgotten how to separate mealtimes from technology and all the other activities that contribute to our hyperdemanding lives.

In *Mindless Eating*, Brian Wansink outlines research that shows how watching television or using the internet while eating increases food intake and contributes to weight gain.[156] We also eat much too quickly, often gulping our food down in five or ten minutes as our minds are busy thinking about other things. This is a problem because it takes around twenty minutes for our stomach to tell our brains we are full, by which time we have eaten far more than our body really needs. The bigger the plate of food, the more we eat because rather than tuning in to our body, we rely on visual cues to tell us when to stop eating. Dinner plates are now, on average, six centimeters bigger than they were fifty years ago.[157] Wasink cites studies which found that people can eat anywhere from 25 percent to 50 percent more food just because it is served on a larger plate. We gauge portion size based on packaging and food containers, which are often oversized. Marketers are well aware of our reliance on visual cues and have contributed to the "supersize" culture by packaging food in "family-sized" portions so that we believe we are getting better value for money. Such ploys are creating bad eating habits, as our brains don't fathom the serving sizes, and we overeat as a result. Food labels can also make us eat too much, with meals labeled as "healthy" or "low fat," encouraging us to overeat by up to 40 percent.

There is a lot of conflicting and misleading information about food and diet in the media. This has created much confusion for people, and—because food is such a gigantic industry—an unhealthy focus on diet culture. Consequently, many people experience fear and anxiety around food choices and are unsure of what to eat. This leads to an intuitive disconnect with their eating habits, which, when combined with the lack of awareness that so often accompanies stress eating, gives marketers an unrivaled opportunity to influence consumers with diet hype and exaggerated food claims.

We are also losing the fine art of the family meal. Due to our overscheduled lives, we are increasingly falling into bad nutritional habits as we eat alone, at different times, in front of the television after a hard day's work. Studies have shown that only around 30 percent of families manage to eat together regularly, which is causing a huge fall in good nutrition, as well as limiting opportunities for social bonding.[158] In some families, basic cooking skills are not being passed down from parents to children, resulting in an inability to plan and cook meals when young adults leave home. Our modern, fast-paced lifestyles often lead families to be overly reliant on ready meals and delivery food. Many children are so used to living on takeouts that research shows an alarming number are growing up without the ability to use a knife and fork. We have a new generation of kids who have never been taught to cook or even use cutlery. One study of 1,500 British families found that 54 percent of youngsters between the ages of four and ten did not use a knife and fork properly at mealtimes, and 60 percent often just ate with their hands.[159]

Mindless eating habits are also augmented by the fact that our food is so processed and unnatural that we no longer know what we are consuming or how it got to be on our plates. It is full of a myriad of additives and artificial foods we've never heard of, so the ingredients list on the back of the pack sounds like gobbledegook. We are uneducated about the global food supply and its grave impact on the planet. We have no idea of the ecological degradation caused by each mouthful or how it affects distant countries and people. We have become so disconnected from nature that children don't know where food comes from or how it is grown. They think it all comes from the supermarket. According to a poll of two thousand people by Leaf (Linking Environment and Farming), more than half of young adults in the UK don't know that butter comes from a cow, and a third don't know that eggs come from hens or that bacon comes from pigs.[160] We do not know what is in season because we are used to eating supermarket food that comes from all over the world at all times of the year. All this has only served to increase our disconnect from nature's hand that feeds us.

It has also made us profoundly ungrateful. We rarely give thanks for our food or truly take the time to appreciate the blessings of Mother Nature. There was a time when saying a small prayer of gratitude before each meal was commonplace. We thanked the animals for sacrificing their lives and the plants and the farmers who grew them. We thanked the cook for making the meal and nature or the God of our understanding, for all the blessings we were about to receive. This made us think deeply about the food we were eating and its significance in our lives, including all the labor and love that went into it. It made us feel lucky. In this age of abundance, we have forgotten what it feels like to go hungry, so we waste our food—1.3 billion tons globally, in fact, which is a whopping one-third of all the food produced for human consumption. The impact of food waste is devastating for the planet, contributing 10 percent of total greenhouse gases due to the methane that it produces as it rots in landfills—never mind the resources and energy it took to grow, package, and distribute all that produce.

The Good News

A key solution to these problems is simply to become more mindful of what we consume and how we consume it. Mindful eating means slowing down and savoring the taste, becoming aware of our body as we eat. This tuning-in process helps us to become more thoughtful about portion size and food waste, as well as our waistline. We are also more inclined to think deeply about where our food comes from and what impact it has on our health and the planet. Becoming mindful of the ingredients in our meals can support the right food choices for our health and make us more aware of the carbon footprint of our diets, as well as ethical considerations such as animal cruelty and fair trade. As we become more thoughtful consumers, we are far more likely to buy food that is nurturing for ourselves as well as the world.

Savoring the flavor and fragrance of food delights our senses, makes us more present, and creates more enjoyment in the moment. It makes food one of the joys of life, helping us to feel thankful for nature's bounty. Giving a silent prayer of gratitude lifts our mood and reinforces wise food choices in the future. Slowing our eating also helps us to calm our nervous systems, which enhances digestion, reduces calorie intake, and helps us lose weight. As we become more aware of our own bodies and how we are feeling, we are more likely to stop when we are full, and to distinguish between emotional and physical hunger. Mindful eating also involves becoming more aware of the people around us and the opportunity for social connection at mealtimes. It makes us more likely to prioritize family meals and shared experiences around food.

Reinstating the primacy of the family meal would be a huge health boon, particularly for our children. One Harvard study found that families who eat together are twice as likely to eat five servings of fruit and vegetables a day as those who do not.[161] They found that children who eat family meals also have fewer psychological problems and a reduced chance of indulging in risky behaviors such as substance abuse and violence. They have healthier eating habits and broader palettes and are less likely to be picky eaters. Family meals encourage better academic performance, fitness, and lower the risk of eating disorders in youths. They help to grow the vocabulary of preschoolers and offer huge benefits in terms of social connection, strengthening bonds and building better relationships for everyone at the table. Family meals offer an opportunity for parents to listen to their kids and vice versa. Parents can be role models for healthy eating, good conversation, and polite table manners. The sense of belonging engendered by the family meal leads to better self-esteem and greater self-confidence all around. And because we talk more, we eat less, taking time over our meal, which helps us to listen to our body's cues for satiety. Family meals thus have a significant role to play in reducing weight gain.

There is an abundance of research on the benefits of mindful eating, including its capacity for reducing anxiety and depression, food cravings, and weight management issues.[162] Studies show that it is a useful tool in controlling chronic health conditions like diabetes and eating disorders. Mindfulness inhibits automatic responses and improves emotional flexibility for people who suffer from compulsive eating. It helps broaden the palates of finicky eaters, improves the perception of taste, and helps stop habitual, unhealthy snacking. It also improves self-awareness, focus, and self-control around food, crucially reducing stress levels and increasing self-compassion.[163] Mindful eating makes us kinder to ourselves and increases joi de vivre.

Mindful eating also helps us to become more intuitive eaters, consuming what our bodies really need rather than what our routines dictate. Instead of "Taco Tuesdays," we are more likely to decide what healthy foods we require in the moment, mindful of what our bodies are asking for. Intuitive eaters are in sync with the rhythms of their body, knowing when to have mealtimes, what and how much to eat. They are more likely to front-load their calories by eating more during the day and foregoing late-night meals that cause digestion problems, sleep issues, and increased waistlines. As we shall see in Chapter 7, sleep and nutrition are deeply intertwined—if we eat the right things at the right time, we sleep well and feel rejuvenated. Equally, it can go the other way. If our nutrition impacts our sleep, we wake up tired and grumpy the next day, which makes us more likely to stress eat. Mindful eating involves timing meals so that we are not digesting our food while we sleep, which impacts the quantity and quality of our rest.

In terms of timing our meals for optimum health, intermittent fasting has become increasingly popular, with many health professionals advocating a gap of fourteen to sixteen hours between dinner and breakfast the following day. In popular books such as *The Complete Guide to Fasting* by Jason Fung MD[164] and *Fast, Feast, Repeat* by Gin Stephens,[165] the authors cite research which suggests that allowing the body to take a break from digestion for extended periods of time helps us to detoxify and increases autophagy (literally meaning "self-eating"). Autophagy breaks down and removes waste materials from cells, significantly contributing to longevity and good health. Intermittent fasting also helps people to lose weight by encouraging them to eat fewer calories while boosting their metabolism. Fasting has been found to be particularly beneficial in reducing dangerous visceral fat. Studies show that intermittent fasting has innumerable health benefits, such as improving glucose control, lowering blood pressure, reducing liver fat, cholesterol, oxidative damage, and inflammation in the body. It also has important benefits for brain health, preventing brain damage, and encouraging the growth of neurons.

Eating mindfully also means chiming in with the seasons, favoring lighter foods in summer and warm, heavier meals in winter, according to the needs of our bodies as the weather changes. Eating seasonal produce also encourages people to buy from nearby farms, which supports local communities and reduces food miles. Mindful eating is a practice that impacts all the other pillars of health. It is a way of tuning in to our bodies, relaxing our minds and connecting to the world around us in a more conscious and ethical way. As Hippocrates once said: "Let food be thy medicine, and thy medicine be thy food."

In ancient times, the kitchen was often considered the most sacred room in the house because it was where the family was nourished and revitalized. Cooking was seen as a shared activity that united not only relatives but the community, as families came together to prepare and eat meals together. Today, if we cultivate the joy of healthy food, we can reinspire the ancient truth that cooking and eating are important ways to celebrate life.

Key to mindful eating practices is the understanding that no one size fits all. The way that we eat, no matter where we live in the world, will differ from person to person depending on our age, body type, health, family and upbringing, genetic, cultural and religious customs, the geography of where we live, the climate, and what resources are available. Taking this myriad of things into consideration requires us to develop our own set of principles that can be applied to our individual needs and unique set of circumstances. The cumulative effect of such a mindful approach may be to make us less susceptible to the exaggerated claims and misinformation rife in the food industry while increasing healthy food choices not just for ourselves but for our families, communities, and the environment.

CONCLUSIONS

While there is much fault to be found with typical Western food choices, there is also light at the end of the tunnel, as science has shown that a Mediterranean diet full of diverse, organic whole foods is extremely good for body, mind, and soul. Eating mindfully and choosing food from sustainable sources is not only good for our health but for the health of the planet, the subject of our next chapter.

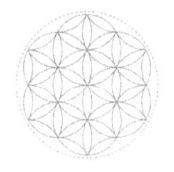

CHAPTER 6

NUTRITION AND PLANETARY HEALTH

A small change in our diet can make a big change in the world
—Frances Moore Lappé

This chapter focuses on how our nutrition is intimately linked with the global food system and its impact on the planet. Since the postwar modern era began nearly eighty years ago, our food system has contributed to the wholesale destruction of the environment, contributing to about a third of all greenhouse gas emissions and triggering biodiversity loss on a scale not seen since the dinosaurs were wiped from the Earth.[166] Our food system has also led to enormous structural inequalities between developing and developed countries and an ever-widening gap between rich and poor as farming is increasingly geared toward profits, not people.

Like the last chapter, the sections below outline the problem, followed by the good news. It gives a hopeful account of how sustainable food choices can support biodiversity, the climate, and more equitable power dynamics between the Global North and South. Ditching our addiction to chemical agriculture, industrial meat farming, and overfishing is paramount, and new models of agroecology are already gaining steam, with the potential to birth a new age of organic, regenerative farming that could restore our own health and the health of the planet.

DIETARY DIVERSITY SUPPORTS BIODIVERSITY

One of the most insidious aspects of the Western diet is that the lack of diversity in our food choices has led to the decimation of biodiversity on our planet. Our repetitive eating habits have created enormous strains on the environment, with vast swathes of monocultures sweeping the land and causing a staggering decline in wildlife. In fact, in the last century, we have lost an eye-watering 75 percent of all the genetic plant diversity in agriculture.[167]

This has caused a vicious cycle. Monocrops involve the repeated farming of a single species, which reduces diversity. Because diversity is fundamental to ecosystem health, this leads to a buildup of pests and diseases. Monocrops are thus weaker and more at risk than other crops, leading to the need for pesticides to bolster their growth. The use of synthetic chemicals kills not only pests but also the soil microbiome and pollinating insects, leaching into water systems and causing a gigantic ripple effect throughout the food web, as the growth of plants and trees is affected and wildlife deteriorates. The resultant loss in biodiversity and soil health weakens crops further, so more chemicals are needed to fertilize the soil and fight weeds and pests.

This addictive cycle goes round and round, causing soil degradation and biodiversity loss on such a scale that wildlife has declined by 69 percent since 1970 and insect species by more than 40 percent, suggesting that our pollinators could vanish within a century.[168] Without pollinators like bees and butterflies, there are no plants, and without plants, the entire web of life disintegrates. Agricultural chemicals also run off into rivers and streams, which end up in the oceans and create algal blooms that suffocate aquatic life, killing biodiversity in the world's great marine ecosystems. The use of agrochemicals to combat the inherent weaknesses of monoculture crops has come at a grave cost to the planet.

It is important not to underestimate the regenerative powers of nature. After Rachel Carson's landmark book *Silent Spring*[169] in the 1960s, which explored the disastrous impacts of DDT on bird populations, the chemical was later banned, and species previously threatened with extinction (like hawks, raptors, and the bald eagle) made a dramatic comeback. Unfortunately, DDT was just one of hundreds of chemicals used to keep crop-eating insects at bay, and the number of pesticides has continued to grow ever since. Today, more than a thousand different pesticides are used in industrial agriculture, and around two million tons are used on a global basis annually, almost double that of 1990 levels.[170]

Chemical farming has been devastating not just for the natural biodiversity of the planet but also for the climate. Soil is the planet's fragile skin from which all life springs, yet a staggering 75 percent of the world's land is now substantially degraded.[171] This has depleted the soil's ability to absorb carbon from the atmosphere—a truly catastrophic loss when you consider that it is second only to the ocean as a carbon sink, absorbing four times more than all the world's forests put together.

To make matters worse, land degradation is responsible for some of the biggest emissions contributing to climate change. This is because when land is degraded, soil carbon and nitrous oxide are released back into the atmosphere, turning our precious carbon sinks into sources. Agriculture emits copious amounts of greenhouse gases (GHGs) at the same time as destroying nature's ability to absorb them. Industrial farming, with its reductionist solutions to increasing monocrop yields, has contributed to systemic environmental problems that dwarf anything humankind has ever experienced. Everything from global warming to the sixth mass extinction can be traced back to soil health and chemical agriculture's role in denuding the unique microscopic life that resides within it.

The lack of diversity in our food supply has also caused major problems for farmers, with monocultures and monopolies dominating Big Agriculture (dubbed "Big Ag"). Everything from growing crops to animal farming and food processing is controlled by a handful of corporations that command the global food industry. Over the past three decades, a series of mergers and acquisitions created the "Big Four" in agriculture: Bayer, Corteva, ChemChina, and BASF. These companies now own more than half of the world's seed supply. Patents mean that farmers cannot save seeds to be used for planting the next year and instead must buy them annually at premium prices, allowing the seed companies to monopolize the market. Insidiously, the top seed companies are also the major pesticide producers of the world, with big stakes in genetically modified technology. This concentration of portfolios has created a circle of dependency for farmers, as the heavy marketing of GM seeds tolerant to pesticides in turn stimulates pesticide sales, and these sales then stimulate demand for more pesticide-tolerant seeds, driving prices up for farmers and sending profit margins soaring for Big Ag.

Around half the crops in the world are grown, processed, and shipped by fewer than two dozen companies, and these products are then manufactured and distributed by another dozen or so companies, with many key players overlapping. Disturbingly, Big Ag is also "Big Pharma," with Bayer being one of the largest pharmaceutical companies in the world. The very companies creating unhealthy, chemical-laden food are also the ones treating the maladies that come from consuming it, creating little incentive to find healthier ways to farm or invest in nutrition-based preventive healthcare measures. Like Big Pharma, Big Ag has enormous lobbying power, perfecting strategies for keeping consumers in the dark about the dangers of pesticides, animal hormones, antibiotic usage, factory farming, animal cruelty, and the devastating environmental impacts of agriculture.

Consolidation of power in the global food system has meant that retailers and manufacturers (a.k.a. "Big Food") have considerable leeway to dictate what crops farmers should grow at what price, simplifying their supply chains by focusing on the few varieties in demand. There is thus a circular relationship between retailers and consumers, disincentivizing diversity. This has created intense competition for farmers, who are forced to churn out the same old export crops with few market opportunities to branch out, encouraging low returns. Commodity crops are traded on the stock market with high price volatility, so farmers risk having their profit margins wiped out by low prices while the cost of seeds and pesticides keeps going up. This has caused increasing numbers of small, independent farmers to go bankrupt as the whole agricultural value chain is increasingly condensed into the hands of the few.

Much of what is consumed in the Global North is made in the South, where labor and production are cheapest. As world-renowned environmental activist Vandana Shiva highlights in books such as *Stolen Harvest*[172] and *Seed Sovereignty, Food Security*,[173] traditional farmers have been the biggest losers in this system. In fact, there has been a national catastrophe of farmer suicides in India, where nearly three hundred thousand people have taken their own lives since the 1990s, often—in a cruel twist of fate—by drinking pesticides because they cannot repay loans for increasingly expensive seeds and chemical farming inputs. Moreover, poor countries that are particularly reliant on export crops often fund exports at the expense of local food production and so are exposed to the fickle profits of volatile global markets for grain, which can lead to a spiraling chain of poverty and food insecurity. What used to be a sustainable circular economy on family-run farms with few external inputs sold locally is now a hegemonic global system based on a model of excessive growth, greed, and profit, with devastating consequences for local communities, ecology, and health.

The Good News

This situation is depressing, to say the least, until we realize that diversifying our diets is one of the most impactful—and easiest—things we can do to protect both our health and the planet. Diversified diets mean less monocultures, which in turn means healthier soil microbiomes, flourishing biodiversity, and mitigating (perhaps even reversing) climate change. Eating a wider range of foods may also help to overcome food insecurity and poverty in the Global South by changing demand and supply, which in turn transforms the power dynamics in the global food system.

There are new varieties of produce that are burgeoning in niche markets, which could become more mainstream if enough people ate them. These range from different varieties of grains (such as buckwheat, barley, and amaranth) to plant-based proteins, which have recently enjoyed a surge in popularity thanks to the increasing acceptance of veganism. There is also a plethora of weird and wonderful vegetables (such as oca, romanesco, kohlrabi, and brusselberry sprouts) to more exotic foods such as seaweed, algae, tubers, cacti, jellyfish, and edible insects. It may sound strange to Western palates, but in Asian countries, many of these foods are the norm; for instance, jellyfish and seaweed salads are commonplace on Chinese or Japanese menus. Edible insects may sound repulsive to the average Westerner but go down a treat in many places all over the world—fried crickets and grasshoppers in Thailand, caterpillar ice-cream in South Africa, chocolate queen ants in Brazil, and tortillas filled with roasted maguey worms in Mexico, to name but a few. Even in the West, there are some tentative signs of bug-eating culture; for instance, in the Netherlands, a government-backed drive to market insects as a healthy source of protein with low environmental impacts has led to 21 percent of the population having tried insect-based food, and 47 percent being open to the idea.[174] As climate impacts increase, what seems unusual now may well be the go-to foods of the future.

As the global population is estimated to reach 10.7 billion by 2080, we need to find ways of feeding the world with a changing climate. Adaptation is one of the three pillars of climate policy (the others being mitigation and compensation for poorer countries). Agriculture will clearly play a crucial role in future climate action, and one of the ways to adapt to a warmer world is by switching to diverse crops that can adapt to challenging weather conditions. The WWF's 2019 "Future 50 Foods" report highlights a variety of produce that could help to achieve these aims.[175] It promotes ancient grains like spelt (a variety of wheat), wild rice, and less common types of quinoas. It also lists different variants of fruits and vegetables, beans and pulses, algae, tubers, and cacti. The foods were selected for their high nutritional value and low environmental impact, as well as taste, price, and accessibility. Many have higher yields than normal crops, and some are more tolerant of extreme weather, which could be invaluable in the years of climate volatility to come.

Along with diversifying our diet, buying locally and decentralizing our food systems would go a long way toward increasing food security and empowering local people, creating self-sufficient communities that are connected to the global network. In the acclaimed book *Agroecology: The Science of Sustainable Agriculture*,[176] Miguel Altieri discusses decentralized food system networks as integral components of agroecological practices. These networks involve smaller-scale production, distribution, and consumption systems that prioritize local resources and knowledge. Altieri highlights the benefits of decentralization, including increased food sovereignty, reduced dependence on external inputs, and enhanced resilience to external shocks such as climate change or economic instability. By fostering connections between producers and consumers at the local level, decentralized community networks promote social cohesion, economic viability for small-scale farmers, and cultural preservation.

Decentralized food systems can also contribute to environmental sustainability by minimizing transportation distances, reducing greenhouse gas emissions, and preserving biodiversity through diversified agricultural practices. This offers farmers the opportunity for innovation and experimentation, as local communities adapt agricultural techniques to suit their specific environment and cultural contexts. Along with diversifying our diets then, we need agricultural policies that empower communities to shape their own food futures in the manner of "Think global, act local."

MAKING THE SWITCH TO REGENERATIVE FARMING

As we discussed in the last chapter, a key reason why our nutrition is causing an exponential rise in chronic disease is the ingestion of environmental toxins. Due to its enormous profitability, Big Ag has been particularly vociferous about quashing public information on the side effects of pesticides. Pesticides are like antibiotics—they are designed to kill bugs. In doing so, they decimate the microbes in both our soil and our gut, with severe environmental and health repercussions.

The potential health effects of the herbicide glyphosate (more commonly known as Roundup) have caused huge global contention because it is the most widely and heavily used agrochemical in the world, regularly sprayed on crops, parks, and amenities as well as gardens.

Research has found ample evidence for a strong link between glyphosate and cancer,[177] as well as endocrine, developmental, and reproductive issues, liver and kidney problems, gut dysbiosis, and leaky gut.[178] The US Environmental Protection Agency and the European Food Safety Authority have declared glyphosate as safe, but most of their research has been provided by the maker of the herbicide, Monsanto (now Bayer). Independent studies highlight "a compelling link" between glyphosate and non-Hodgkin lymphoma, with people exposed to glyphosate at higher levels having a 41 percent increased risk of developing the disease.[179]

In 2015, the WHO's International Agency for Research on Cancer categorized glyphosate as "probably carcinogenic in humans," and many countries put in place bans (such as Germany, France, Australia, Thailand, and several states in the US). However, most of the world still uses Roundup in enormous quantities. In 2018, a US jury ruled that glyphosate contributed to the terminal illness of a groundskeeper diagnosed with non-Hodgkin lymphoma. In subsequent court cases, Monsanto was ordered to pay over two billion dollars in damages to cancer-afflicted claimants, and by 2022, over one hundred thousand lawsuits were settled, worth eleven billion dollars in total.[180] Monsanto was also found guilty of suppressing information on the toxicity of its glyphosate products, using deceptive efforts to defend its safety record (such as ghostwriting scientific papers), and quashing conflicting research findings.[181] There has also been public outrage over evidence of Monsanto's cozy relationship with regulators.

The Good News

Chemical farming, while still the norm, is being challenged by new models of pioneering, eco-friendly agriculture. Organic food has become increasingly popular around the world, and supply is responding to demand. A survey by IFOAM-Organics International found that globally, organic farmland had grown by two million hectares in 2018.[182] In the US, organically certified farms grew by 17 percent between 2016 and 2019,[183] and in Europe, organic farming has increased by 56 percent since 2012, with France, Spain, Italy, and Germany leading the way.[184]

Apart from its obvious health benefits, the biggest boon of organic farming is that it enriches rather than depletes the soil. According to a meta-analysis of fifty-six different studies, organic farming enhances the soil microbiome by anywhere between 32 percent and 84 percent, making it a crucial step toward a more sustainable agricultural model.[185] However, even organic produce has been found to contain pesticide and herbicide residues because chemicals are blown in the wind from conventional farms onto neighboring organic ones. Because so many pollutants are in the air and water cycle, they fall onto plants and soils everywhere and find their way into the food web, organic or not. Because of this, washing both organic and conventionally farmed produce is highly recommended. The Environmental Working Group offers a guide to the "Dirty Dozen" and "Clean Fifteen," which lists the most and the least likely foods to contain pesticide residues annually.[186]

Many farms—both organic and conventional—still plow the topsoil to prepare seedbeds, bringing fresh nutrients to the surface and burying weeds. This practice is highly destructive as it disrupts the soil microbiome, creating erosion and releasing carbon dioxide back into the atmosphere. There is now growing support for "regenerative agriculture," which goes beyond organic farming by putting the restoration of soil health and biodiversity at the heart of its model. As George Monbiot highlights in his bestseller *Regenesis*,[187] regenerative agriculture protects the soil by drilling seeds into the earth, thereby avoiding pernicious plowing practices that kill the soil microbiome. Instead of planting the same monocrop year after year, "no-till" farms use diverse cover crops and crop rotation to restore the earth, increasing its ability to absorb carbon, store water, and encourage biodiversity. Crop rotation decreases pests and disease, reducing the need for chemical inputs. A 2019 special report by the International Panel on Climate Change (IPCC) lent its support to regenerative agriculture by describing it as a "sustainable land management practice" that can be "effective in building the resilience of agroecosystems."[188] Animal welfare and fair trade are also a part of the model, which the Rodale Institute in the US is now certifying under their "regenerative organic certified" (ROC) scheme.

Because no-tillage supports the soil's ability to cycle enormous amounts of carbon from the atmosphere, regenerative agriculture has sometimes been referred to as "carbon farming" and is increasingly being seen as a key solution to the climate crisis. In fact, the nongovernmental organization Regeneration International claims that transitioning to regenerative agriculture could sequester enough carbon dioxide to reverse climate change.[189] Regenerative agriculture is also more profitable for farmers, producing higher yields and better quality, nutrient-dense food because it works with nature rather than against it. By shifting away from single crops to produce a diversity of goods that complement each other, farmers create more revenue streams. In her acclaimed book *For the Love of Soil*,[190] agroecologist Nicole Masters highlights studies that show regenerative agriculture can be up to 78 percent more profitable than industrial agriculture. Carbon farming, therefore, has the potential to revolutionize our food system by feeding the growing global population in an environmentally friendly, commercially viable manner. As such, regenerative agriculture is slowly gaining steam and is now being picked up all over the world.

There are other innovations, too, such as regenerative agroforestry, which combines agriculture with trees. Rewilding is an essential aspect of mitigating climate change, and major tree-planting schemes are already underway in many parts of the globe. In fact, the first authoritative study on global tree restoration by Zurich University's Crowther Lab has calculated that there are 1.7 billion hectares of land ripe for tree-planting (the size of the US and China combined) that does not encroach on urban and agricultural areas. This could remove an incredible two-thirds of all man-made carbon emissions from the atmosphere.[191] The potential for carbon capture makes agroforestry a brilliant systemic solution to the climate crisis because it combines farming with rewilding. Agroforestry not only reduces emissions but creates healthier soils and higher yields, not to mention vital homes for wildlife. Crops grown underneath trees benefit from the nutrients cycled into the soil by the tree roots. Animals can also graze under the trees (called "silvopasture"), enriching the soil with their manure, while the trees in turn provide shelter and fodder for the animals. Farms using the agroforestry model therefore become sustainable ecosystems, foregoing monocultures and pesticides in favor of crop diversity and organics and utilizing animals symbiotically to create rich natural environments that support biodiversity and soil health. This ancient land management method is undergoing a huge renaissance across the globe because of these amazing benefits.

Inspired by nature, small-scale farms are also adopting "permaculture" food systems based on crop diversity, resilience, natural productivity, and sustainability. These small-scale solutions ensure food autonomy for communities and neighborhoods, making it vital for adapting to the years of climate change ahead. There are also revolutionary new developments in agriculture, such as hydroponics and aeroponics, which are a potential light in the dark as land degradation and climate change pick up pace.

Hydroponics is a new method of vertical farming that grows plants in stacks on top of one another without the use of soil, using water-based nutrient solutions and substitutes such as peat moss for the roots to hold on to. This allows farmers to grow food anywhere in the world, at any time of year, which means fewer resources and higher yields—and most importantly, avoiding the problems associated with changing climate and soil conditions, as well as disappearing arable land. Because roots are nourished with all the nutrients they need from the start, plants spend more time and energy growing up than spreading roots down into the earth in search of food. The method also uses less water because hydroponic containers are closed systems with lower rates of evaporation. Some hydroponic systems, such as Vertical Roots, claim to use up to 98 percent less water than traditional soil-based agriculture.[192] Hydroponics means local food systems can be created without having to ship produce from a far, with container farms potentially even set up directly next to food retailers so that the freshest possible produce is available to consumers on the spot.

Aeroponics is a similar model, but instead of suspending plants in water full-time, they are fed nutrients from a mist sprayed onto their roots. While vertical farming models such as these have clear benefits in terms of land use, they have drawn criticism from the more ardent proponents of organics. Although these plants require no pesticides and hardly any land, they are fed with artificial nutrients, grown on fabricated substrates, and may be in buildings without windows or natural light. Critics question whether vertical farming can therefore be defined as sustainable as they are not exactly "organic," and some even go so far as to call it "wet" chemical farming, given that chemicals are simply added to water rather than the soil. There is also the potential for human error in getting the mix of nutrients exactly right to replicate nature.

In contrast, regenerative agriculture and agroforestry draw on the science of agroecology, which looks at how ecological principles can be applied to farming so that yields can be increased at the same time as contributing to rewilding and reducing environmental impacts. While the jury is still out on some of the newer ideas emerging on how to grow the food of the future, agroecology and its variants certainly gives hope to a systems view of health, where our food system works with nature rather than against it.

The "Single Biggest Way To Reduce Your Impact On Earth"
Of all the issues with the Western diet and its links with ill-health, industrial meat production is perhaps the worst culprit. Disease is rife on factory farms where animals are kept in crowded and unsanitary conditions, requiring regular doses of antibiotics to keep disease at bay. Around three-quarters of all antibiotics in the world are used for livestock rather than people, with drugs used routinely to prevent infection and speed growth rather than to treat sickness. This has led to the problem of antimicrobial resistance, which has nearly tripled the occurrence of disease-causing bacteria easily transmitted from animals to humans, such as E.coli and salmonella. Drug-resistant strains can be passed on to humans either through food consumption or through animal excretions, which contaminate the environment. According to the latest comprehensive study in 2019 covering over two hundred countries, antimicrobial resistance is now a leading cause of death worldwide, with millions dying of antibiotic-resistant infections every year.[193]

Another pressing concern is the risk of pandemics from farmed animals, which has grown exponentially because of the atrocious conditions they are often kept in. In fact, SARS, MERS, BSE (mad cows' disease), bovine tuberculosis, Nipah virus, and several strains of bird and swine flu have occurred as a direct result of industrial animal farming. UNEP estimates that factory farming is linked with up to a quarter of all infectious illnesses in the world.[194]

Our over-reliance on meat has not just caused disease, but it has also created grave consequences for the environment. There are many popular books, such as *Fast Food Nation* by Eric Schlosser,[195] *Food Fix* by Dr. Mark Hyman,[196] and *Eating Animals* by Jonathan Saffron Foer,[197] that detail how industrial animal agriculture harms not only humans but animals and the planet. Leaving aside the appalling ethics of factory farming, which creates needless suffering with the inhumane rearing and slaughtering of countless livestock, animal farming accounts for nearly 60 percent of agriculture's greenhouse gas emissions and at least 16.5 percent of global greenhouse gases.[198] That makes agriculture the world's second highest source of emissions after fossil fuels, in large part due to humanity's penchant for eating animals, particularly cows.

The Worldwatch Institute audited the carbon footprint from animal agriculture in 2009 and found that uncounted emissions made livestock's contribution to global greenhouse gases considerably higher when weighed for lifetime and potency.[199] This is because methane is included in the GHG mix, which is released when livestock digest food. Methane is up to eighty-four times more potent as a heat-trapping gas than carbon dioxide. It also includes nitrous oxide from manure and urine, which is 310 times more potent. To make matters worse, the animal products we eat are also a key driver of deforestation, which destroys the Earth's carbon sinks. When you add these two factors together—significantly adding to GHGs while simultaneously taking away our carbon sinks—it becomes clear that agriculture may indeed rival fossil fuels for climate impact.

Animal farming is polluting not just in terms of greenhouse gases either. As the 2014 Netflix documentary *Cowspiracy* highlights, every minute, seven million pounds of excrement are produced by livestock, 130 times more than the entire human population of the USA.[200] This staggering amount of animal waste pollutes the water cycle and affects human health, as well as having devastating consequences for marine life.

Another grave problem is that animal farming is exceptionally resource intensive, with vast amounts of land-use changes for pasture and feed driving environmental destruction. Half of all habitable land in the world is used for agriculture, and 77 percent of this is used for animal farming.[201] This is equivalent to the size of the United States, Russia, China, and India combined, making animal agriculture the leading cause of deforestation and biodiversity loss across the globe. Deforestation is a double whammy for the climate; not only do we lose our carbon sinks, but the trees burned for land clearance release huge amounts of carbon dioxide into the atmosphere. In fact, there are reports that the Amazon rainforest may be reaching a tipping point where it starts to emit more carbon dioxide than it absorbs.[202]

The expansion of agriculture has transformed the environment to such an extent that farming is responsible for 80 percent of all the species threatened with extinction in the International Union for Conservation of Nature (IUCN) red list.[203] Cattle ranching in particular has caused grave ecological damage, with great expanses of forests, grasslands and wetlands destroyed to feed livestock. The demand for beef causes a staggering 80 percent of the deforestation in the Amazon, and scientists now warn that it is in fact close to the point of collapse, which means that devastatingly, the "lungs of the earth" could disappear in less than fifty years.[204]

Animal farming is resource intensive in other ways, too, with more than a third of the world's cereal grains used to feed livestock. The UN's Food and Agriculture Organization estimates that there is enough cropland to feed the world if the crops produced for animal feed were used directly for human consumption.[205] This means we could eliminate world hunger if we stopped animal farming—yet even in terrible famines, the food continues to go to animals. An article in the Guardian newspaper entitled "Avoiding Meat and Dairy is 'Single Biggest Way' to Reduce your Impact on Earth" highlights that despite animal farming's extreme resource intensity, it is a surprisingly inefficient way of feeding the world, producing just 18 percent of global calories and 37 percent of total protein.[206]

Meat production also accounts for nearly a third of the world's freshwater consumption, requiring ten times the amount of water per calorie than vegetables or grains. Producing just one kilogram of beef takes around 13,000 liters of water, equivalent to a small swimming pool.[207] Animal farming is thus a major contributor to water scarcity, which raises the specter of "water wars," as the world's reserves of groundwater are being depleted at twice the rate they were in the 1960s.[208]

The Good News

Despite these shocking statistics, there is much to be hopeful for. As individuals who care about the environment, it may even be a cause for celebration that something as simple as reducing meat and dairy consumption can have such a momentous impact on the climate and biodiversity. Recent research by the University of Oxford highlights that plant-based diets have about 10 percent of the environmental footprint of animal agriculture and that cutting out meat and dairy can reduce individual carbon footprints from food by up to 73 percent.[209] Eating more plant-based foods also has a positive effect on gut flora and human health, as well as increasing animal welfare by reducing the amount of factory farming.

In their 2019 special report, the IPCC made a policy recommendation for a global reduction in meat consumption, describing plant-based diets as a major opportunity for achieving climate goals.[210] In 2021, the WHO recommended a plant-based diet for a healthy lifestyle.[211] Numerous celebrities have championed plant-based diets in the media in recent years, from Natalie Portman to Bella Hadid, changing the old vegan stereotype of anemic virtue signalers to a more media-friendly version that has captured the hearts and minds of the public. Veganism has been gathering momentum ever since, going from fringe to mainstream in a few short years in countries like the UK, where meat consumption has declined by 17 percent over the last decade.[212]

There is no denying that for many people, meat is an ingrained part of their diet, with cultural significance that may make it difficult to cut out entirely. Nevertheless, simply reducing meat consumption—particularly beef—would create huge changes that could even reverse climate change and biodiversity loss if enough people acted. In *We are the Weather: Saving the Planet Begins at Breakfast*,[213] Jonathan Saffron Foer suggests that cutting out meat for breakfast and lunch while allowing it for dinner is one way that people could reduce consumption in a way that is more agreeable to them. He cites a study by the Johns Hopkins Center for a Livable Future, which found that people who stopped eating animal products for two out of three meals a day had smaller carbon footprints than the average vegetarian who consumed lots of cheese and milk. The onus is thus not all on meat-eaters; for vegetarians, reducing cheese consumption is a particular priority, as studies have found it to be the third most carbon-intensive food after beef and lamb.[214] And while dairy is best avoided, if it must be eaten, it is better to be 100 percent grass-fed and organic, with sheep and goat products preferable to dairy from cattle.

There is another reason to be optimistic if you are a dedicated carnivore. Eating a small amount of meat and dairy from animals raised in the right way might actually be part of the solution to climate change. In regenerative agriculture, livestock is integrated symbiotically into the ecosystem. Rotational grazing moves a diversity of animals around the farm so that hooves break up the soil to allow more nutrients and sunlight to enter, while manure enriches the soil organically, making chemical fertilizers unnecessary. Livestock is thus a key part of the farm ecology, which cannot work without animals being part of the system. In fact, the eating, movement, and bodily waste of grazing animals are vital to the health of many wild areas, including grasslands. Regenerative systems thus ensure that animal farming is life-enhancing rather than destructive, helping to reverse climate change, biodiversity loss and water scarcity while protecting human health.

Veganism and its variants are also not a panacea for environmental problems—conventional crops still require land that displaces wildlife, are water and energy intensive, and use pesticides and chemical fertilizers. Vegans still need to opt for organics where they can. There are exciting ideas in the offing for how to make protein consumption less resource-intensive and more compatible with rewilding, such as precision fermentation, which involves replacing animal farms with micro-organism tanks. These are tanks that brew bacteria and yeast to make biologically identical proteins in a way that is 40,900 times more land-efficient than beef—which means we could take care of all the protein needs of the globe on an area of land smaller than the size of Greater London.[215] The sustainable farming of the future may well add such innovations into the mix of regenerative agriculture and agroforestry, working alongside tree planting and rewilding campaigns to transform the countryside, protect biodiversity, and restore the Earth's carbon sinks.

A WHALE OF A PROBLEM: OVERFISHING

We have yet another problem with our food supply that threatens the health of our planet—overfishing. If, as discussed in the previous chapter, fish oils really are what gives us our evolutionary advantage, we are doing everything in our power to drive the extraordinary source of our brain food to extinction. Decades of industrial fishing using destructive techniques such as trawling have ensured that a whopping 90 percent of the world's fish stocks are now fully exploited, overexploited, or depleted.[216] There have also been huge collateral impacts on other marine life due to collapsing food webs and the vast amounts of bycatch (aquatic life other than the target species caught in fishing nets).

This predicament has led to the rise of aquaculture, with around one hundred billion fish farmed each year—more than all the livestock slaughtered in the world. Unfortunately, fish farming has very similar problems to industrial meat farming. Aquatic farms cramp fish into pens with up to sixty kilograms of fish per cubic meter of water, equivalent to twenty-seven trout, each about one foot long, sharing a bathtub. These crowded conditions create rampant disease; in fact, as many as a quarter of salmon die before they can be eaten.[217] Like animal farming, the prevalence of disease creates the need for antibiotics, leading to the familiar problem of drug-resistant strains spreading to wild populations. Sea lice are a regular issue in overcrowded fish pens, and pesticides are used to kill them. Pesticides, along with other chemicals and waste products, are then flushed into surrounding waters, where they contaminate the water supply. Uneaten food and fish feces degrade the water quality and can lead to destructive algal blooms.

Organically farmed fish live in less crowded conditions without the need for antibiotics. However, they still cause problems because fishmeal (also used to feed livestock) is made from smaller wild fish, pejoratively called "trash fish," which are lower down the food chain. Trash fish are caught in such numbers (37 percent of global seafood catch) that food webs have started to collapse.[218] Fish farms can also have a negative effect on biodiversity by introducing invasive farmed species bred for size and quick growth into the wild. Farm-raised fish are not only bad for ecosystems, but they are also less healthy for us, with studies consistently finding them to have lower levels of omega-3 and higher levels of omega-6, as well as higher amounts of PCBs and mercury.[219]

Rather than farming, the real solution to the problem of overfishing is to let fish stocks recover. In David Attenborough's bestselling book *A Life on Our Planet*,[220] he argues that to protect marine ecosystems, we need to ban all fishing in international waters and create a network of "no-fish zones" in coastal waters throughout the world. This is a contentious political issue, as many seaside communities rely on fishing for their income. Yet, we may have little choice if we are to protect future generations. Dr Barry Sears, a leading authority on creating hormonal balance with good nutrition, argues that if humans become deficient in omega-3 for any length of time, our evolutionary advantages in terms of brain power could be severely diminished.[221] He suggests that while there is still enough reserve capacity present to maintain the same level of human brain capacity for a while, by the second and third generation, severe neurological deficits may manifest themselves. Apart from protecting marine ecosystems, banning overfishing is clearly a major priority for human health.

The Good News

Fortunately, there are solutions at hand, and progress is being made that may put humanity on a path toward living in harmony with nature. In 2022, a historic ruling by the World Trade Organization prohibited harmful fisheries subsidies, which were a key factor in the depletion of fish stocks.[222] In December of 2022, governments around the world made a landmark deal at COP15 to halt biodiversity loss, pushing through an agreement twenty years in the making known as 30x30, which aims to conserve at least 30 percent of the Earth's land and oceans by 2030. In 2023, the High Seas Treaty was finalized, enforcing the 30x30 pledge to protect the ocean outside of national boundaries—a legal mechanism without which the target would almost certainly fail.

Sustainable fishing practices used by local fishing communities can alleviate the pressure on wild fish species. Sustainable fishing is a more artisanal and small-scale method that protects marine ecosystems by adapting to the reproductive rate of fish, thereby maintaining ecosystem balance. It uses selective methods to minimize bycatch and avoid waste, which creates the basis for small fishing communities to thrive. Sustainable fishing offers a triple win of protecting marine ecosystems at the same time as feeding a growing global population with protein-rich food that also happens to have a low carbon footprint.

A new report called the "Blue Food Assessment" highlights that foods such as fish, shellfish, seaweed, and algae are lower in carbon emissions and require far fewer resources than land-based animal protein.[223] The report estimates that if wild capture fisheries were operated sustainably, an extra sixteen million tons of catch could be generated annually to feed seventy-two million extra mouths, as well as swelling fisheries employment. "More Fish, More Jobs, More Money" is the title of the most comprehensive study on rebuilding EU Fisheries, aptly highlighting the triple bottom line of sustainable fishing, benefiting not only profits but people and the planet.[224]

One of the keys to future success in protecting marine ecosystems is to educate consumers on buying fish from sustainable sources. Currently, food labeling lacks standardization, which makes this somewhat challenging, as there are so many different guidelines and voluntary codes of practice which can confuse people. Food labels can have generic claims of being "responsible" or "sustainable," but in fact the latest research by the Marine Conservation Society (MCS) may say otherwise, as species numbers continually fluctuate, and population data is a moving feast. For this reason, the MCS publishes an annual "Good Fish Guide," which has a traffic light system to show which fish to choose and which to avoid in any given year.[225] There are also concerns that certified fisheries sometimes breach the rules, so constant monitoring is needed, and the onus is on both authorities and consumers to stay up to date. The recently agreed marine reserves covering 30 percent of the oceans will allow fish stocks to recover and populate other areas. The problem lies in policing them.

CONCLUSIONS

To end this chapter on the most hopeful note possible, this excerpt from Christina Figueres's acclaimed book *The Future We Choose* paints a heartwarming picture of what can be achieved if we make sustainable nutrition a top priority:[226]

> [Imagine that] the forest cover worldwide is now 50 percent, and agriculture has evolved to become more tree based . . . Now we have shady groves of nut and fruit orchards, timberland interspersed with grazing, parkland areas that spread for miles, new havens for our regenerated pollinators . . . We [have] transitioned quickly to regenerative farming practices—mixing perennial crops, sustainable grazing, and improved crop rotation on large-scale farms, with increased community reliance on small farms. Instead of going to a big supermarket for food flown in from hundreds, if not thousands, of miles away, we buy most of our food from small local farmers and producers. . . . The most resource-depleting foods of all—animal protein and dairy products—have practically disappeared from our diets. Fish is still available, but it is [sustainably] farmed, and yields are better

managed by improved technology. We make smarter choices about bad foods, which have become an ever-diminishing part of our diets. Government taxes on processed meats, sugars, and fatty foods [have] helped us reduce the carbon emissions from farming. The biggest boon of all is to our health, (as) people are living longer, and health services around the world cost less. In fact, a huge proportion of the costs of combating climate change are recuperated by government savings on public health.

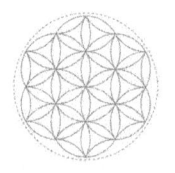

CHAPTER 7

SLEEP

Sleep is the cure for waking troubles.
—Miguel de Cervantes

A key pillar of health, but one that is most frequently underrated, is sleep. It is incredible to think that we spend a third of our lives sleeping—that means if we live to the age of eighty, we will have been asleep for around twenty-six years. But while everybody knows that a good night's rest is important for well-being, unfortunately, most of us don't get enough of it. Sleep is almost as important as breathing or eating, yet in our fast-paced modern world, getting adequate rest is not always our biggest priority. Life has gotten so busy that many of us feel that there simply isn't enough time in our day to get a decent amount of shut-eye, as living in the fast lane demands our continual attention and our to-do lists grow ever longer. Some people even boast about how little sleep they need, as if being sleep-deprived somehow makes us "tough." Yet sleep is arguably the most important pillar of health in terms of ensuring that we are productive and useful human beings, so it is hugely counterintuitive to downplay its importance in the name of living life to the fullest.

Numerous bestselling books such as *Why We Sleep* by Dr. Mathew Walker,[227] *The Sleep Revolution* by Arianna Huffington,[228] *The Secret Life of Sleep* by Kat Duff,[229] and *Sleep Smarter* by Shawn Stevenson[230] describe a silent sleep-loss epidemic occurring in modern society caused by our hectic schedules, workaholic culture, twenty-four-hour internet technology, and cities that never sleep. In *Why We Sleep*, the renowned neuroscientist Mathew Walker claims that two-thirds of adults in the developed world do not get the eight hours of sleep a night recommended by the WHO and the National Sleep Foundation. Moreover, one in three people try to survive on six hours or less. This is a major problem because scientific research consistently shows that any less than eight hours of sleep a night has major consequences for our health.

Science has also shown that quality of sleep is as important—if not more—than quantity, yet our busy lives have caused sleep hygiene habits to go out the window. As sleep quality is eroded, our quality of life suffers. Good-quality sleep may well be one of the greatest medicines on earth— yet doctors get almost no training on the importance of sleep or sleep hygiene at medical school.

In the following sections, we look at why we are not sleeping enough, what the health consequences of sleep deprivation are and how it affects the other key pillars of health. We also cover the different stages of sleep and their benefits, including the power of our dreams and how they help us to process thoughts and emotions. The chapter closes with a discussion of good sleep hygiene and tips for sleeping smarter.

WHY ARE WE NOT GETTING ENOUGH SLEEP?

When Thomas Eddison invented the lightbulb in 1879, he probably had no idea the full impact his pioneering work would have on the world— let alone human health—in the years that followed. Edison apparently considered sleep to be a waste of time, and his frustration with working by candlelight at night was a key motivator for his invention of the lightbulb. What ensued with this innovation was nothing short of a sleep revolution as a new kind of nightlife arose, and people began to socialize till the wee hours of the morning. With the advent of the modern era, sleep deprivation became commonplace as people gained access to twenty-four-hour television and the internet. Now smart phones, tablets, and laptops rule our lives and keep us working away till all hours of the night. This has taken an extreme toll on our nervous systems, as we are still hardwired to get sleepy soon after dusk and wake up with the sun.

Our circadian rhythms are our body's internal biological clock and are responsible for our natural sleep-wake cycle. This master clock is triggered by environmental cues, especially light, which is why the lightbulb has had such a devastating effect on our sleep patterns. Our circadian rhythms are critical to health because they catalyze essential bodily functions over the course of the day. All of nature's organisms have this master clock, which is why nocturnal animals become active at night when there are fewer predators and why flowers open to the sunshine during the day. The rhythms of nature are cyclical, and circadian rhythms are no different—the term *circadian* comes from the Latin phrase *circa diem*, which means "around a day."

The biological clocks of humans are triggered by both internal and external factors. Internal factors include things like social activity and exercise, while the main external cues are light and temperature. Our biological clocks are particularly sensitive to light because, for most of human history, we've been hunter-gatherers. Our ancestors were programmed to sleep at night because taking a nap during the day was a great invitation to be lunch for a lion. Human evolution over millions of years has conditioned us to respond to the Earth's orbit around the sun, which gives us light and dark, and it is only in the last 150 years that we have started to override this natural programming with modern technology. This has meant that we are no longer in sync with nature, as our bodies simply haven't had time to catch up. With our new nocturnal habits, we are ignoring a central aspect of our well-being—in fact, in *Why We Sleep*, Dr. Mathew Walker[231] maintains that sleep is not just a key pillar of health but the foundation on which all other pillars sit.

In *The Secret Life of Sleep*, Kat Duff [232] highlights the problem of "social jet lag," a term first coined by the chronobiologist Till Roenneberg, which refers to the imbalance that occurs when our busy work and school schedules cause us to be out of sync with our circadian rhythms, resulting in sleep issues. In *The Sleep Revolution*, Ariana Huffington[233] cites studies highlighting that Americans have reduced their vacation time by 28 percent in the last twenty years as society has become ever more addicted to a work-spend cycle that involves long hours at the office to pay for high-consumption lifestyles. And it is not only the well-off that get insufficient sleep—in fact, those in lower-income brackets may be even more sleep-deprived if they are working double shifts and moonlighting with extra jobs just to make ends meet. Poorer neighborhoods are also often noisier, so sleep may be more disturbed and irregular. Huffington cites a 2013 study by the University of Chicago that found a person's quality of sleep has a direct correlation with their wealth, diminishing progressively as income decreases.

Our workaholic culture is also having a major effect on children, who start school in the early hours of the morning so that their parents can get to work on time. Yet children need more sleep than adults, and early morning rises are particularly challenging for teenagers, whose hormonal changes encourage them to stay up late and sleep in the next day. Numerous studies have shown that students are pathologically tired due to the timings of school schedules, which dovetail with the commuting workforce, and this is having a detrimental effect on grades. Some schools have experimented with starting classes later, such as high schools in the Seattle School district in 2016, which delayed classes from 07:50 am to 08:45 am and found an increase in median grades as a result, as well as an improvement in attendance.[234] A major piece of research involving the Open University, Harvard Medical School, and the University of Nevada tracked the performance of teenage students over four years and found similar results.[235]

WHAT HAPPENS WHEN WE DON'T GET ENOUGH SLEEP?

The timing of sleep is also important, as there is a magic window for adults between 10 p.m. and 2 a.m. when the production of melatonin and the human growth hormone reaches its peak, resulting in deeper, more rejuvenating sleep—hence the old adage "an hour of sleep before midnight is worth two after." If we stay up later than 10 p.m., our body misses important time to rest and recover, which may contribute to ill-health. A major study published in the journal *Sleep Medicine* found that people who slept later in the night had a 10 percent increased risk of heart attacks, strokes, and death.[236]

So why is the timing of sleep is so crucial? Melatonin is often called the king of hormones because it is crucial to the onset of sleep and the timing of our circadian rhythm, which helps us to synchronize our sleep-wake cycle with the natural rhythms of night and day. Our circadian rhythms coordinate all manner of biological processes, from digestion, detoxification, metabolism and cellular regeneration to brain chemistry, hormonal regulation, and immunity. Circadian rhythms are also crucial to the sleep-wake cycle by triggering the production of the hormone melatonin when the sun goes down, which builds up steadily over the next few hours so that we are sleepy enough to go to bed and stay asleep until daybreak. A disturbed circadian rhythm can give rise to major sleep issues, as people struggle to fall asleep (called sleep-onset insomnia) or struggle to stay asleep, waking at all hours of the night and having difficulty getting back to sleep (called sleep-maintenance insomnia). It can also give rise to shallow and unrejuvenating sleep. All of these issues have a cumulative effect on bodily processes and daytime drowsiness. Disrupted circadian rhythms can result in prolonged insomnia as the body uses adrenaline to get through the day, which then makes it harder to fall asleep because people are too wired and tired to feel drowsy at night. From there, a vicious circle ensues that is hard to break, as the less rest we have, the harder it is to sleep.

Studies have shown that losing even a couple of hours of sleep can cause our reflexes to slow down and result in accidents—particularly on the road, which is a major factor in the soaring rates of traffic deaths worldwide.[237] Sleep deprivation is also a major contributor to chronic disease and morbidity. Because poor sleep contributes to stress, it increases inflammation in the body and compromises our immune system. Dr.

Mathew Walker has made it his life's mission to get the message out that the shorter you sleep, the shorter you live. In *Why We Sleep*, after analyzing more than twenty studies, he found a strong correlation between life expectancy and the number of hours that people slept. For instance, in one study, people who slept less than six hours a night were 200 percent more likely to have a heart attack or stroke than those who got eight hours or more. Other studies have linked lack of sleep with numerous health conditions, from diabetes, cancer, and chronic pain syndrome to Alzheimer's, depression, and obesity. An extremely large and wide-ranging study by the University of Surrey published in the *Journal of Sleep Research* in 2021 examined half a million participants in the UK over seven years, finding that people who consistently stayed up late increased their likelihood of early death by 10 percent, shaving an average of eight years off their life.[238]

The reason why not getting enough sleep makes us sick is that as our internal body clocks go out of whack, the essential bodily processes are not adequately preformed at night. Shifting your sleep patterns affects the metabolic clock of your vital organs and puts you at greater risk of ill-health. For instance, vital cleansing performed by the liver during sleep can be diminished, leading to a decrease in blood filtration and the removal of toxins. Lack of sleep can deprive you of the time your body needs for physical restoration, weakening your immunity so that you are more likely to get infections. Not only that, but a lack of sleep is a risk factor for developing diabetes because it increases insulin resistance and raises blood sugar levels. Sleep deprivation also increases blood pressure and has a major impact on our cardiovascular system, contributing to the soaring rates of heart disease and strokes we see in the world today. A 2014 study by the University of Michigan found staggering statistical correlations with heart attacks around daylight savings; in spring (when we lose an hour of sleep), there is a 24 percent increase in heart attacks, and in autumn (when we gain an hour's sleep) there is a 21 percent decrease.[239]

Sleep deprivation is also linked to a higher risk of developing cancer. This is because it lowers the amount of natural killer cells in our immune system (the body's "soldiers"), diminishing our ability to fight malignant tumors. In a study of people who'd had only four hours of sleep, there was a 70 percent reduction in natural killer cell activity, a very worrying drop in immune function from just a single night of poor sleep.[240] The link between lack of sleep and cancer is now so convincing that the WHO has recently classified night work as a "probable carcinogen." Nightshift workers are particularly at risk of sleep deprivation and its health consequences, with numerous studies highlighting higher rates of cancer as well as obesity and diabetes in this group.

Mathew Walker says that sleep deprivation can even erode the biological fabric of life itself—our DNA. He describes a sleep study where subjects were allowed to sleep for only six hours a night for one week; researchers found that by the end of the study, seven hundred genes had been impaired. Half of these genes had switched off, and half had switched on. The ones that had switched off were related to the immune system, while the genes that had switched on were related to stress, chronic inflammation, cardiovascular disease, and cancer. In a recent TED talk called *Sleep is your Superpower*,[241] Walker says that: "Sleep loss will leak down into every nook and cranny of your physiology, even tampering with the very DNA nucleic alphabet that spells out your daily health narrative."

Sleep deprivation also affects your hormones, impacting testosterone production (which needs at least three hours of uninterrupted sleep) and growth hormone production, which especially affects children and adolescents. Studies have found that men who sleep five hours a night or less have the testosterone levels of someone ten years older, impacting virility, muscle strength, bone mass, and hair loss, as well as causing mood swings and more intense emotional reactions.[242] Women also suffer from deficiencies in their reproductive hormones due to a lack of sleep, which has serious implications for fertility rates. Sleep also halts the production of stress hormones while increasing GABA, the calming hormone, so the less sleep we get, the more likely we are to feel anxious and triggered.

Not only that, but poor sleep drains you of physical and mental energy, leaving both your brain and your body feeling exhausted. The brain is highly energy intensive, using a staggering 25 percent of our daily energy supplies—so if we don't get enough shut-eye, we are left feeling fatigued and foggy-brained. Walker explains that wakefulness causes low-level brain damage—and we need sleep to repair this. Without sleep, we have difficulties problem-solving and decision-making, as well as ensuring we are far less able to cope with stress. It has a particular effect on memory, impairing both short- and long-term recall, shortening concentration spans, and creating learning difficulties. Sleep is like hitting the save button on your computer for all the things you've learned during the day, converting short-term memories into long-term ones. It is essential to prepare you for new learnings, filing away existing emails and deleting unnecessary ones in the inbox of your brain so that it can receive new messages the next day. Without sleep, your brain becomes overloaded, so you can't learn anything new.

Sleep deprivation also diminishes brain function by impairing the glymphatic system, which is responsible for detoxifying the brain. The flushing of toxic waste from the brain occurs in deep sleep, so the less deep sleep that you get, the more toxins remain in your nervous system. Insufficient sleep has such a detrimental effect on the brain that it has been found to be a major determinant of Alzheimer's disease. We all know that as we get on in years, we become more forgetful as our mental cognition starts to decline. Unfortunately, our biological makeup means we also sleep less as we get older so that sleep deprivation and aging become more and more correlated. Older people are thus at greater risk of dementia than any other age group. It also has implications for our sleep patterns in middle age. Studies have found that people in their fifties and sixties who sleep six hours or less are significantly more likely to develop dementia later in life.[243] Margaret Thatcher is famously said to have slept for only four hours a night, yet sadly, for the last twelve years of her life, she suffered from Alzheimer's.

Without sleep, our mental cognition nosedives, as does our emotional intelligence, making us more easily triggered by the challenges of the day. We quickly become irritable and moody, which puts a strain on our social relationships. Sleep is critical for our emotional health, helping us to process negative feelings and feel emotionally stable. If we don't get enough sleep, the amygdala becomes overreactive, so we stress over relatively minor things and turn them into catastrophes. Over time, poor sleep may cause paranoia, depression and even suicidal thoughts. Poor sleep is highly correlated with mental health issues, and conversely mental health problems can cause sleep issues, creating a vicious circle. Good sleep hygiene is thus critical to avoiding a nightmarish spiral.

Insomnia also makes us more prone to "microsleeps" during the day, where we fall asleep for a few seconds without realizing it. These nanonaps can be extremely dangerous, particularly if we are driving or operating heavy machinery, and have led to countless accidents and deaths—indeed, drowsy driving causes more deaths than drugs and alcohol combined. Studies show that being awake for seventeen hours or longer creates physical and mental impairments similar to alcohol intoxication, yet drowsy driving has none of the stigma or legalities attached as being drunk at the wheel does.[244]

HOW DOES SLEEP IMPACT THE OTHER PILLARS OF HEALTH?

Lack of sleep impacts other foundations of health too. As we have seen in the last chapter, sleep and nutrition are intimate bedfellows, with sleep having a major impact on the digestive system and vice versa. While late-night meals can keep us awake at night, a lack of sleep increases the hunger hormone ghrelin, which may cause us to overeat when we wake up tired the next day. It also reduces the hormone leptin, which tells us when we are full. This makes it very easy to put on weight if we are not getting enough sleep. People who sleep five or six hours a night eat two hundred more calories a day on average, which adds up to ten to fifteen pounds of annual weight gain.[245] If people are particularly sleep-deprived, they can eat up to 450 extra calories a day—and it's often sugary, fatty junk food they crave to make up for low energy levels.

In fact, graphs of obesity rates have a direct correlation with society's decreasing hours of sleep over the years.[246] Diets high in sugar and carbs and low in fiber give us less deep and more fragmented sleep. It also affects gut health, which contributes to the stress cycle and makes sleep issues more pronounced. Heavy meals that are difficult to digest can also affect your night's rest, so it's important to finish eating a good two to three hours before bed. Studies have found that just a few nights of bad sleep can cause changes in our microbiome, which leads to a host of digestive issues such as bloating, stomach pains, and food sensitivities.[247]

A lack of sleep also affects exercise, as we may feel too tired to hit the gym, which can cause weight gain over time. On the other hand, if we try to push on through and exercise when we are exhausted, we can suffer from adrenal fatigue and burnout, which only fans the flames of the stress cycle. Research by the National Sleep Foundation says exercise and sleep are bidirectional; that means exercise helps sleep efficiency, and better sleep leads to more energy for exercise.[248] Exercise has a protective function against sleep issues, as studies have found that people who are more physically active are less likely to develop insomnia in later years. The National Sleep Foundation cites research which shows that people suffering from insomnia who begin regular exercise end up falling asleep sooner, staying asleep longer, and improving the quality of their sleep over time.[249]

Sleep deprivation also makes it difficult for us to relax because we are so wired from all the adrenaline our bodies use to overcome daytime drowsiness. Lack of sleep also makes us irritable, which affects our relationships. We are far more likely to overreact to stressful situations if we are tired, and this can lead to conflict with family, friends, and colleagues. A study by Berkley University in California found that a lack of sleep makes people feel less inclined to be sociable, triggering isolation, loneliness, and feelings of rejection.[250]

Poor sleep also affects our work relationships and productivity. The Rand Corporation, a nonprofit global policy think tank, claims that the US loses a staggering 1.23 million working days a year due to insufficient sleep.[251] Japan loses around 604 thousand workdays a year, and the UK and Germany around 200 thousand. This equates to around 2 percent of global GDP—that's a staggering $1.7 trillion a year. This obviously has a huge effect on work performance, impacting productivity and quality, not to mention team dynamics, absenteeism, career progression, and job satisfaction. Meta studies show how sleep-deprived employees take on fewer work challenges, produce fewer creative solutions, focus on easier tasks such as answering emails instead of project work, and slack off in groupwork (called "social loafing," where they ride on the coattails of other more efficient employees).[252] Moreover, business leaders who get less sleep are rated as less capable and charismatic by their staff. It is curious, then, that long work hours are still considered to be a hallmark of motivation and success in the office when these studies point to the exact opposite. Working yourself to the bone by burning the midnight oil is simply pointless—science shows that we are far more productive and efficient with more sleep and fewer hours on the job.

Ariana Huffington is an outspoken proponent of napping at work so that employees can catch up on sleep. Her company, *The Huffington Post*, together with other major companies such as Google, Ben & Jerry's, Nike, Uber, and Facebook, have trailblazed the implementation of office sleep pods for workers who need to take a power nap. In fact, according to a survey in 2008 by the National Sleep Foundation, 34 percent of US companies were "pro-nap," allowing napping during breaks at work.[253] Naps have the benefit of recharging your system and increasing your overall health—as long as they are no longer than thirty minutes. Any more, and they may affect your sleep at night.

SO HOW DOES SLEEP WORK? THE FIVE STAGES OF SLEEP

Now that we know just how important sleep is, let's take a look at what happens when we nod off at night. There are five different stages to sleep, with different brain waves that occur at each stage.[254] In our normal waking state, our brainwaves are in beta, the fastest of all brain waves. In stage one, the transitional stage, our brain waves slow down to alpha waves as our brain dips into sleep, but we can still hear things and have a sense of awareness, so it feels like we are still awake. Stage two is a stage of light sleep in the slower theta state, and although our body is relaxed, we can still be easily woken. Stage two is a golden time for body maintenance. While deep sleep is thought to be the most restful form of sleep, light sleep is also very important and takes up more than half the night.

In stage three, we go from moderate to deep sleep (also called slow wave sleep—SWS), where our brainwaves move to delta, which is extremely slow, so it is more difficult to wake. Stage three lasts around ten minutes and accounts for only about 7 percent of the night's sleep. We are not dreaming at this point—our brain is offline as it were, and our muscles are completely relaxed. During deep sleep, we excrete growth hormones, which enable our bodies to do all the repair and rebuilding work it needs, as well as strengthening our immune systems. Stage four is the deepest sleep, where breathing, heart rate, and brain temperature is at its lowest. This stage lasts about thirty-five to forty minutes and accounts for 15–20 percent of our sleep time. This is when the body gets the most amount of repair work done. It is also a time when people may sleepwalk or suffer from night terrors.

Stage five is when we get our REM (rapid eye movement) sleep, which is when most dreaming occurs. Whereas deep sleep is about restoring the body, REM sleep is all about the brain, which is very active at this stage. Like defragging a computer, it clears itself of any files that are no longer needed. While the brain is active, the body is very inactive—in fact, we are totally paralyzed during REM sleep. The dream state is very important for emotional regulation, information processing, memory enhancement, problem-solving, and creativity. It is critical to cope with daily challenges as it allows us to work through our anxieties. Nightmares and restless dreams have a function, which is to make us aware of fears and emotions that were previously unconscious so that we can process them. REM sleep is in fact so important that our brain keeps track of whether we are in "REM debt" and seeks to make up for it during subsequent sleeps, which can result in intense dream states—and if we don't catch up, eventually delirium.

In dreams, we use all the information we've previously learned and connect it with new data that we've just taken on board, rewiring the brain to enhance its neuroplasticity. We test new associations and seek out novel ways of doing things, role-playing all the different possibilities at lightning speed to find innovative solutions to previously impenetrable problems, which is why sleeping on a problem is such a great idea. In fact, Mathew Walker calls sleep the greatest performance-enhancing drug known to man. He explains that dreaming helps us to learn by chunking information in one smooth rhythm. We tend to have problem points that stop us from connecting the chunks during the day, but when we dream, we connect the chunks together so that we can perform things seamlessly. Walker highlights studies that consistently show athletes are 20 to 30 percent better at their sport the next day than they were at the end of their training session the day before. This is because in our dreams, we play out skills that we need to learn, practicing them at quantum speed so that we are better at them the following morning. Conversely, sleep deprivation causes a 20 to 30 percent decline in our abilities—a big problem if we have prematch tension, exam nerves, or a big work presentation that stops us from getting a good night's sleep. This is where relaxation techniques like meditation and breathwork are particularly useful; not only do they calm our minds, but they help us sleep, so we can be ready for peak performance the next day.

Our body goes through these five stages multiple times a night, each cycle lasting roughly ninety minutes. The first half of the night is when we get the most amount of deep sleep, which is why it is important to go to bed early for physical rest and regeneration. During the second half of the night, the body alternates between light and REM sleep, which is why early morning wakings may rob us of important dream time and cognitive processing.

SLEEP HYGIENE

As we discussed at the beginning of this chapter, people consistently underestimate their need for sleep despite the shocking effects of sleep deprivation. It is as if we are now where we were in the 1950s with smoking: we have all the facts, but the public hasn't yet woken up to them. There is a lack of education about good sleep hygiene in schools and few government-sponsored public information campaigns. Imagine what savings could be made if just a fraction of the GDP lost from work absenteeism went into public information campaigns and school education about the importance of good sleep hygiene. More importantly, doubling the budget for sleep education could more than pay for itself by slashing the cost of healthcare. So, let's take a look at some key sleep hygiene tips to help us get a better night's rest.

Keep It Dark

Excessive mobile phone, tablet, and laptop use has been linked to insomnia, not just because of the connection between social media and anxiety or depression (particularly among teens and young adults[255]), but because of its impact on the sleep-wake cycle. The blue light emitted from the screens of our devices is a disaster for our circadian rhythms, confusing our brain by flooding it with light to counteract our natural sleep hormones. Mathew Walker cites research which shows that reading on a tablet before bed delays the rise of melatonin by up to three hours and ensures peak melatonin levels are at half their normal level. Because of this, the National Sleep Foundation recommends turning off devices an hour before bed. Apart from disturbing melatonin production, looking at social media or watching an exciting TV show last thing at night can keep you awake at night by boosting adrenaline levels and alertness. Another golden rule of sleep is never to look at your devices if you wake up in the middle of the night because it shuts down the activity of your pineal gland and disturbs your circadian rhythms just when you are trying to get back to sleep. Looking at screens anytime between 11 p.m. and 4 a.m. also reduces dopamine levels, contributing to lower moods the next day.

It's also a good idea to turn on night mode filters or use blue light glasses well before this to minimize the impact of technology on sleep. Studies have found that turning down the lights in the evenings before bedtime gets our body prepped for sleep, so use dimmer switches or turn on soft lighting and lamps as soon as it gets dark. One study found that campers in the Rockies denied access to electrical lights and gadgets ended up going to bed two hours earlier than usual because their melatonin levels rose as soon as it got dark. This helped reset people's body clocks, leading scientists to recommend camping as a way of reversing the effects of social jet lag.[256]

Keep It Cool

Sleep studies have found that our core body temperature needs to drop two to three degrees Fahrenheit in order to sleep, which is why people find it much easier to get a good night's rest in cool rooms. The ideal room temperature is sixty-four to sixty-eight degrees Fahrenheit (eighteen to twenty degrees Celsius). Having a hot bath before bed helps this process by cooling us down as we get out. However, we also need to have warm hands and feet, for when our extremities are cold, they constrict the blood vessels, which affects our blood circulation, hindering body temperature regulation. According to the National Sleep Foundation, warming our feet before we go to bed is a good way to help our brain to cue sleep.

Keep It Quiet

If there is constant noise outside our bedroom window, or we're living with noisy householders who go to bed late, then we are more likely to have problems getting to and staying asleep. Even while we're sleeping, our brain continues to register sounds around us as it goes in and out of the different stages of sleep. A noisy house or neighborhood can lead to restless nights and insomnia. White noise (like the sound of static) can help drown out intrusive sounds by creating a steady background noise that makes it easier to go to sleep. There are recordings available of everything from the hum of air conditioning to fans and hair dryers, depending on your preference. "Green noise" (nature sounds like waterfalls and waves lapping) has been found to be particularly relaxing. Covering floors with rugs to reduce echoes and creaks can also help, and of course, earplugs are a great investment for cutting out external noise.

Get Regular Exercise

Exercise helps insomniacs for many reasons; it realigns their internal body clocks and boosts serotonin levels, which is a precursor to melatonin and, thus, a key hormone in the sleep-wake cycle. Exercise also relieves anxiety and depression, which may affect sleep. However, for some, it is best to avoid exercising too close to bedtime, as this can increase heart rate, body temperature, and adrenaline levels, as well as release endorphins that energize the brain, leading to delayed sleep onset. For this reason, experts recommend avoiding exercising at least two hours before bed.

Keep a Regular Routine

It's a good idea to go to bed within thirty minutes of the same time every night. Sticking to the same bedtime helps to keep our body clocks in sync so that we get enough sleep—after all, our bodies don't know what day of the week it is, which is why many of us still wake up early at the weekend even when we would really like to sleep in. Just like children need a prebedtime routine to give them the necessary cues for sleep, adults too can help themselves in the same way to feel drowsy at the right time for sleep. A good routine might include turning off technology and having a hot bath before bed, opening the window a crack for some fresh air before closing the curtains, turning down the lights and putting a bedside table lamp on to read, listening to some relaxing music or a guided meditation to help calm the mind. Once you are ready for sleep, it's lights off, and if you live in a loud house or neighborhood, you might want to turn on some white noise. Eating early is also helpful to a good night's sleep, as our prehistoric digestive system is naturally programmed to switch off after 8 p.m. to help us wind down for bed.

Create a Sleep Sanctuary

Another hot tip is to make a "sleep sanctuary" that creates a relaxing atmosphere in your bedroom. Introducing plants into the room is a great way to create the right ambience, not only because they are pleasing to the eye but because they perform the all-important function of filtering the air.

If we don't have our windows open regularly, the air inside gets stale; plants can reinvigorate us by oxygenating the room and recharging the air with negative ions. Negative ions improve our health by getting rid of bacteria and viruses, as well as cigarette smoke, pet dander, and dust. Diffusing essential oils from trees such as cedar, pine, and sandalwood can also help create a calming atmosphere, as they contain phytoncides (covered in Chapter 4), which are antimicrobial aromas that boost immunity and relax us. Studies also show that lavender and jasmine oil can also help some people to sleep.[257] Others swear by putting crystals such as amethyst, moonstone, and rose quartz under their pillow.

It also cannot be understated how important it is to have a good mattress that supports the spine, along with comfortable pillows—but beware of having too many, as they can put your neck at an awkward angle and contribute to sleep problems. To support your neck, experts recommend two pillows if you sleep on your side, one if you sleep on your back, and either a slim one or none if you sleep on your front.

Perhaps the most important rule of all in creating a sleep sanctuary is to keep work out of the bedroom. Bringing technology into your sleeping space is not just bad from the perspective of blue light; they also emit electromagnetic frequencies (EMFs) that add to our background stress. Although studies are not yet conclusive, there is enough evidence of a correlation between cell phones and brain tumors that the WHO has classified EMFs as a possible carcinogen. Technology can also create spikes in your cortisol levels if you are looking at work emails or social media last thing before bed. This can also lead to negative associations with your bedroom, which subconsciously make it harder to sleep.

Avoid Stimulants

Most people know that having a late-night espresso is likely to make them stay up till the wee hours of the morning, which is why coffee is such a popular drink for those needing to pull an all-nighter in the office. Coffee is a stimulant, that much is commonly known; its effects are felt almost immediately as it energizes the brain and raises our alertness and mental focus by increasing the stress hormone cortisol. Apart from the fact that elevated cortisol levels over long periods impair our immune system, caffeine can contribute to chronic disease and shorter lifespans by messing with our sleep. What most people don't realize about caffeine is that it takes a long time for the body to process. It has a half-life of three to five hours, which means it can take up to ten hours to clear out of our system. So, that morning cup of coffee may have only just cleared through by nightfall, while having a cup of coffee after lunch means caffeine will still be in our systems well into the night. Caffeine can be highly detrimental to sleep, causing insomnia and affecting the amount of both REM and deep restorative sleep we clock through the night. For this reason, experts say it is a good idea to avoid caffeine in the afternoon (and definitely after 2 p.m.)—this includes not just coffee but all caffeinated drinks such as Coca-Cola, energy drinks, and black or green tea. In addition, caffeine can cause anxiety in some people, which may contribute to sleep problems.

It goes without saying that stimulant drugs like cocaine and amphetamines impair sleep cycles. Cigarettes are also stimulants, as nicotine makes it more difficult to fall asleep and may cause sleep to be lighter and less restorative. Another drug that definitely affects our sleep is alcohol. Many people view alcohol as a relaxing drink, and while it may initially reduce the time it takes to fall asleep, it has a very disruptive effect on our sleep cycles, especially REM sleep. It triggers more frequent night wakings and can create difficulties getting back to sleep. Anyone who has had one too many knows it can also lead to night sweats, nightmares, and more. Alcohol affects virtually every part of our body, including the central nervous system, the circulatory system, and the liver, which has to process the poisonous effects of ethanol on top of its normal cleansing functions during our sleep. If you have sleep issues, drinking is an anathema to getting good-quality rest.

Natural Sleep Aids Can Help

There are many natural sleep aids on the market, including nature sound alarm clocks (which mimic the soothing sounds of nature), sunrise alarm clocks (which gradually emit light over a period of time to simulate the sun rise and help us wake gently), binaural beats (which contain frequencies that entrain our brains to reach particular mental states, such as calm or sleepiness), guided meditations, sleep hypnosis videos, and subliminals (which can train the mind with subconscious messages conducive to sleep). And if you're still finding insomnia a problem, there are all sorts of alternative therapies that can help, including massage, reflexology, acupuncture, acupressure, yoga, Ayurveda, hypnosis, Reiki, chiropractic treatment, herbal medicine, and homeopathy. Perhaps the most powerful alternative medicine of all is meditation, which research suggests is a particularly effective way of treating insomnia.[258]

CONCLUSIONS

Thanks to a growing body of scientific evidence on its benefits, now more than ever, we know that a good night's sleep is vital to human health and well-being. A side effect of our hectic modern lives has been an epidemic of sleep deprivation that has direct links with the explosion of chronic disease we see in the world today. Thankfully, it is one of the consequences of modernity we can solve most easily, with simple sleep hygiene tips enabling us to sleep smarter, live healthier, and feel happier.

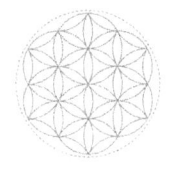

CHAPTER 8

EXERCISE

To enjoy the glow of good health, you must exercise.
—Gene Tunny

As humans are part of the animal kingdom, we were born to be outdoor creatures. Our hunter-gatherer ancestors lived in physically demanding environments and were constantly on the move, so our anatomy is designed to walk, run, and play. The human body has been evolutionarily adapted to intersperse light exercises like walking with high-intensity activities such as sprinting, jumping, and climbing, which require fitness, flexibility, balance, and strength. Cardiorespiratory fitness has consistently been shown to be one of the strongest determinants of long-term health, so we can assume that our nomadic ancestors were very fit and healthy indeed. Unsurprisingly, chronic illnesses such as heart disease are rare among hunter-gatherer tribes, yet in today's modern society, it is the world's number one killer.

Shockingly, our sedentary lifestyles are now the fourth leading factor in mortality worldwide, according to the latest WHO statistics.[259] It is simply not healthy for the human body to be physically inactive, yet as modern living has given us effort-saving technology at the same time as ramping up long hours at the office, we have become increasingly immobile. Research shows that hunter-gatherers typically cover around eight miles a day (around sixteen- to seventeen-thousand steps), whereas the average American now gets about five thousand steps a day,[260] and the average Brit only three- to four-thousand steps.[261] We spend most of our time indoors, sitting at desks glued to screens and devices. According to research by the British Heart Foundation, Brits spend around 9.5 hours a day sitting, which equates to a staggering sixty-seven hours per week.[262] Excessive sitting—dubbed "the new smoking"—is linked to around fifty thousand deaths a year in the UK. Our sedentary lifestyles are indeed killing us.

So, what exactly is it about exercise that makes it so enormously beneficial for our health? In the following sections, we take a look at the effects of physical activity on both our body and mind before describing how important exercise is for the other pillars of health.

THE PHYSICAL BENEFITS OF EXERCISE

Exercise—defined as any activity that involves movement and burns calories—is perhaps most widely known for its weight loss benefits, which help to reduce obesity and related health risks. Certainly, exercise can help to boost our metabolism so that we burn more calories, and when combined with strength training, it can maximize fat loss while increasing muscle mass. The more muscle we have, the more calories we burn, which helps to keep the weight off for good. But the health gains of being physically active certainly do not end there. Exercise does everything from improving heart health to enhancing our gut microbiome and strengthening our immune system, regulating hormonal function, increasing muscle and bone strength, boosting energy levels, and increasing lifespans.

Heart Health

Let's start with the role exercise plays in heart health. The fitter we are, the better our muscles are at pulling oxygen out of the blood, reducing the need for our heart to pump more blood around the body. This lowers our resting heart rate, which puts less stress on this vital organ. Exercise also lowers blood pressure and cholesterol levels, which reduces the risk of cardiovascular disease and stroke while protecting the kidneys and aiding blood filtration. A strong heart helps us to detoxify, as the more we pump blood around our bodies, the easier it is for the liver and lymphatic system to do their job. Physical activity increases blood circulation, sweat production, and lymphatic flow, as well as cleansing the skin as we work up a sweat.

Microbiome Health

Another important (but little-known) benefit of exercise is that it is very beneficial for our gut. Exercise helps us to increase our good bacteria, enriching microbial diversity, which in turn helps us to stay healthy. It does this by increasing blood flow to the muscles in our digestive system so that food is metabolized more efficiently while boosting intestinal activity so that we are better able to get rid of waste. By supporting our digestive system, physical activity can help to reduce constipation, bloating, gas, and IBS symptoms. Studies show that within as little as six weeks, exercise can improve our microbiome independent of diet and other factors—and the healthier our gut flora, the healthier our immune systems become.[263]

Immune System Health

Exercise has been shown to have a hugely positive impact on our immune system, increasing antibodies that fight bacteria and viruses. As we breathe harder, physical activity flushes bacteria out of our lungs, making us less susceptible to respiratory illnesses. Exercise also raises our body temperature, which can help fight bacteria in a similar way to a fever. Moreover, physical activity promotes natural killer cells that protect against disease—so much so that the American Cancer Society has linked exercise to a lower risk of thirteen different types of cancer.[264] Because physical activity has such a positive impact on our gut and immune system, overall inflammation is reduced, which dramatically lowers the risk of chronic disease. In contrast, a lack of regular exercise—even in the short term—can lead to significant increases in visceral (belly) fat, which may increase the risk of a chronic condition.

However, there is an important caveat here: the frequency, duration and intensity of physical activity makes a big difference to inflammation levels. Moderate exercise for an hour or less has been found to be optimal for reducing inflammation, but any more than this can actually contribute to it. Chronic inflammation not only correlates with chronic disease but has been associated with less muscle mass and strength, so endurance athletes must be careful to balance their intense workouts with strategic rests, restorative movement, and a strict anti-inflammatory diet.

Muscle and Bone Strength

Another important function of exercise is that it increases muscle and bone strength. Bones can be strengthened by both resistance training, such as lifting weights, and weight-bearing exercises, such as walking, running, hiking, climbing or dancing. Such activities are especially important the older we get, as bone density decreases after around fifty years of age, particularly among women (when estrogen, a hormone that protects bones, decreases sharply). As we age, we need weight-bearing exercise to prevent osteoporosis (thinning of bones) and fractures.

Energy Boosting

Exercise also raises energy levels, improving mitochondrial biogenesis where new mitochondria, the energy factories of our bodies, are created. Aerobic activity boosts heart and lung health, which helps us to feel significantly more energized and vital. Research has found exercise to be better than anything else at reducing chronic fatigue syndrome and has even been able to raise the energy levels of people with chronic diseases such as cancer and heart disease.[265]

Increased Longevity

Finally, because of its numerous health benefits, exercise increases longevity. As we have seen, it dramatically lowers the risk of disease, and it also reduces oxidative stress, decreasing free radicals and tissue damage in the body. Research has found that all-cause mortality is decreased by a staggering 30 to 35 percent just by exercising.[266] Simply taking the recommended amount of exercise of 150 minutes or more per week, life expectancy can be increased by about seven years compared to people who are not regularly active.

EXERCISE AND MENTAL HEALTH

Being active is key to living not only longer but happier. Because of its positive impact on our gut, exercise leads to the release of happy hormones, which greatly benefit our mental health. Books such as *The Joy of Movement* by Kelly McGonigal,[267] *Move!* by Caroline Willams[268] and *Spark* by Dr John Ratey[269] reveal just how important exercise is for brain health and mental well-being.

Brain Benefits

Exercise increases blood flow and oxygen to the brain, with amazing results for our cognitive health. With lots of available blood nutrients, our brains are fueled for optimal performance, triggering biochemical changes that allow new brain cells to develop (called "neurogenesis") while creating neuroplasticity by encouraging new neural connections. A key benefit of exercise is that it increases the size of the hippocampus, the area of the brain responsible for learning and memory. Our brains literally grow the more physically active we are. The fact that we can bolster the hippocampus with exercise is important because it is the first region of our brain to decline with age. Forget crosswords; if we want to keep our memory and cognitive skills sharp as we get older, a short burst of exercise—even just ten minutes a day—is one of the best ways to do this.

Aerobic exercise also triggers the release of growth factors, which are proteins necessary for your brain to create neural connections. Movement thus triggers proteins that help your brain to generate new cells and preserve aging ones. Exercise also helps to create new blood vessels in and around the brain, which increases the circulation of nutrients that help us to stay smart. Regular movement also slows down the aging of the brain. Research shows that older people who are physically active in their youth consistently outperform their peers in cognitive skills and memory tests, with scores that match other test-takers ten years younger.[270] Exercising in midlife is an important way of lowering the risk of dementia, which reduces by 30 percent with regular physical activity—for Alzheimer's specifically, exercise can reduce the risks by an incredible 45 percent.[271] Exercise also lowers blood pressure and stretches blood vessels, which helps prevent blood clots and brain aneurysms.

Interestingly, it is not just aerobic exercise that has cognitive benefits—resistance and strength training can also have brain-boosting results, as well as low-impact activities such as yoga and tai chi, which reduce stress while honing concentration skills. Varying activities between high- and low-impact exercise, aerobic, resistance, and balance training all have amazing benefits for the brain.

For optimal results, it is better to exercise more often—but not more intensely. Even twenty to thirty minutes a day can help to increase cognitive function and mental health, which means just having a good stretch, dancing to your favorite song, or walking to work can lift your mood and "future-proof" your brain in old age. The main thing is to get active—after all, we were born to move.

The Feel-Good Factor

Our brain and body need physical activity to relax. One of the amazing benefits of exercise is that it regulates hormonal function and keeps cortisol in check. This means that exercise can lower our stress levels, which makes it essential to help us rise to the challenges of modern living. Crucially, though, this only applies if we don't overexercise, as too much high-intensity activity actually increases cortisol, making us more stressed, not less. Exercise stimulates the production of endorphins, which are the body's natural mood elevators and painkillers, making us less susceptible to anxiety, depression, and pain. In the olden days, the recommendation for treating chronic pain was rest, but now research suggests that light exercise not only helps to reduce pain but raises pain tolerance and decreases pain perception.[272]

The endorphins released in the brain clear away anxiety and boost our mood, which is why exercise makes us feel so good and plays a major role in good mental health. Because it is so beneficial for our gut and brain, exercise also increases our levels of serotonin, GABA, oxytocin, and dopamine, which means that regular physical activity ensures we are awash with feel-good chemicals. This why some people become exercise fanatics—physical activity is addictive! Recent research suggests that the euphoric feeling that you get after a great workout (commonly known as "runner's high") is the result not just of endorphins but "endocannabinoids," which are a class of neurochemicals that mimic the effects of cannabis.[273] Studies show that endocannabinoids not only reduce anxiety and depression but also make us more social, generous, and cooperative.

In *The Joy of Movement*, Kelly McGonigal[274] explains that enterprising initiatives like the GoodGym in London capitalize on the social benefits of exercise by organizing communal runs where members volunteer to plant trees, clean up communal areas, and help elderly people with house maintenance and gardening. McGonigal explains that the feel-good factor of exercise would have had an evolutionary benefit by keeping us hunting and gathering for longer periods, which would have made it more likely we would survive. The increased feelings of cooperation and generosity after a hunt would have also encouraged people to share their spoils with the tribe.

Building Self-Esteem and Mental Strength Through Exercise

Exercise can also enhance self-esteem. This is not just because of its body-sculpting benefits; setting ourselves physical challenges like running a marathon encourages us to face our fears and overcome limiting beliefs. This empowers us to see what we are truly capable of and helps us to gain huge confidence by achieving what we once considered impossible. Physical challenges can even help people overcome phobias such as a fear of heights or cold. Wim Hoff has famously trained thousands of people to swim in freezing waters by teaching them the power of the mind to face physical challenges.

McGonigal explains that the reason challenging exercise works so well in building self-esteem is that it gives people a sense of control. By setting themselves a challenge, people can experience their own fortitude and resilience in a controlled way, which sets them up to believe in themselves when life's unexpected ups and downs arise. Challenges help us grow, and physical challenges are no different. Performing a powerful or courageous feat sends a message to your brain that you are strong. In this way, exercise can transform our deepest understanding of ourselves, helping us transcend limiting mindsets. Statistically, an unusually high proportion of ultramarathon runners and Iron Man athletes have experienced depression in the past; this is because many choose these intense activities to overcome mental health issues. They know that as well as increasing feelings of well-being, endurance sports enhance mental strength, stamina, and resilience that carries over to other aspects of life.

Green Exercise

An even more impactful way of boosting the positive benefits of physical activity is exercising outside. So-called green exercise combines the brain-boosting effects of movement with the power of nature to lift our mood and invigorate us. As we discussed in Chapter 4, nature has a very soothing effect on both body and mind, helping us relax by activating the parasympathetic nervous system and filling us with detoxifying airborne chemicals (such as phytoncides from plants and trees or negative ions from moving water). Combined with the stress-relieving benefits of exercise, being active outdoors can have enormous benefits for our mental as well as physical health. A plethora of studies have shown that outdoor exercise is much better for our physical and mental well-being than exercising indoors, with greater reductions in emotional tension, anger, and depression.[275]

McGonigal cites research that shows the natural brain states of people indoors versus outdoors lean toward negativity, making us more prone to anxiety, rumination, and self-criticism. Conversely, when we are in nature, our default brain state is more relaxed and calmer—we slip into a mindful state researchers call "soft fascination," where our brain patterns more closely resemble those seen in regular meditators. According to psychologist Alexandra Rosati, these two brain states, indoor rumination and outdoor mindfulness, correspond to the distinct types of cognition that were essential for our ancestors' survival. The ruminating state helps us to think about people and relationships within small groups, while the mindful state derives from a "foraging cognition," which enables us to be alert while hunting and gathering food. People who spend more time exercising in nature develop more of this foraging condition, which leads to greater happiness and life purpose.

As mentioned in Chapter 4, the numerous studies on shinrin-yoku (forest bathing) in Japan have shown that people who engage in green exercise have lower levels of cortisol, blood pressure, and heart rates.[276] A breath of fresh air also helps us to sleep better, which helps our body recover from exercise.[277] Exposure to direct sunlight can also have benefits for our health. Sunshine provides vitamin D, invigorating the body by oxidating muscles and boosting energy levels while lifting our spirits and making us feel happier. Sunshine is also a natural antimicrobial, with a die-off rate for bacteria and viruses of a staggering 90 to 99 percent within just a few minutes of sunning ourselves.[278]

The benefits of green exercise have given rise to what is known as ecotherapy (also called nature therapy), which is rooted in the idea that people are part of the web of life, and so our well-being is intimately connected with our relationship to nature. Ecotherapy combines forest bathing and nature meditations with green exercise and conservation activities to support physical and mental health. Cited as one of the biggest wellness trends of the last few years, the healing power of nature is far from new, but ecotherapy is gaining traction among conventional and alternative medicine practitioners alike as the evidence for the benefits of green exercise grows.

Synchronized Movement

As the name of McGonigal's book[279] suggests, the joy of movement goes far beyond hitting the gym or training for ultramarathons. She describes the remarkable effects of synchronized movement, such as line dancing, crew rowing, or simply walking in step for community spirit and bonding. It is actually an ancient human reflex to align our breathing, heartbeat, and brainwaves to another person close to us because it encourages feelings of unity and harmony. Coordinated rhythmic movement entrains the brain to be in harmony with another person, acting as a sign of similarity that promotes a feeling of connection, belonging, and common purpose.

A 2023 article in the Scientific American explains that when people feel connected with each other, their brain waves actually sync up. This process, known as "interbrain synchrony," happens when neurons in different brains activate at the same time, forming identical patterns. As the interaction goes on, neurons become increasingly aligned. become increasingly aligned.[280]

Moving in unison helps people to feel in sync and therefore more bonded, which heightens feelings of empathy, cooperation, kindness, and trust. It is also a key factor in creating collective joy; the sociologist Emile Durkheim called this "collective effervescence" because it helps us leave our separate egos behind and find a more transcendent state of unity. Exercise can thus benefit us socially and spiritually as well as boost our health.

EXERCISE SUPPORTS THE OTHER PILLARS OF HEALTH

As we have discussed, exercise is vital for stress management because it helps us to relax—but crucially, only if we don't overdo it. One of the problems with a "work hard, play hard" approach to life is that it can lead to adrenal fatigue, and overexercising can seriously contribute to burnout if we push ourselves too far. Modern life can be exhausting, so it is often counterproductive to hit the gym when we are at our lowest ebb. When we feel stressed, activities such as walking in nature or doing a yoga class can help to create a deep relaxation response that is far better for body and mind than a punishing workout. As with everything in life, moderation is key, although today, most people do need to ramp up their exercise routines, not downsize them.

Another recommendation for stress management is to be less rigid about our exercise regime. In *The Four Pillar Plan*,[281] Dr. Rangan Chatterjee highlights that compartmentalizing physical activity into structured workouts at the beginning or end of the day while being sedentary for the rest of the time is not as helpful as moving regularly throughout the day, as our hunter-gatherer ancestors once did. While we may not be so free to roam as they were, we can still take time out for brief walks or get up from our desks and stretch at regular intervals so that our bodies do not become too tight. Poor posture only fuels the stress we feel, and over time, the increased inflammation, aches, and pains in our body will have a compound effect on exhaustion levels and corresponding mood. Chatterjee concludes that the antidote to sitting is not necessarily going to the gym but simply getting up and moving around. Moving unlocks stress in our bodies, and if we can marry that with a breath of fresh air outdoors, we feel all the better for it. A simple walk in the woods can be all it takes to create a sense of mental well-being that improves the way we handle the stresses and strains of everyday life.

Another reason why exercise is so crucial to our health is that it helps us to sleep better. The energy loss that occurs during exercise stimulates restorative processes during sleep, helping to improve the quality of our rest. Moreover, because exercise increases our body temperature, this can help to improve sleep quality when our temperature drops during sleep. Because we sleep better, we inevitably have more energy when we wake, which increases our motivation to exercise. This becomes a virtuous circle, encouraging a cascade of health benefits as our mood lifts and we feel more prepared to take on the challenges of the day.

There is also an obvious relationship between exercise and nutrition. Exercise burns energy; food provides it. However, the link goes much further than that. As we discussed in Chapter 4, the nutrition we give our bodies has a direct correlation with how much energy we have and how stressed we feel. If we are eating poorly, we may not have the motivation to work out, and even if we do manage to drag ourselves out for a jog or bike ride, poor food choices may mean our body does not have the nutrients it needs to build and repair our muscles, so progress is slow. Moreover, if our postworkout meal is of the fast-food variety, we can easily cancel out all the stress-relieving, mood-elevating effects of our physical activity, not to mention the calories we just burned. Most people underestimate the calories in snack foods, so grabbing a chocolate bar as we leave the gym can easily wipe out the weight loss benefits of a single exercise session.

It is important to note that considering food and exercises as simply "calories in minus calories out" can also have its problems, leading to restrictive eating habits and obsessive exercising, which does little to nourish or honor the body. What we need to focus on is getting the balance right. Good nutrition can give us more energy and encourage a regular fitness program. A healthy meal plan that dovetails with our exercise regime can give us greater motivation to go for that power walk on a cold winter's morning, and conversely, regular exercise helsp us to feel more like eating nutritiously. Moreover, the combination of a balanced diet and regular exercise can make us feel better about ourselves, helping us to build self-esteem and feel more positive about life in general.

CONCLUSIONS

This chapter has highlighted the crucial role that exercise plays in a healthy lifestyle. Being active not only brings us physical benefits, it creates mental health that cascades into other areas of our life, bringing us emotional well-being and resilience, as well as potential social, environmental, and spiritual connection. This leads us to the third section of the book, where we offer a big-picture view of health from an individual, societal, and planetary perspective.

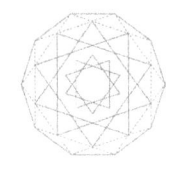

PART 3:
THE FIFTH PILLAR OF HEALTH—CONNECTION

When people go within and connect to themselves, they realise they are connected to the universe and to all living beings.
—Armand Dimele

As we have seen from our discussion, the key pillars of health impact each other in profound ways, creating virtuous—or vicious—circles, depending on our choices. Each pillar exerts an influence on every other aspect of our health, highlighting how our bodies are a miraculous web of relationships and interactions. Clearly, it's folly to see our health issues in isolation because this kind of reductionist thinking has unintended consequences. For instance, a stressful job with long work hours can ruin our sleep hygiene, causing us to stress eat and put on weight. This can increase feelings of anxiety and body consciousness, which creates more stress and starts a vicious cycle. To take off the pounds, we might add in a boot camp exercise regimen that exhausts us further, so we end up stress eating more. As our waistline continues to expand, we might go on a crash diet that feeds the wrong gut bacteria, weakening our immune systems and causing us to become ill. Now we are bedridden and sick, and none the slimmer, fitter, or healthier for it.

We need to stop looking for fast and easy solutions and instead honor our bodies by educating ourselves on the key pillars of health so that we can make wiser choices. Understanding how exercise, nutrition, sleep, and relaxation all interact together can help us to lead healthier, happier lives and reach our full potential in life. Moreover, having a solid foundation of health is essential for maintaining our flexibility and adaptability in the face of change. When these pillars are balanced, we have a sturdy base, so we can withstand the pressures of modern living, dance with the challenges of life and adapt easily to unforeseen triggers that come our way. All this means looking at our health more holistically. When you think about it, it's not necessarily illness that causes the collapse of our health, but the collapse of our health that causes illness. Flexibility and adaptability are skills we need to hone, as they are vital to ensuring that we stay within our stress thresholds and avoid the lifestyle diseases that are so common today. This simple insight has been known since antiquity. Lao Tzu put it simply in *Tao Te Ching*, verse 76: "Stiffness is a companion of death, flexibility a companion of life . . . An army without flexibility never wins a battle. A tree that is unbending is easily broken."

The four pillars discussed so far are so intertwined that it is obvious that the overarching fifth pillar is connection. This pillar is often overlooked in health models despite its obvious importance to well-being, and when it is acknowledged, it is usually limited to social connection. However, as this book is based on a systems view of health, the next section takes a much broader view, looking at the importance of the mind-body connection in healing before delving into the role of social, environmental, and spiritual connection in the well-being of humanity and the planet.

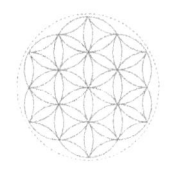

CHAPTER 9

THE MIND-BODY CONNECTION

Your mind is in every cell of your body.
—Candace Pert

In the last few chapters, we have seen the crucial interplay between our biology and our psychology, how our health has a significant impact on our state of mind and vice versa. In the next sections, we discuss the growing body of research on the mind-body connection, including a plethora of compelling evidence for the power of the mind in healing. The mind-body medicine revolution of the last half-century has provided the final nail in the coffin for outmoded dualistic beliefs about mind versus matter, ushering in a more systemic approach to healing that will no doubt have huge reverberations for the pioneering healthcare solutions of the future.

Because the mind-body connection is such a huge subject, it is split into two chapters. In this chapter, we look at the remarkable implications of the placebo effect and the profound impact that our attitudes and beliefs have on our physical as well as mental well-being. The role of positive thinking and visualization on neuroplasticity and health is explored, including the importance of dealing with any past traumas at the root of our health concerns. The next chapter explores mind-body medicine techniques, including the efficacy of meditation and mindfulness, yoga, breathwork, and hypnosis, as well as psychotherapy and alternative medicine techniques for encouraging health and well-being.

MIND OVER MATTER: THE PLACEBO EFFECT

So, just how powerful is our mind in healing our bodies? Well, a great deal, if the placebo effect is anything to go by. The placebo effect is the most tried and tested response there is, because every clinical drug trial in the world has to show that the drug outperforms a placebo to be approved. A placebo is a dummy treatment, such as a sugar pill, that is not designed to have any therapeutic effect. Yet because patients believe they are being given a real drug, it works—in anywhere from 15 percent to a staggering 72 percent of cases.[282]

The placebo effect is an undisputed medical fact. The implications of it are profound because it highlights just how important our beliefs are in determining our health and well-being. The mere thought that something is going to heal us creates an expectation that has tangible therapeutic effects, as the anticipation causes chemical reactions in our brain that cascade into biological changes in the cells of our bodies.

Studies have found that placebos believed to be painkillers increase the production of endorphins, the body's natural pain relievers. A 2016 metastudy of thirty-nine drug trials for neurological issues such as spinal cord injuries, strokes and multiple sclerosis found that placebos produced the same pain-relieving effect as pharmaceuticals, with no difference between the severity or type of condition.[283] In Jo Marchant's bestselling book *Cure*,[284] she highlights research that found that placebo pills can alleviate cancer pain as much as the powerful sedative ketamine.

The placebo effect is so impactful that in the book *Supernature*,[285] author Lyall Watson cites a study where the test group were told they were being given a sleeping pill, but one of the participants was secretly given a stimulant. Despite this, he or she slept soundly through the night with the rest of the group. In another experiment, the reverse happened; the group were told they were being given a stimulant, but one was secretly given a sleeping pill. True to form, everyone stayed up all night, including the placebo taker.

The placebo effect has been shown to work on all manner of diseases and ailments—and they are not just limited to pills. In one meta-analysis of seventy-nine studies, maladies were reduced by sugar pills in 22 percent of cases, fake acupuncture in 38 percent of cases, and sham surgery in a staggering 58 percent of cases.[286] Fake surgeries are perhaps the most astonishing indicator of the power of the mind, with studies finding placebos to be just as effective as state-of-the-art operations in treating a range of conditions, from angina to arthritis. A meta-analysis of fifty-three sham surgeries showed that an astounding twenty-seven trials were just as effective as a real operation, and a similar number showed comparative improvements.[287]

A well-known study of sham surgeries was published in the New England Journal of Medicine in 2002, when 180 patients with degenerative osteoarthritis of the knee were put into three groups and told they were receiving surgery. Two groups received the surgery as expected, and the third one received a fake surgery. The sham patients were put under anesthetic, received an incision (so it seemed as though they'd had an operation) and then revived. At a postsurgery follow-up two years later, all three groups were better, walking and climbing up the stairs with no discernible difference between them.[288] In another study published in the journal *Radiology* in 2011, the practice of "vertebroplasty," whereby fractured bones are injected with cement to reduce pain, was later found to be entirely due to the placebo effect.[289] The researchers concluded that: "'Placebo efficacy' does not imply that there is anything fake about the effectiveness of an intervention that works by means of the placebo response. On the contrary, extensive scientific experiments elucidating placebo effects, especially with respect to pain, have demonstrated that the placebo response is a real neurobiological phenomenon with potential for clinically meaningful benefit."

Placebos are so effective that many doctors have admitted to regularly prescribing them for a range of health conditions.[290] Interestingly, the shape and color of a tablet can make a difference. Larger pills tend to produce a stronger effect than small pills. Red, orange, and yellow are associated with stimulants, while blue and green are associated with tranquilizers. More expensive packaging increases the effect of the placebo, as does branded versus generic medication, which gives people the expectation that it will be more effective. There is also a relationship between the strength of a person's expectations and the effect; the stronger the anticipation, the bigger the impact. The more we believe in our medicine, the more it works. The same is true for side effects; if people expect to experience negative reactions such as nausea or headaches, the more likely these will occur.

Neuroscientist Joe Dispenza is a leading authority on the mind-body connection and has written extensively on the subject. In his acclaimed book *You Are the Placebo*,[291] he describes the results of a drug trial for depression, where the placebo group were told they were receiving an antidepressant with nausea as a potential side effect. After a few weeks, the placebo group reported a more uplifted mood and electroencephalogram (EEG) measurements showed increased activity in the prefrontal cortex of the brain (which is normally reduced in people with depression). Interestingly, the placebo group also reported nausea as a side effect. In other studies, cancer patients who were told they would feel nausea after chemotherapy treatment often started to feel sick even before the treatment started.

Dispenza makes an impressive case for the power of the mind in healing. In one case, a man suffering from cancer was given a placebo, which reduced his tumors, but as soon as he was told that he'd received a placebo, the tumors tragically returned, and he died shortly after. This is indicative of just how much people underestimate the mind-body connection—because we equate placebos with the word *fake*, the power of the mind in healing is somehow considered an illusion. Yet the key is in Dispenza's title—*You are the placebo*. He makes the case that our consciousness can shrink tumors and cure cancer—the external remedy may simply be a prop with which to harness the power of the mind to get well.

Nocebos

As well as placebos, there is also a "nocebo" effect, where people believe that something benign will have a negative impact. A classic example is a case published in the British Medical Journal in 1995,[292] where a builder was admitted to the hospital in agony after jumping down onto a six-inch nail that penetrated all the way through his boot. He was in so much pain that he was administered fentanyl, the most powerful painkiller known to man. When doctors removed the nail and took his boot off to examine the damage, to their surprise, they found that it had slipped between his toes. His foot was completely uninjured; the pain had been entirely psychological. This is not to say that it wasn't real—the builder's lived experience was exactly how it would have felt like to have your foot pierced from a great height by a sharp object. But the pain was created by his beliefs and expectations about what had happened, demonstrating just how powerful our mind is in creating our reality. Pain, in particular, is never purely biological—it has so much to do with our thoughts, perceptions, and emotions.

In *Cure*, Jo Marchant describes another incredible case, where a man in the placebo group for a clinical trial for antidepressants got into an argument with his girlfriend and tried to commit suicide by taking all his antidepressants at once. He was rushed to the hospital with a racing heartbeat and plummeting blood pressure, but when he was told that he'd only been taking sugar pills, all his symptoms disappeared. The man had created the experience of a drug overdose simply with the power of his beliefs.

Honest Placebos

Because placebos can impact the same biochemical pathways as drugs, they have been known to have an effect even when the person knows they are taking them. These are called honest placebos and have been used to treat everything from pain, sleep disorders, depression, and menopause to irritable bowel syndrome. There are now promising lines of research into "placebo-controlled dose reduction" (PCDR), where medication is swapped for placebos over time to lower the dosage of drug treatments. PCDR can reduce the risk of side effects and dramatically reduce the cost of healthcare, not to mention empower people by showing them the potency of their minds.

Positive Consultation

The patient, doctor, and situation all have an effect in creating the right conditions for placebos to work. Our expectations are influenced by what we are told about a treatment, as well as its nature. For instance, sham surgeries often have a larger placebo effect than sugar pills because there is a ceremony and gravitas to the procedure that increases the expectation of the patient. The attitude of the doctor also plays a big role. Studies have found that the way a doctor frames a treatment or therapy has a major effect on the outcome; if they seem confident that a treatment will work, it is more likely to be a success than if they seem doubtful or unsure. In his bestseller *Why Woo-Woo Works*, Dr. David Hamilton talks about the power of positive consultation.[293] He cites a study in the British Medical Journal that compared patients who were given a firm diagnosis and a confident prognosis of a speedy recovery with those whose doctor seemed uncertain of what was wrong and how to treat it. Both positive and nonpositive consultation groups were given a placebo. After a couple of weeks, almost double the amount of people in the positive group were better compared with the nonpositive group, highlighting just how much our healing is influenced by the perceived expectations of others, as well as the way healthcare providers communicate with us.

Words can be self-fulfilling prophesies; they cast spells (hence the word *spelling*), which is why there are ethical considerations for doctors who have the unenviable task of telling people how long they may have to live. In one tragic case, Joe Dispenza describes a man who died from cancer after receiving a false positive on a scan, despite the autopsy showing that his cancer was nowhere near the fatal stage. As Dispenza puts it, "he died, quite simply, because everyone in his immediate environment thought he was dying."

SPONTANEOUS HEALINGS

All this highlights just how incredible the mind-body connection is in healing, as well as in our experience of reality. We can harness the power of our minds by having a strong intention to transform our health and, with self-belief and determination, make breakthroughs that might have otherwise been considered impossible. We've all heard of athletes with irreversible injuries who have fully recovered, or people with life-threatening cancers that have miraculously disappeared a few months later. Our biology and psychology are in fact so powerful that spontaneous healings have happened since the days of antiquity, with reports of paraplegics walking again and the blind suddenly regaining their sight. While these were once attributed to supernatural causes, science shows that the higher intelligence of our body and mind is indeed capable of miraculous things.

In fact, there is much evidence to suggest that the body has its own wisdom. In the ground-breaking book *Molecules of Emotion*,[294] the pioneering work of renowned neuroscientist Candace Pert in the 1980s showed that human intelligence human intelligence, once thought to be located purely in the brain, actually exists all over the body. Every thought and emotion we have creates messenger molecules (known as "neuropeptides") which attach to our cells. The brain then reads this information and converts it into innumerable streams of neurochemicals, which our bodies harmonise like a genius conductor of a world-class symphony orchestra, ensuring that everything from our heart and lungs to our muscles and nerves works in perfect unison. Deepak Chopra, in his foreword to Amit Goswami's *The Quantum Doctor*,[295] writes: "Thanks to hundreds of thousands of receptor sites on the outer membrane of each cell, we have no doubt that the qualities once ascribed to the brain—including intelligence and conscious awareness—are shared with the rest of the body."

Thanks to such scientific discoveries, the mind-body connection is now irrefutable. In his book *Evolve Your Brain*, Dispenza describes how the proteins of our body scan 3.2 billion DNA sequences for mutations, reading our biology better than any supercomputer.[296] Dispenza makes the case that when we tap into this higher intelligence, we can heal our ailments at the deepest level—sometimes even spontaneously.

The mind-body connection is so extraordinary that people suffering from multiple personality disorders can display biological changes with each personality. In Barry Cohen's book *Multiple Personality Disorder from the Inside Out*,[297] he describes cases where the medical conditions of one personality, such as epilepsy, diabetes, or an allergy to wasp stings, disappear when another personality takes over. Similarly, a drugged personality can become instantly sober when the switch is made, and visual acuity can differ, with one personality needing glasses while another does not. Incredibly, even the eye color of different personalities can change, and moles can appear and disappear at will. Each personality has a unique brainwave pattern and even a unique voice print that is impossible to mimic. Multiple personalities challenge all our preconceptions of the inevitability of our physical as well as mental states, suggesting that somewhere deep in our psyche, we can change our reality by consciousness alone. What we call miracles start in our own minds.

THE POWER OF POSITIVE THINKING

If our thoughts are really that potent, can we heal ourselves simply with the power of positive thinking? This is a question that numerous bestsellers have attempted to answer, including *How Your Mind Can Heal Your Body* by Dr. David Hamilton,[298] *The Power of Positive Thinking* by Norman Vincent Peale,[299] and *When the Body Says No* by Dr. Gabor Mate.[300]

In *How Your Mind Can Heal Your Body*, Hamilton highlights numerous studies which show that optimists live longer than pessimists. One study spanning thirty years by the Mayo Clinic found that those who saw the bright side of life had an astonishing 50 percent lower risk of early death.[301] Positive thinking seems to have a protective function, boosting our immunity and making us less susceptible to getting sick or suffering pain. Optimists have more energy and zest for life, as well as being generally happier and calmer than pessimists. Having a good giggle with friends and family acts like a natural antidepressant, lifting our spirits, releasing stress, increasing friendliness, and enhancing cognitive function.[302] Laughing and taking ourselves less seriously can also help us to step out of egoistic behavioral patterns, encouraging different perspectives and a new, more uplifting attitude toward life.

Studies show that our mental attitude particularly affects our heart, with a positive outlook giving us up to a 77 percent reduced risk of death from heart disease.[303] Considering that it's the world's number one killer, this is an incredible statistic. Hamilton highlights how hostility impacts our heart—"Hard Marriage, Hard Heart" is the title of one review paper he cites, which found that anger and bitterness in relationships can lead to hardened arteries. In fact, according to scientific research, hostility is just as reliable an indicator of heart disease as diet and lifestyle. Conversely, kind-hearted people have huge reductions in inflammation, better stress responses, and much healthier immune systems.[304]

Heart Wisdom

Research by the HeartMath Institute builds on these findings, highlighting that there is not just a gut-brain axis but a heart-brain connection too.[305] A little-known fact is that our heart sends more signals to the brain than the brain does to the heart, and consequently, the activity of this vital organ has a major impact on the way we think and feel. Negative emotions like anger and frustration make our hearts beat erratically, which sends disordered neural signals to the brain, resulting in an inability to think clearly, learn, or remember things under duress. Conversely, a coherent heart rhythm (a regular sine-wave form) occurs when we are experiencing uplifting emotions such as joy and appreciation, which in turn encourages peak performance thinking. A coherent heart rhythm is not to be confused with the relaxation response, which entails a lower heart rate. Instead, heart coherency is predicated on sustained positive emotions, which create harmony in our brain and nervous system. Research shows that positive emotions like love and gratitude not only make us happier and healthier but wiser, too, because our brains actually work better when we feel this way. It is interesting to note that historically, people in every culture have referred to the "wisdom of the heart," and the pioneering work of HeartMath suggests that this link may be more than merely metaphorical. As mentioned in Chapter 3, our mental and physical states are so intertwined that just thinking of things that annoy us will produce stress hormones in the body. Whether or not we act on our frustrations, ruminating or complaining about them has a similarly malefic effect. And not only that, but complaining is a sure way to raise not just our own stress levels but those of the people around us, making them more likely to see things negatively too. Emotions are often more contagious than disease—but luckily, studies show that positive feelings are far more catching than negative ones.[306]

As Hamilton points out, the good news is that just as we can change our lifestyles, we can also change our attitudes. Kind thoughts and compassionate acts produce hormones like the love hormone oxytocin, which reduces cortisol and boosts our immune system. Research shows that a simple hug that lasts for twenty seconds or more is enough to produce oxytocin, reducing inflammation in the body as well as creating a stronger bond between huggers.[307] Pets can keep us healthy, too, by triggering the love hormone. A Japanese study found that people who spent half an hour with their dogs, including time spent gazing into their eyes, produced an astounding 300 percent spike in oxytocin.[308] Many hospitals employ therapy dogs to visit patients for this reason.

According to scientific research, the idea that "love cures all" may have real truth to it. A recent study by UCLA found that women who had recently fallen in love had higher levels of activity in the genes involved in viral defense.[309] Self-love also has a powerful impact on health; a 2019 study by Oxford and Exeter University found that self-compassion switches off the stress response, which damages our immune systems.[310] As the Dalai Lama reminds us, "love and compassion are necessities, not luxuries. Without them, humanity cannot survive."

In his acclaimed book *The Power of Positive Thinking*, Norman Vincent Peale explains why pessimism can result in a spiral effect. When we think negatively, we are more likely to experience negative outcomes, including a decline in health. If we then complain and blame others because of those outcomes, we start a vicious cycle that can spiral into a victim mentality, causing us to live in perpeta survival state. When we live in perpetual survival mode, we create more stress and suffering, which means we are more likely to miss the opportunities that life presents us with. These destructive thought patterns can make us feel stuck in a rut, playing out as constant negative experiences and life circumstances.

While it is true that some people face more difficulties and challenges than others, it is equally true that we can choose how adverse circumstances affect us and, therefore, how much stress we feel about them. Instead of blaming others for our problems, when we realize that our lived experience is nothing more than the thoughts we have about those experiences, we create the possibility for a new way of living, one that is infinitely healthier and more contented. As Vincent Peale highlights, it is not the situation but our reaction to it that defines our perception of life. If we think positively, we are more likely to feel good things, which leads to a happier, more fulfilling experience of reality. In the deeply inspiring book *Man's Search for Meaning*,[311] Victor Frankl, an Auschwitz survivor, highlights this point poignantly: "We who lived in concentration camps can remember the men who walked through huts comforting others, giving away their last piece of bread. They may have been few in number, but they offer sufficient proof that everything can be taken from a man but one thing: the last of the human freedoms—to choose one's attitude in any given set of circumstances, to choose one's own way."

Neuroplasticity

One of the reasons why positive thinking works so well to keep us healthy is due to neuroplasticity. First coined by Polish neuroscientist Jerzy Konorski in 1948, neuroplasticity has become a well-studied phenomenon. Celebrated books such as *Soft-wired*[312] by pioneering neuroscientist Dr. Michael Merzenich and *The Brain That Changes Itself*[13] by Dr Norman Doidge highlight that humans have a tremendous capacity to adapt and evolve, and this includes our brain. Contrary to previous beliefs that our brains were hardwired after childhood, neuroscience has shown that the brain is constantly rewiring itself. In *Evolve Your Brain*,[314] Dispenza argues: "Just as thoughts are the language of the brain, feelings are the language of the body. And how you think and how you feel create a state of being. A state of being is when your mind and body are working together."

According to Hebb's Rule, each thought we have makes certain neurons fire, and "nerves that fire together, wire together," creating networks of neural pathways.[315] The more often we have the same thought, the stronger that neural pathway becomes until it is a well-worn track in our minds. If this is a negative track, it can lead to constant worrying, anxiety, and depression that leads to an addictive cycle of stress hormones being released, followed by more negativity. If it is positive, it leads to feelings of happiness and well-being, which releases dopamine and oxytocin, continuing the feel-good cycle. This is why regular gratitude practices and positive affirmations can be so powerful. If we can break negative mental habits and replace them with positive ones, we not only burn new neural pathways in the brain that lead to greater contentment, but we also create tangible effects in our bodies that result in flourishing health and vitality.

Our thoughts not only sculpt our brains, but they can also change our DNA. In the acclaimed bestseller *The Biology of Belief*,[316] epigenetics expert Bruce Lipton highlights that every thought you have sends a message to your genes. Our genetic activity—all the proteins, enzymes, and chemicals that regulate our cells—is significantly influenced by our beliefs and attitudes; in fact, our bodies are constantly changing in response to our internal monologues as genes are switched on or off depending on our thoughts about our life experiences. This highlights the critical importance of mental self-care because it directly impacts the very fabric of our physical health.

As we have seen from the placebo effect, what we expect tends to happen, so when we believe in ourselves and our powers of self-healing, we allow for the possibility of transformation in our lives. According to so many scientific studies, it is our beliefs and attitudes toward health that make all the difference, and when we have self-belief, crisis can become opportunity. If we acknowledge the learning and growth that occurs from our difficulties, we can start to appreciate their role in our life and how challenges help us to reach our true potential. If we actively appreciate what we've learned from hard times, we can look back and reinspire the past by seeing how good came from bad. This fuels a more optimistic outlook on life, which then attracts more positive circumstances our way. The American poet E. E. Cummings put this idea beautifully: "Once we believe in ourselves, we can risk curiosity, wonder, spontaneous delight, or any experience that reveals the human spirit."

Visualization and the Power of Our Imagination

To make the most of our inherent neuroplasticity, Dispenza highlights that there are two important ways we can evolve our brain. The first is novelty. If we want to change our lives, we need to have new experiences and learn different information so that new neural pathways are created. The second is repetition. When we consistently repeat positive thoughts or mental imagery, we strengthen those neural connections until they become solidified in our minds. We are who we think we are, so if we want to be healthy and happy, we need to consistently see ourselves that way. If we focus on happiness, we strengthen our happiness pathways; but equally, if we focus on stress, we strengthen the stress pathways in our brain.

Visual imagery is now a key aspect of mind-body medicine because our brain—and therefore our experience of reality—becomes what it habitually perceives. This is how affirmations and mental rehearsals work; repetition plants the seeds of positivity in our minds and rewires the brain for success. Visualization can make a dramatic difference to our mental health; instead of experiencing depression, frustration, or victimization, we can mentally rehearse being happy, calm, and empowered and thus train our brain to experience these states. According to Dispenza, visualization requires consistency (daily rehearsal) and depth—engaging as many emotions and senses as possible to activate more neural connections.

The reason visual imagery is so effective is because the brain does not distinguish between what is real and what is imagined. MRI scans show that whether you experience something or just visualize it, the same neural networks are fired. In *Why Woo-Woo Works,* Hamilton describes the "piano study" of 1995 by Harvard Medical School, where one group of volunteers were asked to play five notes on a piano every day for five days, while another group was asked to simply visualize playing these notes. Brain scans of the participants showed that at the end of the five days, both groups had comparable changes in the brain regions correlated to their finger muscles—to the point where it was impossible to tell the difference between those who had played the piano and those who had merely visualized it. It is incredible to think that when we practice something, our brain cannot tell the difference between mentally rehearsing and actually doing the activity. The implications are huge; it means our imagination is the key player in unlocking the human potential. When we see ourselves a certain way, we literally burn neural pathways in our brain to become that person. To quote the Buddha again: "All experience is preceded by mind, led by mind, made by mind."[317]

Sportspeople have known this for years and regularly use visualization techniques to enhance their performance. This not only improves motivation and concentration but also trains their brain for victory. It is well-known that much of an athlete's success is mental, so mastering the mind is crucial to being at the top of their game. Meta studies have found that mental rehearsal creates the neural pathways that allow sportspeople to build confidence and skill under pressure, training their muscles to perform exactly as they are supposed to. Mental training has been shown to improve motor skills while enhancing motivation and mental toughness, all of which elevate performance.[318]

This can also be applied to health and well-being. Research has shown that visualization and guided imagery reduce pain, fatigue, anxiety, and depression in people with fibromyalgia.[319] Systematic reviews on insomnia show that guided imagery is an effective way of improving sleep quality,[320] and there is also evidence that it can decrease pain in patients with cancer.[321] But it does not stop there. When we consistently visualize ourselves as healthy, we create neural connections that encourage healing. Guided visualizations have been shown to bolster the immune system—and not just because they reduce stress. Meta studies highlight compelling evidence that visualizations targeting specific cells in the immune system actually have an effect on those cells.[322] For instance, in *How Your Mind Can Heal Your Body*,[323] Hamilton cites a study by the University of Texas that found people who used imagery to increase particular antibodies known as "secretory immunoglobulin A," had more than double the levels of them in their body after six weeks compared to the control group who had just performed relaxation imagery. In another study of targeted imagery, the white blood cells of patients suffering from a range of conditions, including cancer, AIDs, endometriosis, and viral infections, increased significantly over a three-month period. Hamilton is such a proponent of the power of visualization in healing that at the end of his book he includes an A-Z of visualizations for common ailments and disease. He concludes that: "Visualization can change the microscopic structure of the brain. . . . It can impact the immune system, and in so many cases, perhaps even change the course of disease. Placing your attention on your breathing, in the case of meditation, impacts over 1,000 of your genes. Thinking of someone you love dilates arteries, reduces blood pressure, and gives the immune system a boost. If you can do all these things, I wonder what else you can achieve."

RELEASING NEGATIVE EMOTIONS

Does this mean that positive thinking is a panacea for all our health problems? Seeing the positive in every situation certainly changes negative stress into positive stress—from threat to challenge, as we discussed in Chapter 4. However, as Gabor Mate highlights in *When the Body Says No*,[324] constant positive thinking can do more harm than good if it leads to repressed emotions. Only allowing yourself to think happy thoughts while pushing away negative ones can become a destructive defense mechanism because when you repress negative emotions, you create resistance. Resistance requires a great deal of energy and increases stress in the body, which can result in ill-health. Embracing all of reality—"feeling all the feels"—is an important aspect of healthy living because it opens us up and allows emotions that no longer serve us to be released. Letting go of negative emotions promotes well-being, increasing our emotional intelligence and encouraging us to be more empathetic with others, as well as increasing our own levels of self-love and self-care.

While emotional challenges take us out of our comfort zones, they show us what we are capable of, and so they can empower us. Awareness and acceptance of negative emotions can help us lean into our feelings and process them, thereby making problems feel less scary. Releasing negativity helps us to reframe our beliefs and perceptions, reinspiring the past by transmuting painful memories so that we can see our present circumstances in a more positive light.

One of the tricky things about releasing negative emotions is that they are often based on unconscious beliefs, which are determined by our conditioning. This means that when it comes to health, being optimistic about getting better won't work if we have a subconscious belief that our illness is serious or life-threatening. For instance, if we have a disease that runs in the family, we may have a subconscious belief that we are going to die from it because it caused the death of our father or grandfather. Thinking happy thoughts about ourselves or visualizing the success of a potential treatment is highly unlikely to work if this is the case. Instead, we need to get to the root of our fears and work on releasing them before being consciously optimistic can work.

Subconscious beliefs may be difficult to dislodge, but it is not impossible. First, we must make them conscious—we need to look our fears squarely in the face and acknowledge them. This opens us up to the possibility of change, which can lead to deep healing and personal transformation. Releasing suppressed emotions and facing our fears may require therapy, which is where mind-body medicine, psychotherapy, and alternative healing come in.

CONCLUSIONS

This chapter has highlighted the remarkable power of our beliefs and attitudes on our physical and mental well-being. The evidence presented underscores the importance of positive thinking and visualization in promoting health, as well as the necessity of addressing past traumas to achieve holistic healing. The next chapter delves into various mind-body medicine techniques, offering practical approaches such as meditation, mindfulness, yoga, breathwork, hypnosis, psychotherapy, and alternative medicine. These methods further illustrate the transformative potential of the mind-body connection, paving the way for innovative healthcare solutions that integrate both mental and physical health for optimal well-being.

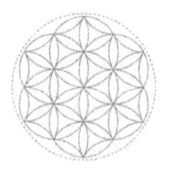

CHAPTER 10

MIND-BODY MEDICINE

Health does not always come from medicine. Most of the time it comes from peace of mind, peace in the heart, peace in the soul.
—Belinda Wilcox

The mind and body are clearly not separate but one integrated system. Mind-body medicine includes a variety of therapies that facilitate healing. Called "mind-body interventions" (MBIs) by scientific researchers, MBI programs have now been established at prestigious medical schools such as Harvard, Johns Hopkins, and Stanford University, with detailed studies to confirm their efficacy. The following discussion examines the latest findings on the benefits of MBIs, including meditation, mindfulness, yoga, breathwork, biofeedback, and hypnosis. The important contribution that psychotherapy has made to mental well-being is also reviewed, and the chapter ends with a discussion of the mind-body-spirit connection in healing, exploring the scientific evidence for the power of spiritual practice, faith, and alternative therapies in well-being.

MIND-BODY INTERVENTIONS

Meditation

Once dismissed as a cult-like mystical practice, meditation has now become one of the fastest-growing wellness trends in the world. After Maharishi Mahesh Yogi first taught meditation to the Beatles in the 1960s, the practice has quickly become mainstream and is now practiced by millions of people across the globe. A key reason for its popularity is because it helps people to relax. Highly acclaimed books such as *The Relaxation Response* by Dr Herbert Benson,[325] *The Science of Meditation* by Goleman and Davidson[326] and *Siddhartha's Brain* by journalist James Kingsland[327] showcase the abundance of scientific evidence for meditation's health benefits. These include stress management and mental health gains, improved immunity and sleep quality, boosted digestion and energy levels, reduced pain and addictions, as well as cognitive benefits such as greater focus, productivity, and creativity. The benefits of meditation seem endless, so it is little wonder that countless people from all walks of life have embraced this ancient spiritual practice.

The efficacy of meditation as a stress-management technique is now well-established, and there are meta studies galore on the subject.[328] The reason for its stressing-busting effect is that it limits incoming sensory stimuli and increases internal self-awareness, allowing the mind to ease up and become more restful. As we stop thinking about our endless daily tasks, the brain moves from its normal busy betawave state to the slower alpha waves, which activate the parasympathetic nervous system and induce relaxation. Meditators can also dip into the deeper theta state, which normally occurs during sleep. Research has found that the practice triggers a kind of "hypometabolic" state similar to animals hibernating, which creates the opportunity for deep healing and rejuvenation.[329] This makes meditation a highly effective—as well as time-efficient—way of overcoming the burnout that so often accompanies the hustle and bustle of modern life. For instance, a 2020 study by Oregon State University found that just ten minutes of meditation replaced forty-four minutes of sleep in exhausted business entrepreneurs.[330] Other studies have found that just fifteen minutes of meditation is comparative to the relaxing effects of a whole day's vacation.[331]

Research has found that meditation not only lowers our "sleep debt" (the difference between the amount of sleep we get and what we actually need), but it also helps us to get better quality sleep. A 2019 meta-analysis of 1645 people by the National Institute of Health found that sleep quality was significantly improved with meditation, concluding that the practice is an effective way of treating insomnia and other sleep disturbances.[332] By allocating time during the day to lower stress levels before bed, the practice means people have less trouble falling asleep and staying asleep at night. It may also mean you need less sleep, so you wake earlier and are more productive the next day. Many people resist meditation because they feel they just don't have the time, but paradoxically, regular practice can increase the hours in one's day due to its many beneficial effects.

Research has found that meditation has countless physical health benefits, the most notable of which include strengthened immune systems, decreased inflammation, and improved gut health.[333] Meditation makes us feel generally healthier, more relaxed, and vibrant. Because it helps the gut, it can increase energy levels, regulate the metabolism, modulate hormones, and even increase fertility by aiding the rest-and-digest process.[334] Because it reduces the stress hormone cortisol and corresponding blood pressure, studies have found that meditation lowers our heart rate and improves heart rate variability (a measure of stress), thus boosting heart health and reducing the risk of type 2 diabetes.[335] Meta studies show that meditation reduces pain and improves the quality of life for sufferers of chronic conditions such as cancer, fibromyalgia, and arthritis.[336] Meditation can also decrease the recovery time of athletes and help injuries heal faster.[337]

In the acclaimed book, *Super Brain*,[338] Deepak Chopra and Alzheimer's expert Professor Randolph E. Tanzi highlight that meditation can even slow down the aging process. Not only does meditation encourage the growth of new brain cells and therefore help to prevent brain disorders like dementia in old age, but studies by the University of California have found that intensive meditation increases "telomerase," which are the tips at the ends of our DNA strands that deteriorate as we get older, leading to cell damage. Meditation can slow down this deterioration, leading to greater longevity and rejuvenation. In the book *The Telomere Effect*,[339]

Nobel Prize-winning scientist Elizabeth Blackburn and psychologist Elissa Epel describe their research into the effects of stress-related thinking on telomerase and how it speeds up cellular aging and disease. As epigenetics has shown us, negative thoughts can do serious damage to our DNA, and meditation can reverse this.

Interestingly, according to MRI scans, long-term meditators have brains that look quite different from nonmeditators.[340] One of the most fascinating findings of meditation studies is that the practice synchronizes the left and right sides of the brain.[341] While the different brain hemispheres clearly have an intimate working relationship, they work somewhat independently, the left brain being associated with language and logic and the right being associated with creativity and intuition. Any activity that increases coherence between these two spheres gives major boosts to cognition. In *The Effortless Mind*,[342] Will Williamson describes this as "peak performance thinking," when your brain is firing on all cylinders, creativity is flowing, and brainstorming, problem-solving, and decision-making come easily. When the mind is relaxed in an alpha wave state, our brain capability is significantly enhanced, which means we can focus better, think sharper and process more information. Interestingly, of all the cognitive functions, Williams explains that meditation has the biggest impact on creativity.[343] This is because the corpus callosum (the bridge between the two hemispheres of the brain) becomes thicker and stronger the more meditation we do, which in turn helps to increase brain connectivity. Because of this, researchers have found that meditation cultivates a "creative brain dance" of spontaneous connections, eureka moments, divergent thinking (thinking outside the box), and openness to new ideas and possibilities.[344]

Studies have discovered that meditation changes the physiological structure of the brain in other ways too. Research by Harvard Medical School found that it shrinks the amygdala (responsible for the flight-or-fight response) and thus reduces people's reactivity to stressful situations.[345] Meditation really does make us feel more "zen." It also increases cells in the hippocampus (responsible for learning and memory), in the prefrontal cortex (responsible for reasoning, emotional regulation, and empathy), and in the limbic system (which processes emotions). Meditation not only makes us sharper learners and thinkers, it makes us kinder, more emotionally intelligent people too. Another key finding is that meditation makes us feel good. Because it floods the brain with the happy hormones serotonin, dopamine, and endorphins, it creates positive moods, which can increase self-esteem while reducing anxiety and depression.[346] In Candace Pert's book *Everything You Need to Know to Feel Go(o)d*,[347] she asserts that we are "hardwired for bliss," which is why the body makes its own natural opiates in the first place, drenching the prefrontal cortex (the highest, most intelligent part of our brain) with receptors for endorphins. Science has proven the old yogis right—one of the best ways to experience a blissful life is to meditate.

Meditation also reduces activity in the brain's "me center," what scientists call the "default mode network," responsible for mind-wandering—also known as the "monkey mind."[348] A journal article from Harvard University cites research that found that, incredibly, the mind wanders almost half of all our waking hours—and, according to the author, "a wandering mind is an unhappy mind."[349] The monkey mind plays a major role in feelings of self-consciousness and social awareness, as well as in emotions such as anger, fear, and disgust.[350] The monkey mind thus has a bad reputation for rumination, worrying, and other potentially destructive thought patterns. Regular meditation is instrumental in dialing the monkey mind down, allowing us to be less self-absorbed and more emotionally intelligent.

The healing effect of meditation doesn't end there. Will Williamson describes how meditation allows us to process layers of accumulated stress, not just from our normal daily routines but from the backlog of negative experiences and trauma from our past. As the nervous system "de-excites," it gives the body the bandwidth it needs to rid itself of old baggage stored in our cellular memory. When the nervous system is in its least excited state, it goes to work like a computer, deleting old files and creating order in our system. This allows the brain to use more of its computing power for the task at hand because we are no longer using up our precious energy, keeping a lid on built-up stress and repressing emotions. Meditation thus gives us more "adaptation energy," which means we are better able to go with the flow and roll with life's ups and downs.

Regular meditators can even reach a state that yogis call *samadhi*, which means "at one with God" in Sanskrit—a state of pure bliss where the deepest levels of self-awareness and enlightenment can be realized. Experienced meditators regularly report feeling this bliss state, which results in feeling less reactive to external events and more relaxed in the present moment. There is less desire to push hard to "be someone" or "be somewhere," which means that meditators are not only less stressed but more nonchalant and therefore less likely to be rigidly attached to timings and outcomes. Because they are content to move in a general direction without worrying so much about exactly when and how things will turn out, self-esteem becomes less predicated on external achievement or validation and more about self-compassion and a state of inner nonjudgment. Calmer nervous systems also allow for greater enjoyment of the simple things, so life becomes altogether more joyful and fulfilling.

Mindfulness

Another MBI which is similar to meditation is mindfulness. Mindfulness also aims to quiet the mind, but it does so without needing to be still—for instance, the practice can be done on a walk, eating, or doing a task. The goal of mindfulness is to be present so that we become more aware of our surroundings, as well as bodily sensations, feelings, and thoughts. Being present slows your mind down, releases stress, and calms the nervous system. Key to these techniques is to observe your thoughts and feelings without judging them. The idea is that awareness without judgment weakens and overcomes negative thought patterns over time, helping to promote mind-body healing.

While it has its roots in Buddhist meditation, mindfulness practices have now entered the mainstream and are regularly practiced by people all over the world. The popularity of mindfulness is in part due to the work of Jon Kabat-Zinn and his mindfulness-based stress reduction (MBSR) approach. The efficacy of MBSR has been documented by thousands of studies and has inspired countless programs, including those adapted for hospitals, prisons, schools, and veteran centers. Hundreds of medical centers around the world now offer MBSR programs, including leading pain management programs in prestigious hospitals such as Johns Hopkins in the US and St Thomas's Hospital in London.

MBSR includes focused awareness, awareness of the breath, body scans, mindful observation, mindful eating, and walking meditations, as well as mindful stretching with yoga. A 2015 meta-analysis of twenty-nine studies involving over two thousand participants found that MBSR was a highly effective way of reducing stress, anxiety, and depression.[351] Other meta studies have found it to be a beneficial practice for increasing the quality of life in people with chronic diseases such as cancer.[352] In the *New York Times* bestseller *The Body Keeps the Score*, Bessel Van der Kolk advocates mindfulness as a useful tool for recovery from post-traumatic stress disorder (PTSD) because it requires an awareness of the body and emotions rather than denying and repressing them.[353]

Yoga

Yoga is another popular MBI, having taken off in the West during the hippie era of the 1960s and then promoted by the New Age Movement in the 1970s and '80s. A spiritual practice from India dating back thousands of years, yoga is now a multi-billion-dollar industry endorsed by celebrities such as Gwyneth Paltrow, Madonna, Jennifer Aniston, and Sting and is practiced by millions of people from all walks of life. Yoga is used in MBSR because it encourages an awareness of the breath, creating mindfulness and body awareness through moving and stretching. The aim is to flow between postures in tune with your breathing, increasing flexibility and openness, which helps to soothe the nervous system and reduce stress.

Books such as *The Wisdom of Yoga* by psychotherapist Stephen Cope[354] and *The Science of Yoga* by journalist William Broad[355] highlight a multitude of research showcasing the benefits of this ancient practice. For instance, studies have found that yoga can reduce the risk factors for heart disease, such as high blood pressure, cholesterol, and high body mass index (BMI),[356] as well as lowering levels of anxiety and depression, improving sleep quality, increasing energy levels, decreasing inflammation, alleviating back pain, and improving quality of life for those with conditions such as cancer, stroke, and arthritis.[357] Meta studies have found that yoga is also great for cognition, stimulating brain functions such as working memory and mental flexibility, and preventing cognitive decline in old age.[358]

It is not just adults who benefit from yoga either; children and young people also show improvements in stress alleviation, focus, self-awareness, resilience, mood, and emotional self-regulation.[359] Yoga also helps sufferers of trauma. In *The Body Keeps the Score*, Van der Kolk discusses how yoga can be a useful way for trauma sufferers to become aware of their emotional blockages and understand how the body experiences them so that they can then work on releasing them. There are many studies highlighting that veterans suffering from PTSD find yoga to be an effective way of improving mental health symptoms, sleep, and quality of life.[360]

Breathwork

Breathwork is another popular form of MBI. Celebrated books such as *Breath* by James Nestor[361] and *Do Breathe* by Michael Townsend Williams[362] highlight that what links our body, mind, and emotions is the breath. Our breathing reflects how stressed we are; when we are tense, we breath fast and shallow; when we are calm, we breathe more regularly, taking deeper and slower breaths. Yet breathing is not just a reflection of our emotional state; we can actively use our breath to change the way we feel. We've all been told that taking deep breaths can help to calm us down in stressful situations, but not many people know that deep breathing for just sixty seconds is all it takes to rid our bloodstream of cortisol. When we are anxious, the prefrontal cortex—the part of the brain responsible for rational thinking—becomes impaired, which is why stressed people don't usually react well to being told to "calm down." Stress makes it hard for us to think straight, but with the right breathing techniques, we can regain mastery of our mind and, therefore, our nervous system. All we need to remember is to breathe in through the nose and out through the mouth with a long exhale.

The key to relaxation is to do the kind of abdominal breathing that comes naturally to a baby, inhaling through the nose and filling the belly with air before exhaling through the nose for longer than the inhale. Breathing through the nose allows the nose hairs to filter the air and purify it. The long exhale stimulates the vagus nerve that runs from our brain stem to our abdomen, activating the parasympathetic nervous system and shutting off the stress response. Because of its relaxing effects, breathwork has some impressive health benefits. Scientific studies show that slow breathing can boost the immune system, lower blood pressure, improve sleep and digestion, help blood circulation, increase muscle tone, manage pain, strengthen the lungs, boost the lymphatic system, and remove toxins, as well as mental health benefits such as lowering anxiety and depression, improving mood and self-esteem, and heightening focus and creativity.[363]

Breathwork is not just used for relaxation, however; different breathing exercises do different things. For instance, double breathing (taking fast inhales and exhales) can boost our energy levels, while alternate nostril breathing (breathing through one nostril while blocking the other, then reversing) can increase brain coherence by connecting the two hemispheres of the brain (as the left nostril increases activity in the right side of the brain while the right increases the left.)[364] "Iceman" Wim Hoff has demonstrated how different breathing techniques can even be used to influence supposedly involuntary responses of the nervous system, enabling incredible feats to be performed such as running barefoot marathons in the snow, swimming under ice sheets, and being in full body contact with ice for nearly two hours. His techniques have become so popular that thousands of people have trained in the Wim Hoff Method to withstand extreme cold using a combination of breathwork, meditation, yoga, and frequent cold exposure. Hoff's techniques have similarities to the *pranayama* breathwork practiced in yoga and the Tibetan Buddhist practice *Tummo* (which means "inner fire"), involving a combination of breathing techniques and visualizations to raise body temperature. One Harvard study of meditating monks in the Himalayan mountains found that practicing the Tummo technique raised the temperature of the monks' fingers and toes by an astonishing seventeen degrees while lowering their metabolism by as much as 64 percent (compared to sleeping, when our metabolism drops by 10 to15 percent).[365]

Breathwork is not just a tool for spiritual practitioners, extreme athletes, and wild swimmers, though; it can also be used for emotional release and self-healing. Breathwork has become popular for treating a wide range of issues, including anxiety, depression, anger, chronic pain, grief, and trauma. Research highlights how different emotions correlate with different breathing patterns, so changing how we breathe changes how we feel. The reason why breathwork can help with emotional release may also have something to do with the myelin sheath—the protective layer that surrounds the neurons of the brain. Ayurveda holds that many of our negative memories are stored within the myelin sheath, and that breathing techniques such as yogic breathing move fluid through the channels of the brain to flush out the imprints of those memories.

Because of its popularity, there are various breathwork approaches with the goal of working through repressed emotions. For instance, "vivation" is a technique that uses circular breathing to allow you to feel good while working on releasing negative thoughts and emotions. "Quantum healing," developed by Joshua Bloom, uses strong outward breaths (like blowing out a candle) to release emotions trapped in the body, and "rebirthing," created by psychotherapist Leonard Orr, uses "conscious energy breathing" to access the unconscious mind and uncover negative memories. "Holotropic breathwork," developed in the 1970s by the transpersonal psychologist Stanislav Grof, is a technique that uses intense breathing to lower levels of carbon dioxide and decrease blood flow to the brain, causing visions and higher states of consciousness to release painful memories. Shamanic breathwork is yet another technique which induces altered states of consciousness to elicit mind-body healing.

Biofeedback

A popular MBI technique known as biofeedback displays patients' brainwaves on a screen in real time so they can see how stressed they are. This encourages them to make a conscious effort to relax with slow breaths. Once they do, they are rewarded by seeing their brain producing alpha waves, which trigger the rest-and-digest response. A 2020 meta-analysis of fifty-eight studies involving over two thousand patients found that heart rate variability (a measure of relaxation and overall health) improved with biofeedback, resulting in a wide range of mental and physical health benefits.[366]

Hypnosis

Hypnosis is another widely used MBI method, with evidence showing it to be highly effective for treating people with addictions, phobias, pain, IBS, anxiety, depression, PTSD, and more.[367] Accredited clinical hypnotherapists guide clients into a trance-like state similar to meditation and then use autosuggestion to input positive cues into their subconscious mind. Therapists also guide clients to bring unconscious beliefs and memories up to the surface so that they can be processed and released. Some people are particularly responsive to autosuggestion, and hypnotherapists are well-placed to help them overcome their issues and replace negative beliefs with positive ones.

PSYCHOTHERAPY

Along with MBIs, there are many psychotherapy techniques to facilitate mind-body healing. Psychological research has created huge inroads into understanding the role of emotional stressors in the development of disease, and the innumerable therapies that have been developed since the founding days of Sigmund Freud in the nineteenth century have provided lots of different ways to release negative thought patterns and emotions to create well-being. While it is beyond the scope of this chapter to explain all the different approaches, an overview is given here to elucidate the enormous contribution psychotherapy has made to our understanding of the mind-body connection.

Psychoanalysis and Psychodynamic Therapies

First developed by Sigmund Freud in 1896, the focus of psychoanalysis is to use talking therapy to discover the unconscious meanings and motivations behind negative behaviors, feelings, and thoughts. There is a close working partnership between therapist and client, with clients exploring repressed fears and conflicts they've had since early childhood with the aim of experiencing a catharsis. Psychoanalysis has since been extended and modified to include a wide range of psychodynamic therapies, with the four main schools being Freudian, Ego Psychology, Object Relations, and Self Psychology.

Behavioral Therapy

Behavioral therapy is based on the idea of "classic conditioning" or "associative learning," first discovered by Ivan Pavlov and his well-known salivating dogs who drooled at the sound of a dinner bell when they got fed. Behavioral therapy has the premise that all behaviors are learned responses, and therefore, we can learn desirable behaviors through positive reinforcement while eliminating self-destructive ones through negative associations. E. L. Thorndike, another pioneer of this approach, coined the term "operant conditioning," which relies on rewards and punishments to shape people's behavior.

Cognitive Therapy

While behavioral therapy focuses on manipulating the external environment to cause behavioral changes, cognitive therapy focuses on thinking as the basis for change. One popular type is CBT, or cognitive behavioral therapy. CBT emphasizes what people think rather than what they do. Under the guidance of a therapist, CBT helps people recognize and change negative thoughts and replace them with positive ones so that they learn new behavioral patterns. CBT uses techniques such as cognitive reframing (where you change negative thoughts into more productive ones), guided discovery (where a therapist challenges your beliefs in an attempt to broaden your thinking), behavioral experiments (where to reduce catastrophizing you predict what will happen and then later talk with a therapist about whether or not it came true), and exposure therapy (where people overcome phobias by being deliberately exposed to their fears under controlled conditions). CBT also uses time-honored tools such as journalling and role-playing to help clients overcome issues and trauma.

Humanistic Therapy

Humanistic therapy focuses on free will, self-discovery, and true potential to help people develop self-confidence and self-worth. Clients are encouraged to recognize their strengths, creativity, and freedom of choice, with care and respect for others being important themes. Humanistic philosophers include Jean-Paul Sartre, Martin Buber, and Søren Kierkegaard. Three types of humanistic therapies that are particularly influential include client-centered therapy, gestalt, and existential therapy. Client-centered therapy negates the idea that therapists are authorities on their clients' mental health and instead encourages them to take the lead while the therapist listens supportively and acts as a guide. Gestalt therapy focuses on a person's present life challenges rather than delving into the past, stressing the broader context of the client's issues and encouraging them to take responsibility rather than blaming others. Existential therapy focuses on finding the meaning and purpose of the client's life and releasing fear of the unknown.

Integrative Therapy

Many therapists don't adhere to a single approach and instead mix and match different techniques to suit their strengths and client's needs. Like integrative medicine, integrative psychotherapy (also called holistic or body-centered psychotherapy) incorporates traditional and alternative approaches so that the client is treated in a more comprehensive way, exploring not just mental and emotional issues but physical and spiritual factors as well. Integrative therapy combines traditional talking therapy with things like meditation, breathwork, bodywork, dance, art, music, or spiritual therapy to heal emotional trauma.

THE MIND-BODY-SPIRIT APPROACH TO HEALING

Spiritual therapy is an approach that acknowledges a person's soul as well as their mind and body in healing by accessing their faith in a higher power. Prayer has often been used in spiritual therapy, and it has been shown to have a major effect on health. Prayer, like meditation, has brain-boosting benefits, such as soothing the amygdala, creating an alpha wave response that relaxes the body, and increasing serotonin levels, which makes people feel happier.[368] Because it activates the parasympathetic nervous system, prayer can reduce blood pressure and heart rate, lower anxiety and depression, stabilize sleep patterns, and impact autonomic nervous system functions like breathing and digestion. Prayer has also been correlated with a reduction in inflammatory markers, which reduces the risk of chronic disease.[369]

In *The Handbook for Religion and Health*, Harold Koenig argues that people who pray and are religiously active tend to live longer and are healthier overall, with lower rates of illnesses such as heart disease and cancer.[370] Studies have found a strong correlation between spiritual practice and positive emotional states like happiness, self-esteem, purpose, optimism, hope, and a sense of control, which all have a cumulative effect on physical health. In *Cure*, Jo Marchant cites studies which show that people who go to church regularly have a 20 percent reduced risk of dying within the following five years. In another study, she describes how 45 percent of people with HIV who developed faith in a higher power after their diagnosis were found to have lower viral loads in their bloodstream. It appears that faith really does have the power to heal.

Of course, prayer is not the only form of spiritual therapy. There are alternative approaches to suit people of all spiritual inclinations, from Ayurveda to Shamanism to traditional Chinese medicine (TCM), all founded on different religious and philosophical beliefs. For instance,

TCM uses a variety of mind-body-spirit methods such as qigong, tai chi, herbal remedies, and acupuncture to treat a range of physical and mental ailments. Due to the mounting evidence for its health benefits, acupuncture has become a particularly popular therapeutic approach. In England, acupuncture has been prescribed by around half of all medical doctors, and the National Health Service spends around twenty-five million pounds a year on it.[371] The acupuncture boom in the UK has been mirrored in Europe, particularly Switzerland, where, along with traditional Chinese medicine, it has been included in the country's basic health insurance package.[372]

Studies of acupuncture show a demonstrable physiological effect, including reduction of chronic pain, arthritis, migraines, allergies, and high blood pressure.[373] Research has found that acupuncture stimulates immune function and enhances cancer-fighting natural killer cells. It has also been used in cancer treatments to reduce the effect of chemotherapy and radiation. Acupuncture has been shown to aid postoperative recovery and is effective in treating digestive, neurological, respiratory, gynecologic, and sleep disorders, as well as mental health issues like anxiety, depression, neurosis, and PTSD. In fact, the WHO credits acupuncture with treating everything from strokes and arthritis to flu, panic disorders, and addiction.[374] Acupuncture is now available at reputable hospitals throughout the US including Duke University Medical Center, the Mayo Clinic, and the University of California. It is particularly popular in cancer treatments, with eight out of the top ten cancer hospitals in the US offering acupuncture therapy.

Another popular spiritual therapy is Reiki. Numerous studies show that Reiki increases levels of relaxation, reduces pain and anxiety, boosts energy levels, and strengthens overall well-being. It has even been found to diminish the side effects of surgery and cancer treatments. A 2017 meta-analysis of thirteen large studies found that in the majority of cases, Reiki was more effective than a placebo at alleviating the symptoms of chronic disease and postoperative recovery.[375] Similarly, a 2018 meta-analysis concluded that Reiki produces significant reductions in pain over a range of conditions,[376] and another concluded that Reiki reduces the side effects of chemotherapy.[377] The British Medical Journal of Supportive and Palliative Care review in 2019 concluded that "Reiki therapy is useful for relieving pain, decreasing anxiety/depression, and improving quality of life in several conditions."[378] Such findings, combined with the fact that Reiki (like acupuncture) is relatively inexpensive, with no side effects, have encouraged some medical centers to offer the therapy as part of their treatment plans, including prestigious hospitals like the New York Presbyterian, the Yale Cancer Center, and the Mayo Clinic. This points to an increasing willingness to consider alternative approaches in conventional medicine toward a more integrative model of health, which includes mind-body-spirit healing.

CONCLUSIONS

There is no longer any doubt that the mind-body connection is as important to our health as nutrition, exercise, sleep, or relaxation. The abundance of evidence for the therapeutic benefits of MBIs has led to a slow but steady sea-change in attitudes toward alternative therapies at the frontiers of conventional medicine. The power of the mind in healing is now irrefutable thanks to the much-studied placebo effect, and our new understanding of neuroplasticity has heralded a far more empowering view of our ability to turn our health around with positive mindsets and habits. The ideas behind so many of the holistic therapies mentioned in this chapter have been around for millennia, and now the growing evidence for their efficacy is giving them increasing credibility in the eyes of doctors and scientists who only a few years ago might have dismissed them as quackery. This is significant progress, given the enormous challenges we face in combating the pandemic of chronic disease and mental health issues arising from the stress of modern living. The pharmaceutical approach to health is clearly not the only way to deal with our maladies, and as healthcare costs continue to mushroom, the pioneering therapeutic solutions of the future may well focus increasingly on harnessing the miraculous power of the mind to heal our body.

You have powers you never dreamed of. You can do things you never thought you could do. There are no limitations in what you can do except the limitations of your own mind.
—Darwin P. Kingsley

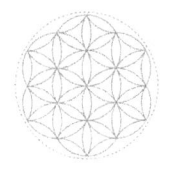

CHAPTER 11

SOCIAL CONNECTION

Community connectedness is not just about warm fuzzy tales of civic triumph. In measurable and well-documented ways, social capital makes an enormous difference in our lives . . . Social capital makes us smarter, healthier, safer, richer, and better able to govern a just and stable democracy.
—Robert D. Putnam

This chapter explores the social determinants of health, which are the societal and economic conditions that influence the well-being of different individuals and groups in society. Social determinants are crucial for well-being because they encompass the conditions in which people are born, grow, live, work, and age. These factors shape our lives and significantly influence our health. In fact, numerous studies suggest that social determinants account for as much as 30 to 55 percent of health outcomes.[379]

The following discussion focuses on how social networks, housing, education, and socioeconomic status affect our well-being. The growing gap between rich and poor is discussed in terms of its health impacts and how addressing health disparities can create more equitable and just societies. The health inequalities between the Global North and South are highlighted, and how social justice relates to environmental justice in sustainability debates. The chapter concludes that the social determinants of health are intimately entwined with each other, as well as with ecological health, the subject of the next chapter.

SOCIAL NETWORKS

Human beings are social animals—we are built to thrive in collaborative networks, which is why social connection is so foundational to our well-being. Social networks such as family, friends, and neighbors have a significant influence on our health in various ways. Being part of a community makes us feel loved and supported, providing emotional support that can help to reduce stress, anxiety, and ill-health. Having good relationships and strong support networks helps us to cope with life's challenges, improving our resilience in difficult times. People with strong social connections tend to have better emotional well-being and are more likely to seek help and support during times of stress or illness. Being part of a community fosters a sense of belonging and purpose, which contributes to a positive outlook on life and a feeling of fulfillment. This innate sense of connection is an essential aspect of healthy living.

Social connection is so important for health outcomes that researchers have coined the term "social capital" because our relationships are what give us the resources, cooperation, trust, and mutual support that help us to thrive in life.[380] The more social capital we have, the more we are likely to flourish—the less we have, the more isolated, impoverished, and disease-prone we feel. Communities with high levels of social capital have better health outcomes overall, which can help bridge the gap between different socioeconomic groups. Social capital can also enable collective action to address health issues, as communities with strong social capital are better equipped to mobilize and advocate for improvements in healthcare services and policies.

Longitudinal research has found that people who feel socially isolated are 30 percent more likely to develop heart disease or stroke.[381] When people feel isolated and lonely, they experience high levels of stress, leading to poor sleep and weakened immune systems. Studies show that social exclusion lowers self-esteem and is linked to an increased risk of mental health disorders such as depression, anxiety, and even suicidal tendencies.[382] It can also lead to faster cognitive decline and a higher risk of conditions like dementia and Alzheimer's disease. Social isolation may lead to unhealthy coping mechanisms such as excessive drinking, smoking, or drug use, which can lead to chronic diseases and a shorter life expectancy.

Loneliness is, in fact, a major health problem not just among those who are objectively isolated but among those with seemingly ample friends and family. In an article in the *Economist* entitled "Loneliness is a Serious Public Health Problem,"[383] studies show that around 22 percent of people in the US and Britain feel always or often lonely, left out, or isolated. The article reports that there is an increasing concern about a "loneliness epidemic," particularly among the elderly, with research finding that in Americans over the age of forty-five, around 35 percent feel lonely, and in 41 percent of Britons over the age of sixty-five, TV or their pet is cited as their main source of company.

By addressing loneliness and social exclusion, healthcare professionals can identify and intervene early to support people at risk. This may involve connecting them to social services, improving community resources, and fostering social cohesion in local neighborhoods to increase community spirit and social bonding.

Social Networks and Technology

Technology can be considered both a blessing and a curse for tackling social exclusion. The advent of the internet and social media has spawned a paradoxical era of connection and disconnection; on the one hand, we just have to switch on our phones to tap into a worldwide community of people online, yet we have also retreated into virtual worlds, seeing less and less of each other face-to-face. This has had some major health repercussions, with studies showing social media to be causing real damage, particularly to young people, who are now three times more likely to suffer from depression, including suicidal thoughts and behaviors.[384]

Jonathan Haidt, an American social psychologist and author, has drawn attention to the surge of anxiety, depression, and self-harm, particularly in adolescent girls, since the early 2010s when social media platforms proliferated exponentially. In an article in the Atlantic,[385] he explains that: "Much more than for boys, adolescence typically heightens girls' self-consciousness about their changing body and amplifies insecurities about where they fit in their social network. Social media—particularly Instagram, which displaces other forms of interaction among teens, puts the size of their friend group on public display, and subjects their physical appearance to the hard metrics of likes and comment counts—takes the worst parts of middle school and glossy women's magazines and intensifies them."

Social media has some great benefits. We now have access to more information than any other generation in history, and we can join online communities of like-minded individuals at the stroke of a key. Dating apps have transformed the art of romance, linking partners from all walks of life who might otherwise never have met. TikTokers, Instagrammers, Youtubers, and podcasters have quickly become the new thought leaders of the modern era, reaching vast audiences that advertisers of the past could only dream of. Young people today who have never known a world without the internet are natural systems thinkers; they find it normal to talk about networks, patterns of organization and complexity.

However, the internet revolution has also absorbed us in an unprecedented way, leading us to disconnect more and more from real-life social interactions. On average, we now spend three hours and fifteen minutes on our phones, and we check them on average fifty-eight times every day.[386] We also spend around six hours and thirty-seven minutes a day on screens connected to the internet.[387] Increased screen time has made us less active, leading to weight gain and obesity and affecting our sleep habits with late-night blue light exposure, increasing risk factors for chronic diseases and mental health issues.[388] All this screen time can also negatively affect our personal development as we do less-diverse things in our spare time. Instead of socializing, we are scrolling; instead of engaging in sports and hobbies, we are watching TikTok and posting on Snapchat or WhatsApp.

Moreover, short texts and soundbites only give us a snapshot of people's feelings and thoughts, which does little to relay context and can distort our impressions of others. Social media has cultivated a culture of perfectionism as people post pictures and videos of their idealized lives, leading to a new generation obsessed with selfies and public image. People say things on social media that they would never say in person—if internet trolls saw the hurt their comments caused in real life, they might be more remorseful and apologetic. Seeing the negative impact that our actions and words have on others in real life helps us learn to behave in a more respectful and dignified manner.

The well-known Netflix documentary *The Social Dilemma* highlights how the internet age has also led to a lack of control over what content we are exposed to. Social media is engineered to be addictive; the algorithms are designed to hook people in with "clickbait," which brings out negative emotions such as outrage or offense, and motivates the user to click on the next story, thus staying on the platform. Social media has an enormous capacity to polarize people, creating "filter bubbles" whereby feeds are based on past searches and "likes" to show only a narrow range of perspectives similar to that of the user. This creates confirmation bias and echo chambers, as people only see content that reinforces their own views. Because of the way algorithms work, filter bubbles and echo chambers can also lead people down rabbit holes that potentially expose them to fake news and conspiracy theories with no counterweights to act as a reality check.

Social media also reduces complicated issues to hashtags or memes, ignoring complexity and nuance by simplifying things so that we don't get the full picture. This makes us more likely to make snap judgments, reacting in a simplistic, knee-jerk way to convoluted problems and issues so that online mob mentality and cancel culture rules. Combined with a lack of diverse viewpoints being shared on our feeds, constructive debate is often sidelined, eroding free speech and leading to a dangerous path of polarization, prejudice, anger, and hate in the real world. The irony of the internet is that while we have created a global web of social interaction, we have also created more division, increasing feelings of social exclusion and isolation.

Increased use of internet porn has also had a negative impact on gender relations. In *Boys and Sex*,[389] Peggy Orenstein argues that the hostile sexism, frequent violence, and dehumanization of females rife in online porn has led boys to devalue, sexualize, and objectify girls. This lowers girls' self-esteem, encouraging the disempowering belief that they need to act in a demeaning way to attract the opposite sex. Similarly, boys can think that it's quite normal or even desirable to degrade and objectify girls. Gender relations have suffered as a result, leading to further mental health issues for younger generations.

The internet is still new; it is an evolving tool that has the power to connect us in healthy, positive ways. This requires a combination of individual responsibility, community engagement and policy support. A positive internet culture that promotes social inclusion and healthy interaction involves a mix of :

- Digital literacy education (encouraging responsible use of social media and a balance between online and offline communication)
- Online community building (encouraging empathy, kindness, and understanding in online discussions)
- Promotion of platforms that encourage a diversity of views and critical debate (with algorithms to support this)
- Government and corporate collaboration so that technology companies implement policies that promote positive online experiences and address harmful content, as well as protect user data.

In a way, the advent of the internet can be likened to humans discovering fire—in the beginning, we didn't really know what we were doing or how to contain it, so we probably burned down a few forests in the process. We are in the same transitional stage with social media, and likewise, our health is benefiting and suffering at the same time. Just as in the early days of fire, we are learning how to use the internet responsibly so that it becomes a tool for social bonding and well-being rather than stoking exclusion and ill-health.

The Blue Zones Project

The well-known Blue Zones Project conducted by National Geographic explorer and author Dan Buettner, studied regions in the world known for having higher proportions of centenarians and healthier aging populations.[390] The research initially identified five blue zones:

1. Ikara, Greece
2. Sardinia, Italy
3. Nicoya Peninsula, Costa Rica
4. Okinawa, Japan
5. Loma Linda in California, USA.

In these regions, Buettner and his team examined the lifestyle, diet, cultural practices, and social connections of the residents to understand the factors contributing to their longevity and well-being. The study generated multiple books, articles, and documentaries sharing insights into the common lifestyle habits of people living in these regions and inspired many communities around the world to follow their example.

Buettner's research showed that people who have a close connection with family and friends and who feel well-connected within their communities live longer and have fewer health issues. People living in blue zones tend to have close-knit communities where social interaction is a natural part of daily life, and this leads to a general feeling of well-being and contentment. Social norms and peer influence in blue zones encourage healthy lifestyle choices, such as a balanced diet and regular exercise. Shared activities and social engagements make people feel happier and more well-integrated in their communities and increases their levels of physical activity and cognitive stimulation. Social isolation and loneliness, which can negatively impact health, are less prevalent in these areas due to the emphasis on socializing and maintaining strong bonds with family and friends.

HOUSING

Housing is another important social determinant of health. It is not difficult to imagine how poverty-stricken, overcrowded homes lacking in sanitation can encourage disease. Research shows that poor housing conditions, including cold, damp, mold, and noise, are significantly related to physical and mental health issues.[391] For instance, damp, moldy houses have been associated with higher levels of stress and a sense of disempowerment and lack of control in life, which can lead to anxiety and depression. It can also be deadly; in the UK, for instance, living in cold houses leads to thousands of deaths a year, mainly among the elderly.[392]

Adequate housing provides a safe and stable shelter, protecting us from extreme weather conditions, environmental hazards, and exposure to disease. Yet our home isn't just a physical space; it's a hub of human connections that contribute to our well-being. Having a place to call home can reduce stress, anxiety, and feelings of uncertainty, promoting a sense of belonging and better mental health. Conversely, if we don't feel safe at home, this has a major impact on our lives. Homelessness significantly increases health risks due to exposure to harsh conditions, lack of access to healthcare, and increased vulnerability to violence and substance abuse.

Housing location is equally important, as it impacts our access to social support networks and community resources. Does housing allow people to create strong bonds with their local community, or do they live in a location that makes them feel isolated? Are there good schools, shops, and healthcare services nearby? Is it an easy commute to work? Are there plenty of parks, playgrounds, and other communal spaces? Is there are strong sense of community spirit, and do neighbors look out for one another? Access to quality housing in safe neighborhoods has a particularly important impact on social capital, educational opportunities, and employment prospects.[393] Our home isn't just a shelter; it's a gateway to opportunities. In vibrant neighborhoods, doors open to social connections, education, and jobs.

While wealthier people are able to move to more desirable locations, poorer people are less able to afford housing moves, and so the rich and poor become spatially segregated. Deprived areas have higher rates of pollution, overcrowding, unemployment, crime, smoking, substance abuse, and associated health issues. Neighborhood deprivation shows a large inverse correlation with social cohesion, and studies have shown a strong link between residences in deprived neighborhoods and poor infant and child health, chronic disease, violence, homicide, and all-cause mortality.[394] The more deprived the neighborhood, the greater the risk of disease and early death.

Secure housing is a fundamental basic need, a prerequisite of good health on so many levels. In developing countries, housing affects access to food, clean water, and sanitation, with slums and shantytowns becoming breeding grounds for infectious diseases and malnutrition. While most housing stocks in developed countries tend to be of reasonable quality, there are still examples of substandard housing that doesn't meet building regulations, which can lead to health issues like respiratory problems due to poor indoor air quality, dampness, mold, or building materials made from hazardous materials such as asbestos.

The Grenfell Tower fire

The Grenfell Tower fire of 2017 in London was one of the deadliest fires in modern British history. The fire spread rapidly through the twenty-four-story building due to the highly flammable exterior siding, allowing the fire to spread quickly from one floor to another, killing seventy-two people and causing many injuries.

In the aftermath of the fire, investigations revealed several issues and concerns. First, there were serious deficiencies in the building's fire safety measures, including issues with the fire alarm system, the absence of a sprinkler system, and inadequate fire-resistant barriers within the building. The building's renovation and use of flammable siding also raised questions about building regulations and safety standards, raising concerns about building safety practices across the UK. The response from authorities and the government in the immediate aftermath was criticized for being slow and inadequate in providing support to survivors and affected families. Grenfell Tower housed many low-income and vulnerable residents, which brought attention to social inequalities and the disproportionate impact of such disasters on marginalized communities.

The Grenfell Tower fire sparked a significant public outcry and led to calls for changes in building regulations, fire safety standards, and accountability for those responsible for the building's design, construction, and management. The tragedy has also become a symbol of the need for addressing social inequalities and ensuring the safety and well-being of all residents, regardless of their socioeconomic background.

Housing and Eco-design

Eco-designed housing, also known as "eco-homes," is an architectural approach that focuses on creating sustainable, environmentally friendly homes that promote health and well-being. Eco-homes incorporate features like enhanced indoor air quality, natural lighting, and proper ventilation, which creates a healthier living space and reduces the risk of respiratory issues and other health problems. These homes are designed to be energy efficient, using renewable energy sources and sustainable building materials, which lowers carbon footprints and mitigates the impact of climate change on health. Eco-designs prioritize green spaces, gardens, and nature, which reduces stress and improves overall well-being.

Eco-homes are often part of environmentally friendly communities that encourage social interaction, fostering a sense of belonging and support among residents, which can positively impact health. Many eco-home areas are designed to promote physical activity, with features like bike lanes, walking paths, and nearby amenities, encouraging residents to lead an active lifestyle. They are also designed with noise reduction in mind, creating a quieter and more peaceful living environment that can positively impact mental health and well-being. The focus on sustainability and eco-conscious living may also promote responsible consumption, which can lead to a sense of purpose and personal fulfillment. Overall, eco-designed housing aims to create a healthier living environment that considers both the well-being of the residents and the surrounding ecosystem, making it a more sustainable and harmonious way of living.

EDUCATION

Education is a key determinant of health. Research shows that those with the lowest life expectancy are three times more likely to have no educational qualifications.[395] Higher education levels often lead to better job opportunities and income, allowing people to access quality healthcare, nutritious food, and a safer living environment. A good education is correlated not only with higher-income levels and a better quality of life but also with healthy behaviors and positive mental health. Having a good education promotes healthy lifestyles—well-educated people tend to be more health-literate, so they are more likely to maintain balanced diets, understand sleep hygiene, engage in regular exercise, and avoid harmful habits like smoking.[396]

Education can also positively influence mental health by fostering cognitive and emotional development and providing people with better coping skills to manage stress and mental challenges. Education gives people the social skills needed to build strong relationships, feel empowered, and have a sense of control over their lives. Studies show that people with a good education have more social capital; they have strong networks of social and emotional support and are more like to remain married, contributing to a healthier, happier family life, which boosts mental and physical health.[397]

Education is tied not only to social capital and income but also to gender and ecological issues. Meta studies show that low literacy levels in women have a direct correlation with population growth, as lack of education and poverty are linked with higher birth rates, which puts pressure on environmental resources.[398] In developing countries, women with low literacy levels have limited access to information about reproductive health, which can lead to a lack of knowledge about adequate contraception. Low literacy can lead to a lack of access to healthcare facilities and poor awareness of maternal health practices, including prenatal care, proper nutrition during pregnancy, and safe childbirth practices. As a result, maternal mortality rates are higher, impacting both women's health and population stability.

Literacy also plays a crucial role in increasing knowledge about child health and nutrition. Women with low literacy levels may struggle to access and comprehend health-related information, leading to inadequate childcare and increased child mortality rates. Literacy empowers women to make informed decisions about their lives, including health choices and family planning. Better-educated women earn more, have fewer children and dedicate more resources to each child, thus raising their children more effectively.[399] Cultivating gender equality by educating women is one of the best ways of reducing population growth because women who feel they have greater freedom and control over their lives generally choose to have fewer children.[400]

Lack of education can also hinder a person's ability to participate in the workforce, making it challenging to break the cycle of poverty. In the Global South, where female illiteracy is much higher than in the North, women are more reliant on agriculture and other resource-intensive activities, which can exacerbate environmental issues like deforestation, habitat destruction, and overconsumption (discussed in the next chapter). Literacy fosters environmental awareness and an understanding of the impact of human activities on the planet. Addressing low literacy levels in women is essential for sustainable development and environmental preservation. Educated women can become powerful agents of change, playing a crucial role in creating a healthier and more sustainable planet for future generations. In fact, research shows that educated women are more likely to advocate for sustainable practices, conservation, and environmental protection than men. According to studies by "UN women," a wing of the United Nations dedicated to gender equality, females who are in charge are more likely to act on climate change, and female legislators typically vote for climate action almost twice as often as men.[401]

SOCIOECONOMIC STATUS, WORK AND INCOME

Perhaps the most important social determinant of health is socioeconomic status, work, and income. Income is a major determinant of well-being, as it affects so many other factors in our lives. Children growing up in deprived areas often suffer disadvantages throughout their lives, from educational attainment to employment prospects, which in turn affect physical and mental well-being. Early childhood experiences can also have intergenerational effects, as health outcomes and disadvantages experienced during childhood can be transmitted to future generations. On the other hand, children who live in wealthier areas have a higher chance of positive health outcomes as they grow older. All these factors are connected; for instance, good social networks and relationships can boost communication skills and self-esteem, which can help educational attainment and qualifications, which in turn affects income, housing, and access to healthcare.

Socioeconomic status (SES) profoundly influences our health in various ways, shaping our access to resources, opportunities, and living conditions. Employment opportunities and job security impacts financial stability, which in turn affects health. The more affluent you are, the more likely you are to have a stable job with benefits that promote health and well-being, while the poorer you are, the more likely you are to have health problems.[402] Studies show that people who are unemployed have a higher prevalence of ill-health, which forms a vicious circle as those who are ill are less likely to regain employment.[403] Long-term unemployment causes a major deterioration in mental health, with the mental health decline being steepest for those who have recently lost their jobs, particularly those who have to borrow money and are suffering from growing inactivity and social isolation due to financial pressures.[404] Research shows that job loss is a highly stressful event, likened to a form of bereavement.[405] Longitudinal studies have found that unemployment often precipitates other adverse life events, such as loss of home and marriage breakdowns.[406] Conversely, even people in low-paid jobs tend to be more active, integrated, and psychologically healthier.[407]

However, just having a job isn't necessarily a good indicator of well-being, as demeaning work creates stress and corresponding health problems. Having a good job means doing work that makes you feel valued and fulfilled, raising your self-esteem and contentment with life. This facilitates the formation of stable relationships and increases a person's feeling of connection and belonging. The increase of so-called Mc-jobs (after McDonalds, the fast-food chain) has had the effect of sharpening inequalities of income, social isolation, and related health disparities.[408] In the real world, the jobs with the worst working conditions tend to have the lowest rates of pay and the highest rates of job insecurity, resulting in reduced health and well-being.

Studies show that people with a higher socioeconomic status also have more social capital in the form of larger support networks, which contribute to self-confidence, contentment, and good health.[409] Those with good jobs often live in safer neighborhoods with better housing conditions, closer to nature and with a better quality of life. Bigger incomes give you greater access to healthier food options, recreational facilities, fitness, wellness programs, holidays, and so on. In contrast, individuals with a lower SES may have limited resources, leading to unhealthy dietary choices, sedentary lifestyles, and increased risk factors for chronic diseases. The richer you are, the better access to healthcare services you typically get, including regular check-ups, specialist consultations, and medical treatments. Conversely, low-income groups may face barriers such as lack of health insurance, transportation issues, or limited availability of healthcare facilities.

Low SES can lead to chronic stress due to financial insecurity, limited opportunities, and discrimination, contributing to mental health issues and chronic disease.[410] SES disparities can result in unequal healthcare utilization, too, magnifying health inequalities. People with low incomes may delay seeking medical care due to financial constraints, leading to delayed diagnosis and poorer health outcomes. SES can also influence exposure to various health risks. For example, those who are struggling to make ends meet may have limited access to safety nets such as specialist care and health insurance, increasing their vulnerability to physical and mental health issues.[411]

The Social Gradient in Health

While lower socioeconomic status means living in more dangerous, disease-prone neighborhoods with less access to healthcare, the link between SES and poor health goes far beyond this. The "social gradient in health" (first referred to in the seminal "Black Report" on social determinants in the UK in 1980)[412] refers to the correlation between an individual's social position and their health outcomes. In the famous Whitehall Studies (a series of research projects initiated in the 1960s by the renowned epidemiologist Sir Michael Marmot),[413] the health and mortality patterns of civil servants working in the British Civil Service found that there was a clear association between an individual's job rank or grade within the civil service hierarchy and their health status. The studies showed that those in higher job grades, with more control over their work and higher levels of authority, tended to have better health outcomes compared to those in lower job grades with less control and decision-making power. The social gradient in health indicated that even within a relatively homogenous group of civil servants, those at the top of the hierarchy experienced better health than those lower down the ladder, whose subtle feelings of inferiority created psychosocial stress, which resulted in health disparities.

This is not just a quirk of the British civil service; since the Whitehall Studies, research has consistently highlighted that across the globe, how people rate themselves in terms of success relative to others is at least as predictive of health as measures of income.[414] For instance, in his celebrated book *Status Syndrome*,[415] Michael Marmot cites studies which show that in Sweden, people with a PhD have a longer life expectancy than those with a master's, who in turn live longer than those with a bachelor's degree. In the US, Oscar winners live, on average, four years longer than other Hollywood actors. Poor health is clearly as much about feeling poor as being impoverished in absolute terms.

Psychological research has similarly shown that happiness is a relative phenomenon. A 2010 study by the University of Warwick found that living amid the rich, even when you are upper-middle class, is bad for your mental health.[416] The study found that income only increases happiness if it also boosts your social rank. The cost of living in a wealthy area is very high, creating alienating comparisons which can make people feel dissatisfied with their lives and thus more prone to mental and physical health issues. When it comes to happiness, what matters is not so much what you earn but what you earn relative to your neighbors.

The social gradient in health highlights how socioeconomic factors and the distribution of power and resources influence health and well-being. Marmot states that: "The lower in the hierarchy you are, the less likely it is that you will have full control over your life and opportunities for full social participation. Autonomy and social participation are so important for health that their lack leads to deterioration in health."

This suggests that addressing health inequalities requires not only improving overall population health by enhancing access to resources but by creating more equal opportunities in society to tackle both real and perceived social inequities.

The Growing Gap Between Rich and Poor

One of the biggest problems we face in addressing the health consequences of socioeconomic disparities is that, over time, the world has experienced a widening gap between rich and poor. The wealth and income of the richest individuals have grown significantly faster than that of the poorest, resulting in major social and economic challenges both within and between developing and developed nations. Half the world still struggles to meet basic needs; in fact, the poverty line for those in lower-middle-income countries is living on less than $3.20 a day, while in upper-middle-income nations, it is $5.50 a day.[417] In contrast, those living in developed countries have an average income of $39,178 per year, which equates to $107 a day.[418] This is nearly twenty times the average wage in places like Colombia and thirty-three times across half of Africa.

According to the UN World Social Report in 2020, wealth inequality has reached unprecedented levels, with more than 70 percent of the global population living in countries where the gap between rich and poor is growing.[419] In fact, the absolute gap between the average incomes of rich and poor countries has doubled since 1990. The world's richest 1 percent own half the world's wealth and are on target to own two-thirds by 2030.[420] Various factors have contributed to this inequality, including globalization, technological advancements, education disparities, and changes in economic policies. And, of course, rising inequalities create more benefits for the wealthiest, with top income tax rates in rich countries dropping from 66 percent in 1981 to 43 percent in 2018.[421]

Wealth Inequality and the "Occupy Wall Street" Movement

The Occupy Wall Street movement, which began in September 2011, was a grassroots protest movement that emerged in response to growing economic inequality and perceived corporate influence in the US political system. The movement was largely fueled by frustration over the increasing gap between the rich and poor, among other grievances. Several key factors contributed to the rise of the Occupy Wall Street movement:

1. Economic Inequality: The wealth gap between the wealthiest Americans and the rest of the population had been widening for decades. Many people felt that the economic system was favoring the rich while leaving the majority struggling to make ends meet, leading to a sense of injustice and disenfranchisement.
2. Financial Crisis: The movement gained momentum in the aftermath of the 2008 global financial crisis, which was triggered by irresponsible practices within the financial sector. The crisis resulted in widespread job losses, home foreclosures, and a sense that those responsible for the crisis were not being held accountable.

3. Corporate Greed and Influence: Protesters expressed concerns about corporate greed and the influence of big business on government policies, often through lobbying and campaign contributions. They believed that the interests of powerful corporations were prioritized over the needs of ordinary citizens.
4. Lack of Accountability: Perceived lack of accountability and legal consequences for financial institutions and individuals involved in the financial crisis added to the discontent and sense of injustice.
5. Social Media and Grassroots Mobilization: The rise of social media played a significant role in mobilizing and organizing the movement. Activists used platforms like Twitter, Facebook, and livestreams to spread their message and coordinate protests, making it easier to bring together people from diverse backgrounds.

Occupy Wall Street participants staged sit-ins and demonstrations in New York City's Zuccotti Park and various other cities across the country. They used the slogan "We are the 99%" to emphasize the economic disparity between the wealthiest 1 percent and the rest of the population. While the Occupy Wall Street movement didn't result in specific policy changes or legislative actions, it succeeded in drawing attention to income inequality and social injustice. It sparked conversations and debates about the role of finance in society, wealth distribution, and the influence of money in politics. The movement also influenced other social and political movements, inspiring similar protests and discussions around the world.

The Wealth Gap and Social Cohesion

Addressing wealth inequalities is important for every socioeconomic group. Interestingly, research has found that the greater the gap between rich and poor, the worse the health outcomes are for both groups, as the lack of social cohesion in the society creates stress, which affects both lower and higher-income groups alike.[422] In places where inequalities are particularly pronounced, there are higher rates of crime and murder, children are bullied at school more, and there are increased teenage pregnancies, as well as mental health problems and substance abuse.[423] There are also less supportive social networks, as a steep wealth hierarchy does little to nurture community spirit and a sense of belonging. In high crime areas like Johannesburg, South Africa, the rich barricade themselves in gated communities and spend small fortunes on private security guards, increasing levels of social stress and divisiveness. Ultimately, when inequality increases, everyone's health suffers. Studies have found that increasing wealth inequality leads to greater dissatisfaction in society overall, as the "jealousy effect" (where people envy those who are richer than themselves) is stronger than the "proud effect" (where people enjoy feeling superior to those lower down the wealth ladder).[424]

SOCIAL AND ENVIRONMENTAL JUSTICE

As we will discuss in the next chapter, the global wealth gap has been exacerbated by the climate crisis. A 2020 UN report estimated that the gap between the richest and poorest 10 percent of the global population is 25 percent bigger compared to a world without climate change.[425] Increasing numbers of climate refugees are threatening to reverse progress made in reducing inequality, highlighting that social justice is deeply intertwined with environmental justice. Sustainability is not a question of choosing between environmental protection or social equity but of reconciling the relationship between the two so that they are mutually supportive. Social and environmental justice advocates need to work together to address systemic issues, promoting participatory decision-making and seeking solutions that benefit everyone while preserving the planet.

One such advocate is Kate Raworth of Oxford University, who has developed an alternative economic model called Doughnut Economics, which offers a vision for a more equitable and sustainable world. She has challenged traditional economic thinking by proposing a framework that takes into account both social and planetary boundaries in ensuring the health and well-being of our society. The central idea of Doughnut Economics is depicted graphically as a doughnut shape, with two concentric circles:

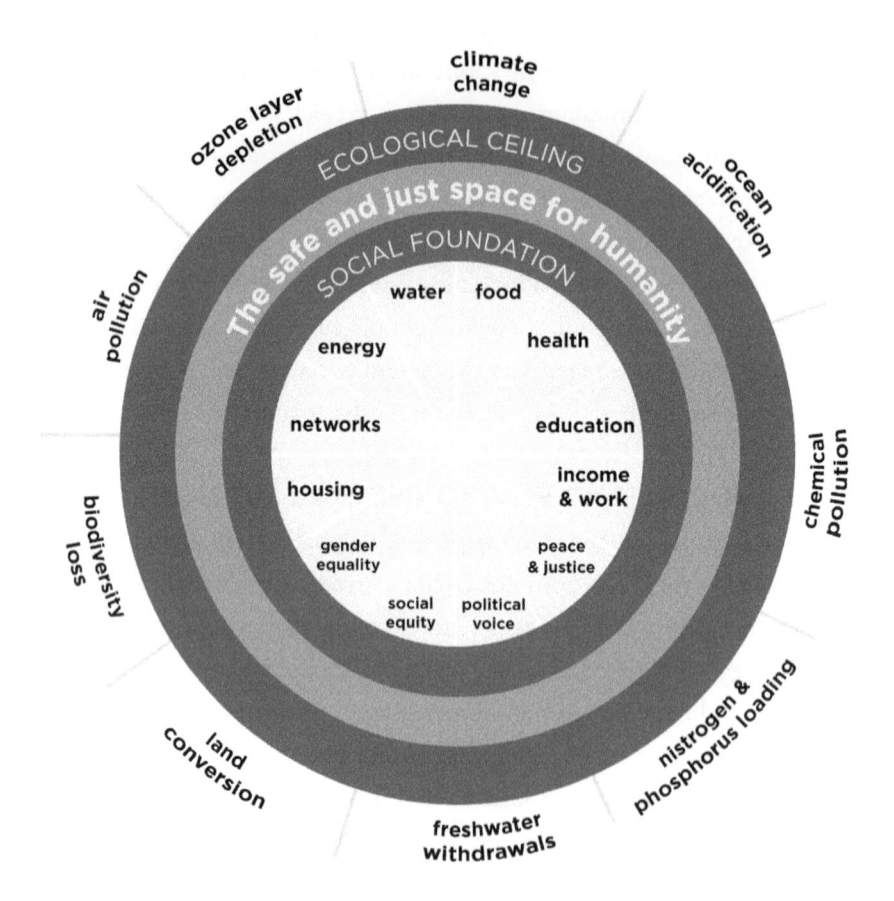

1. **Social Foundation (Inner Circle):** The inner circle represents the "social foundation" and includes essential human needs, such as food, water, housing, healthcare, education, gender equality, income and work, social networks, equity, political voice, and more. The goal is to ensure that no one falls below this minimum

standard of well-being and that everyone has access to a decent quality of life.

2. **Planetary Boundaries (Outer Circle)**: The outer circle represents the "planetary boundaries," which refer to environmental limits and the Earth's capacity to sustain life. These boundaries include issues like climate change, biodiversity loss, deforestation, pollution, and other ecological concerns. The aim is to avoid overshooting these limits to prevent irreversible damage to the planet.

The space between the two circles is referred to as the "safe and just space for humanity." The goal of Doughnut Economics is to create an economic system that operates within this space, allowing society to thrive in a more equitable way while respecting the Earth's ecological boundaries. Certainly, as prosperity spreads, life expectancy rises, fertility rates fall, and education expands, but Raworth proposes rethinking economic growth and development. Instead of pursuing endless GDP growth, she advocates for a balanced approach that promotes sustainable development, social equity, and environmental protection. She argues that the focus of policymakers needs to shift from prioritizing monetary indicators of progress to incorporating a broader set of social and environmental indicators. This encourages a change from the traditional "take-make-dispose" linear economy to a regenerative and circular economy that promotes resource efficiency and reduces waste. Doughnut Economics calls for policies and practices that address inequalities, ensuring basic human needs are met for all while also embracing sustainable technologies and practices. Such alternative models are important because the social determinants of health are intimately entwined with ecological health, the subject of our next chapter.

CONCLUSIONS

Social determinants play a fundamental role in shaping health outcomes and overall well-being for individuals and communities, significantly contributing to inequalities. Factors such as income, education, housing, access to healthcare, employment opportunities, and social support are all interconnected, creating disparities among different population groups. The social determinants of health encompass various aspects of our lives and can have long-lasting effects, often starting from early life.

Addressing the social determinants of health requires policies that go beyond healthcare services to include interventions in areas such as education, housing, employment, and urban planning. Focusing on social determinants is a form of preventive medicine; it may arguably be more effective in improving public health than solely concentrating on treating illnesses because it addresses so many of the root causes of our lifestyle diseases. A holistic approach to health considers the broader context in which people live and recognizes that health is influenced by multidimensional social, economic, and environmental factors.

Recognizing the significance of social determinants helps create comprehensive health strategies that also address environmental and social justice issues. Improving these determinants can lead to fairer opportunities and better health outcomes for all, regardless of their socioeconomic background. Engaging communities in decision-making processes and addressing their unique needs and strengths are essential for effective interventions. By addressing the root causes of health inequalities through social policies, programs, and community engagement, societies can work toward building healthier and more equitable environments, promoting better health and well-being for everyone in the world, not just those who can afford it.

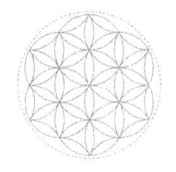

CHAPTER 12

ENVIRONMENTAL CONNECTION

All things are connected like the blood that unites us.
We do not weave the web of life; we are merely a strand in it.
Whatever we do to the web, we do to ourselves.
—Chief Seattle

Connection is critical in maintaining a solid foundation for health in any system, natural or otherwise. We are now facing the greatest threat to humanity since the dawn of our species—the climate crisis—and it will take all our powers of connectivity and collaboration to steer us through the stormy years ahead. We are the first generation to feel the effects of fossil fuel usage and chemical farming on our rapidly changing climate—and the last one to be able to do anything about it. Anthropogenic climate change, deforestation, and habitat loss have combined in a catastrophic trinity to trigger the sixth mass extinction, causing destruction on a potentially unimaginable scale.

The first half of this chapter describes the impact of climate change and biodiversity loss on human health, both now and in the future. Examining the deeper dynamics underlying the climate crisis shows that environmental, social, and economic stressors are deeply interwoven together. The issue of climate justice is highlighted, as the most at risk are in low-and-middle-income countries least able to adapt to climate change and where healthcare is already limited. The second half of the chapter is devoted to a discussion of how we might shift to a more sustainable society. The word *sustainability* is explored, considering what it really means to sustain life. The ecological principles Capra and Luigi Luisi[426] use to define sustainability help us to understand how it might apply to human health and well-being. The chapter concludes that the wisdom of nature provides us with the perfect guide to show us how we can heal ourselves and our planet.

THE ENVIRONMENTAL CRISIS

Over the past four billion years of life on Earth, nature has flourished—not in the steady and inexorable way we might imagine but interspersed with catastrophic mass extinction events. There have been five mass extinctions in the last five hundred million years, the last one wiping out the dinosaurs sixty-five million years ago. We are now entering what is called the "Anthropocene," an age when humans are having a dramatic impact on the planet. Since humans first evolved, we have cut down around half the trees on the planet.[427] Now, every year, we fell approximately ten million hectares of trees—the size of a small country,[428] which means that pretty soon there may not be any forest cover left. Combine this astonishing habitat destruction with fossil fuel burning, and it is little wonder that we are facing a climate crisis of epic proportions, threatening the very survival of life on Earth.

Thanks to a mass of rigorous scientific studies by the Intergovernmental Panel on Climate Change (IPCC),[429] the issue of sustainability has moved to center stage as we grapple with the problem of how human society can be organized in such a way that we don't destroy the planet. We are a global community; everything we do has an impact on everything else, which creates major implications for policymakers and decision-making on all levels. Two hundred years of global capitalism and the pursuit of unlimited economic growth have resulted in a throw-away society based on excessive consumption and production that does not reflect environmental costs in prices. Our increasingly energy- and resource-intensive industrial systems generate pollution and waste on an unprecedented scale, resulting in the ecological mess we are in now.

On top of the imperative for unlimited economic growth, we also have the interrelated problem of population growth, exacerbated by the ever-increasing gap between rich and poor. As the poor continue to get poorer, infant mortality goes up, and so the need for bigger families grows as a fail-safe for survival. This results in a vicious circle of exponential population expansion, fueling further resource depletion. As mentioned in the previous chapter, poverty is often coupled with illiteracy and female disempowerment, with many women in developing countries having limited access to education and family planning, which further increases demographic pressures. Poverty results in growing health pressures and the spread of infectious diseases, as well as environmental degradation.

As these vicious circles play out, we see the familiar interconnected problems of malnutrition, overgrazing, overfishing, deforestation, soil erosion, falling water tables, and so on. Resource depletion also causes social conflict, as problems like water scarcity, food insecurity, energy crises, and forced migration create political tensions, wars, human rights violations, and failed states that fuel tyranny and terrorism, which in turn have a major impact around the globe.[430] All are interrelated, and so as the feedback loops caused by our unsustainable lifestyles and global inequities continue, the web of life begins to break down.

ENVIRONMENTAL IMPACTS ON HEALTH

As pollution and waste continue, the world's climate has started to change dramatically, threatening human health with hazards such as rising sea levels, severe drought, storms, floods, and forest fires. Temperature peaks have caused glaciers and ice sheets to melt in the North and South Poles, causing the ocean to rise by about six to eight inches in the last one hundred years.[431] According to a study published in *Nature Communications*, by 2050, sea level rise could expose three hundred million people to coastal flooding globally, with high tides permanently rising above land occupied by over 150 million people.[432] Some of the most vulnerable cities in the world include London, New York, Miami, Shanghai, Mumbai, Bangkok, and Jakarta.

Extreme weather events have become increasingly common all over the world as global warming picks up pace. Tropical storms and hurricanes have ripped coastal communities apart, floods have caused spikes in waterborne diseases such as cholera, typhoid, dysentery, and hepatitis A, and droughts have caused crop damage and food and water shortages. Heatwaves have become increasingly common, causing heat stroke, chronic kidney disease, and drops in maternal, neonatal, and mental health.[433] In recent years, we have seen record-breaking heatwaves; in fact, 2015 to 2023 were the eight warmest years in recorded history.[434] Heatwaves also contribute to wildfires, such as the tragic 2019 Australian bushfire disaster, which killed 450 people and over a billion native animals. The 2020 Californian wildfires devastated communities and caused more than nineteen billion dollars in damage, and the 2023 wildfires on Maui, Hawaii, killed over a hundred people and razed the historic town of Lahaina. Wildfires lead to spikes in carbon emissions, further contributing to climate change. They also result in chronic health problems such as respiratory and cardiovascular disease, which cause ripple effects for local communities long after the fires have been put out.

Heat is, in fact, one of the biggest environmental threats we face, causing thousands of excess deaths a year—and to date, the planet has only warmed by 0.5–1 degrees Celsius, which is nowhere near the 1.5 degrees Celsius that the IPCC projects by 2050. As temperatures rise, heat hazards are likely to grow dramatically. The elderly and people with preexisting health conditions are particularly vulnerable to heat-related illnesses, so demographic changes such as aging populations will amplify these effects. So will trends like increased urbanization due to the "urban heat island effect," as cities heat up quicker than rural areas because they are so built up. As temperatures rise, so can humidity—and if this reaches close to 100 percent (dubbed "wet bulb temperatures"), it can cause serious health problems such as heart attacks and strokes.[435] Mental health issues soar in the heat, as the physical strain of trying to remain cool results in increased stress, which can push people over the edge mentally and emotionally—particularly if accompanied by hot, sleepless nights.[436]

The impact of rising temperatures depends on the region, the percentage of vulnerable people within that region, and the resources they have to mitigate heat effects. In rich countries, people adapt by ramping up air conditioning and fans, which adds to carbon emissions if powered by fossil fuels, increasing the threat of climate hazards in the future. In low-income areas, air conditioning is prohibitively expensive, so the poor suffer from more heat-related illnesses and mortality, contributing to climate injustice.

Global warming also causes changes in the demographics of infectious diseases such as malaria, dengue fever, Zika, and West Nile virus, which can now survive at higher latitudes.[437] More than 80 percent of the world's population currently live in areas at risk from vector-borne diseases (transmitted by insects such as mosquitoes, ticks, and flies). This percentage is set to rise as climate change increases the number of countries in the "Goldilocks zone," where pathogens thrive in warmer climes.[438] For instance, West Nile virus has sprung up in the US, and dengue fever is now being reported in European countries like Italy, which has historically never suffered from the disease.[439] Malaria is spreading to higher latitudes in Asia, South America, Oceania, Africa, and the Middle East. Places experiencing more rain can also expect a rise in mosquito-borne diseases such as Zika and Chikunga virus, as well as West Nile, dengue, and malaria. As climate change continues, these diseases are likely to spread into temperate areas in Europe as well as the United States.[440] In places where transmission has to date been either zero or historically low, this spells disaster for populations with vulnerable immune systems and public health systems unprepared for new influxes.

Rising temperatures are also causing changes to air quality, increasing ground-level "ozone smog," which is created when pollution from cars and factories reacts to sunlight and heat. It also increases pollen in the air, which results in spikes of allergies and asthma. Dirty air leads to rises in cardiovascular and respiratory illnesses, resulting in chronic conditions such as heart disease and chronic obstructive pulmonary disease (COPD). In fact, fossil fuel–related air pollution is responsible for a staggering one in five deaths worldwide.[441] Poorer urban areas are disproportionately affected by air pollution, so climate change and inequity are inexorably bound together. In developing countries, daily cooking often involves the burning of biofuels indoors, which has terrible health repercussions, particularly for women and children, killing around four million people each year.[442]

The good news is that clean air benefits occur very quickly if we stop burning fossil fuels, as was seen during the Coronavirus pandemic when air pollution plummeted as roads were emptied, planes remained on the ground, and crops were no longer sprayed with pesticides. Indians in the state of Punjab were overjoyed to see the Himalayan Mountains from over a hundred miles away as the mist of pollutants dissipated and blue skies abounded. In the first part of 2020, global carbon emissions dropped by an estimated 7 percent for the first time ever, showing Coronavirus to be more effective at slowing climate change than any of the world's policy initiatives combined (at least temporarily).[443]

CLIMATE JUSTICE

Future climate change will cause sea levels to rise, crops to fail, food systems to be disrupted, and water supplies to dry out, creating ripple effects that will be felt everywhere and hit the most vulnerable populations hardest. Because the most at risk are in low- and middle-income countries least able to adapt to climate change and who are also least responsible for the climate crisis, climate justice has become a hot topic in recent years. Climate justice entails protecting the rights of the most vulnerable to the effects of environmental change, promoting equity, and assured access to basic resources. Addressing environmental issues is an integral part of sustainable development; in fact, the three pillars of sustainability are people, planet, and profits. Poverty alleviation is thus intimately entwined with climate action.

Climate, social, and health justice are linked in the following ways:

Disproportionate Health Burdens: As the planet wrestles with climate change, its effects ripple across regions and communities in very unequal ways. It is often the most poverty-stricken, vulnerable groups in society who find themselves shouldering the weight of these impacts. Marginalized communities are often located closer to polluting industries, power plants, highways, and waste disposal sites, and their health pays the price. Such communities are often populated by ethnic minorities, which exacerbates health disparities and existing inequalities, contributing to environmental racism.

Access to Healthcare: The strains of climate hazards reverberate throughout healthcare systems, particularly in regions already grappling with limited resources. This has dire consequences if access to essential services like emergency care, lifesaving medications, and disease prevention measures is affected.

Migration and Displacement: Climate change can lead to increased migration and displacement as people flee from areas affected by extreme weather events. Climate refugees often face additional challenges, including lack of legal protection, limited access to resources, and difficulties with social integration. The potential for political and social unrest rises as migrant hosts grapple with sudden influxes and wrestle with the pressures of adjusting to demographic shifts and social and healthcare needs in a short space of time.

Limited Access to Healthy Environments: Disadvantaged communities often find themselves denied the infrastructure, resources, and thoughtful planning that promotes access to healthy environments such as beaches, parks, woods, and other green spaces. Thanks to rapid, often unplanned urbanization in low-income areas, marginalized people may live in sinker estates or slums with limited access to nature, perpetuating social and health injustice.

Multiple Stressors: Vulnerable communities may face a combination of environmental, social, and economic stressors that contribute to worsening health. For example, high air pollution rates, lack of access to clean water and nutritious food, limited medical services, and low employment opportunities can all intersect to create a complex web of health problems. The implications extend far beyond individual lives, shaping the very foundations of our global socio-political system, as health inequalities sow the seeds of poverty, substance abuse, crime, conflict, and wars.

Addressing climate justice is clearly critical for protecting both humanity and the planet. It involves not only mitigating greenhouse gas emissions and adapting to changing climate, but supporting vulnerable communities by promoting equitable access to resources, healthcare, and a healthy environment. It also involves participatory and inclusive decision-making so that the voices and perspectives of marginalized people are heard.

Because climate justice is such an essential aspect of sustainability, the 2022 UN Climate Change Conference held in Egypt (COP27) agreed to a loss and damage fund to help developing countries deal with environmental disasters. Policymakers heard from diverse groups, including indigenous people, local communities, and children. The resulting deal marked a turning point in acknowledging the vast inequities people face in adapting to the climate crisis, including the deep disparities in healthcare between developed and developing countries.

The Green Climate Fund (GCF) has also been in operation since the historic Paris Agreement of 2015. It is the world's largest climate fund designed to help developing countries grow their economies while lowering their carbon emissions. Rich countries have agreed to contribute a total of one hundred billion dollars a year to help poorer ones develop more sustainably. However, only some nations have followed through on their commitments, while others have faced challenges in meeting their pledges.[444] Critics contend that the GCF's efforts are insufficient, and much more needs to be done to help the Global South develop sustainably so that the world can meet its net zero targets by 2050.

BIODIVERSITY LOSS AND HEALTH

The staggering degradation of the environment, involving the clear-cutting of rainforests and the invasion of pristine ecosystems in the name of economic development, has fragmented wildlife into ever smaller areas and fractured the web of life. The statistics are sobering; since 1970, we have lost *more than two-thirds* of mammal, fish, bird, reptile, and amphibian populations, mainly due to habitat destruction from logging and industrial farming.[445] In the tropical regions of Latin America, where the Amazon lies, there has been a jaw-dropping 94 percent loss of biodiversity since 1970. This has been largely due to hunting, poaching, logging, and unsustainable farming. In the Amazon jungle, extinction rates are one thousand times faster today than would happen naturally, and there are now over one million species facing extinction.[446] Worldwide, 40 percent of insect species are declining, and a third are endangered, with global populations of pollinators declining at an unprecedented rate of 2 percent a year.[447]

One consequence of these immensely destructive practices for human health is a rise in disease transmission. When creatures that act as natural hosts or predators decline, this can lead to a rise in disease-carrying organisms such as mosquitoes, ticks, or flies, which spread zoonotic illnesses like malaria, dengue fever, or Lyme disease. Because of increasing human encroachment into wilderness areas and a corresponding rise in contact with wildlife, viruses that have lived symbiotically with the surrounding ecology are now jumping from animals to humans, with deadly results. In the past forty years, the world's worst pandemics and epidemics—including COVID-19, HIV, SARS, MERS, Ebola, and Zika virus—have stemmed from habitat destruction and the trade and consumption of wildlife.

Drivers and Effects of Biodiversity Loss

The five biggest drivers of biodiversity loss are habitat loss, climate change, pollution, land degradation, and invasive species. These drivers affect everything from food security, nutrition, and medicinal supply to livelihoods and migration, creating political and economic crises, health breakdowns, and human suffering on a grand scale. Biodiversity loss affects food production, as crops rely on diverse ecosystems for pollination and natural pest control. As covered in Chapter 6, when biodiversity declines, it can result in reduced crop yields, increased vulnerability to pests, and a smaller range of nutrient-dense foods, which leads to malnutrition, vitamin deficiencies, and related health issues.

Biodiversity loss also affects human health in terms of medicinal resources. Plants are a crucial source of medicine, and environmental degradation can lessen our ability to find potentially lifesaving drugs and treatments. In developing countries, it is estimated that around 80 percent of people rely on plant-based medicine for curing ailments, so biodiversity loss makes it harder to combat disease in the very places that have the least access to healthcare resources.[448]

Biodiversity loss affects livelihoods, with many communities relying on their nature-rich local habitats for employment, such as fishing, agriculture, forestry, and tourism. When biodiversity loss impacts job markets, poverty increases, causing grave impacts on health. Green common spaces in the areas we live and work in also contribute to stress reduction, so destroying nature can have a major impact not just on the economy but on our mental well-being. Biodiversity loss has far-reaching and immediate consequences for every level of human health—from individual to community—as well as societal and global well-being. Biodiversity is foundational to the health of the planet and has a direct impact on all our lives, so it urgently needs to be protected.

The Coronavirus Pandemic

In late 2019, COVID-19 reportedly jumped from bats to people in China and quickly spread to every corner of the globe in a matter of months. COVID immediately highlighted the injustices of our society by disproportionately affecting the poor and the marginalized, as the worst hit were those living in densely populated urban areas. Impoverished living conditions, lack of sanitation, inadequate health care, and unprepared governments deepened the spread and increased mortality worldwide. The virus knew no boundaries; the stark truth that rich and poor are only socially—not biologically—separated was evident for all to see.

The health crisis quickly became an economic crisis, as lockdowns all over the world resulted in businesses closing, supply chains breaking down, stock markets crashing, and unemployment soaring. COVID winners and losers soon emerged, as big firms like Pfizer, Amazon, and Netflix reaped huge rewards from the pandemic while small "mom-and-pop" shops suffered. Children had to be homeschooled, widening education gaps as digital divides meant that disadvantaged families without computers and internet access missed out. Mental health issues soared as people dealt with lockdown loneliness, joblessness, financial insecurity, and childcare issues. Relationships were derailed and domestic abuse rose, while anxiety and depression skyrocketed. Alcohol and drug use escalated, as did unhealthy eating habits. Suicidal thoughts rose not just in those with diagnosed mental health conditions, but in young people, ethnic minorities, and lower-income groups.[449] Frontline workers and those in the caregiving industry faced enormous stress, suffering emotional as well as physical exhaustion.

The politics of COVID became extremely fraught as governments were under intense pressure to react quickly and decisively—the political costs of (mis)managing the crisis could not have been higher. Politicians scrambled to formulate policies to handle the crisis in a way that suited their local populations and particular national circumstances, juggling the competing need to curb the virus while protecting the economy from ruin. Policy responses varied significantly across nations, depending on their stance on "health verses the economy," and those who failed to contain the virus were summarily punished with plummeting approval ratings. The balance of power in the world shifted as governments were reshuffled based on their COVID credentials. Later, once the pandemic was over and the wider socioeconomic impacts of lockdowns became evident, politics was reshuffled again as people struggled to deal with the economic recessions and the mental health fallouts of the pandemic.

COVID-19 shook up the world, unmasking the imbalances, injustices, and fragility of our socio-political and economic systems. It also showed the futility of solving any of the world's problems in isolation. The pandemic highlighted how infectious diseases are intimately connected with chronic ones, which are themselves linked with unhealthy, unsustainable modern lifestyles and the corresponding environmental degradation that creates pandemics in the first place. While there is some debate over whether COVID started in a Chinese wet market or in a zoonotic laboratory, the very reason that these labs exist is to research the increasing prevalence of infectious diseases resulting from escalating ecological stress and habitat encroachment by humans.[450] Environmental degradation is a key factor in the global health crisis, and the world can no longer afford to ignore it.

SUSTAINABILITY AND THE WISDOM OF NATURE

So, how might we resolve the environmental crisis and shift to a more sustainable society? In *The Systems View of Life*, Capra and Luigi Luisi[451] explore the word *sustainability*, asking what it truly means to sustain life. The most common definition of sustainable development is taken from the "Brundtland Report" by the World Commission on Environment and Development in 1983, which states that sustainability is: "Development that meets the needs of the present without compromising the ability of future generations to meet their needs."[452]

This is arguably a very human-centric definition, and Capra and Luigi Luisi adopt a more eco-centric perspective, defining sustainability as creating communities and social systems that meet human needs without undermining nature's inherent ability to nurture all life on the planet. They draw from the science of ecology, outlining the fundamental principles that have enabled ecosystems to thrive for millennia. These principles underpin all systems, everywhere, and so are just as applicable to our health and society as they are to the environment. Capra and Luigi Luisi highlight that rather than designing a sustainable community from scratch, all we need do is look to the wisdom of nature to provide us with the perfect guide for what sustainable health and well-being might look like in the years ahead. The authors call this "ecoliteracy," which highlights that sustainable systems share the following essential characteristics:

Interdependence

All living things depend on each other to survive and flourish. Nature is a symbiosis of nested systems that make up a complex, sophisticated web of relationships. Humans are part of this complexity and rely on ecological systems for essential resources such as food, water, air, and climate, as well as disease regulation and cultural values. As humanity has become ever more disconnected from nature, we have forgotten the interdependency and reciprocity at the heart of the web of life, leading to the exploitation of the environment and a feeling of isolation from the natural world that has deep psychological and spiritual connotations (see Chapters 13 and 14).

To have a sustainable society, we must recognize that we are fundamentally at one with nature. As Capra and Luigi Luisi endeavor to highlight, an essential aspect of sustainability is changing our reductionist perspective to a systemic way of thinking so that instead of objectifying the natural world and plundering it for its resources, we see how intimately connected and dependent we are on the web of life. This perspective requires a shift of focus from objects to relationships, and from parts to wholes, so that we see ourselves as part of nature and thus respect our roles as stewards rather than exploiters of the environment.

Because interdependency is so fundamental to life, the systems view sees sustainable ecosystems as based on partnership and collaboration—in contrast to the traditional Darwinian view, which argues that competition is the most pervasive characteristic of nature. While our current global political economy is based largely on competition, a sustainable world will need to have cooperation at its heart.

In Johan Norberg's book *Open: How Collaboration and Curiosity*

Shaped Humankind,[453] he argues that our ancestors needed cooperation to survive, and that partnership and social openness are key to human advancement. He describes every problem as a knowledge problem, including climate change. We know what needs to happen, but what we need to do is find ways of collaborating with each other to spread ideas and get the job done. When we internalize just how interdependent we are, we become more open to the wisdom and perspectives of others so that we can partner with each other to find the best solutions. The ecological principles of cooperation and conservation are thus central to sustainability, replacing the old worldview, which emphasizes competition, expansion, and exploitation.

As highlighted in previous chapters, the principle of interdependence can be seen in terms of our own individual health, too, as our cells and organs are nested within a wider web of interconnections that make up the miracle of our bodies. The interrelationship between the key pillars of health—nutrition, sleep, exercise, relaxation, and connection—shows the folly of isolationist thinking when it comes to well-being and highlights the need for a holistic view with the principle of interdependence at its core.

Cyclical Flow

Another ecological principle that Capra and Luigi Luisi highlight is cyclical flow. Within and between networks, there is always a circular flow of inputs and outputs that ensure the survival and nurturance of all natural systems. Nature recycles everything, so what is waste for one creature is food for another. We are the only species that blatantly disregards this principle, with wasteful systems that allow materials to go from sources to sinks without thought to the natural, regenerative flow of life.

The sustainable communities of the future will need to be built on a circular economy based on the "3 Rs": reduce, reuse, and recycle. Production of goods and services are already being replaced with models based on "services and flow" so that industrial processes reflect pioneering eco-design concepts such as "ecological clustering" (where businesses are clustered together in such a way that the waste of one organization becomes a resource for another). "Waste equals food" will eventually have to become the order of the day in all areas of life, including sustainable agriculture, technology, business, and design. A circular economy also shifts us away from the idea of individual ownership and competition to cooperatives and a "share culture." This means, for instance, that instead of purchasing goods and services outright, we might lease them in a continual flow between suppliers and consumers, which helps to dematerialize society. Sustainable communities based on circular flow know that the success of the whole depends on the success of individual members thriving, so they are partnering and collaborative rather than competitive and controlling.

Individual health also relies on cyclical flow. The cycles of nature are reflected in the seasonal needs of our bodies, as we desire different foods and have different energy levels and sleep patterns at varying times of the year. Sustainable health means taking the cycles of nature into consideration so that we change our routines accordingly, including eating seasonal produce or waking earlier in summer and later in winter as our circadian rhythms adjust to different daylight hours. Healthy lifestyles are in tune with nature's rhythms, and this needs to be reflected in our social and cultural norms to create a healthy work-life balance.

The human body is, of course, its own microcosmic network of cyclical flow, maintaining and regulating itself in dynamic balance with all the relationships that occur both within our physicality and outside in our surrounding environment. Our health is predicated on strong connections, and nurturing ourselves means nourishing these relationships. When connectivity breaks down, ill-health results. Ecosystems have multiple feedback loops that spread out into ever-widening circles, and this may make it difficult to see the original source of the disturbance. Similarly, the complexity of our own bodies and human relationships can obscure the root cause of our health problems. This underlines the need for diagnoses and treatments that take a systemic view, using integrative medical approaches that untangle the web of causality and thread back to the original source of the malady.

Solar Powered

Another key principle of ecology is the fact that nature is solar powered. Food webs depend on plants to transform sunlight into energy-rich organic compounds and oxygen via the process of photosynthesis. The entire web of life is solar powered, and our economies need to reflect this too. Solar energy is, of course, renewable and includes not just photovoltaic electricity but other indirect sources such as biomass, wave, and hydropower. The world is moving toward a renewable energy economy as the cost of green energy becomes ever more competitive, but we are by no means there yet.

Research by the IPCC shows that greenhouse gas emissions need to reach net zero by 2050 if we are to avoid catastrophic climate change resulting from a rise in global temperatures over and above 1.5 degrees Celsius.[454] To hit emissions targets by 2050, up to 80 percent of the world's fossil fuel resources need to stay in the ground.[455] If we are to safeguard our planet for future generations, the days of unrestrained fossil fuel burning are over. Ending our reliance on fossil fuels is a herculean task, requiring systemic policies that utilize both supply-sided and demand-sided approaches. Growing our green energy supply needs huge investment, transforming the global economy in a way not seen since the Industrial Revolution. Reducing demand is equally necessary, as the more we can limit our energy usage, the more efficient and easier it will be to transition to a clean energy supply. Massive changes are needed in our political and business models, such as introducing carbon taxes so that market prices accurately reflect the environmental costs of production, as well as in our lifestyle choices so that green consumption encourages green supply and vice versa.

The fact that the web of life is solar powered has important implications for our health too. Not only do we need to switch to a renewable energy economy to avoid runaway climate change, but we also need to change our eating habits to be more energy efficient. Plant-based diets make the most of the energy harnessed from the sun. However, the higher up the food web we go, this energy decreases, as animals that eat herbivores receive only a small amount of the sun's energy that is stored in their prey. In fact, only a fraction of the energy from one trophic level is transferred to the next—the general rule of thumb is known as the "ten percent rule," where 10 percent of the energy from one level is available for the next one up the food chain. Raising livestock requires huge amounts of plant feed and agricultural land, so plant-based diets are much more energy efficient than meat-based ones, freeing up natural resources and wildlife habitat to boost biodiversity while reducing emissions.

Flexibility and Balance

Other key principles found in nature that can help us navigate our way to a more sustainable society are those of flexibility and balance. While ecosystems tend to remain stable within limits, they are also dynamic, constantly changing in response to natural—and human-induced—disturbances. As Capra and Luigi Luisi explain, "the web of life is a flexible, ever-fluctuating network." However, we are pushing the environment beyond its tolerance thresholds, and nature is beginning to reach irreversible tipping points—hence the alarming rate of polar ice melt and the dwindling Amazon rainforest. Tipping points spell disaster if we do not act quickly to change our ways; when ecosystems lose their balance, it can result in negative feedback loops that dramatically damage environmental services and consequently endanger human health.[456]

Sustainable health from an individual perspective means we need to live balanced, green lifestyles, connecting the dots between the environment and our nutrition, sleep, relaxation, and exercise habits. We need to be flexible and resilient, maximizing our adaptation energy with downtime so that we feel less stressed and more content—and consequently less prone to illness. We also need to ensure that we have strong, resilient relationships and that our communities and cultures are flexible and responsive to the needs of the time. Sustainable societies require versatile institutions so that our communities are adaptable. When institutions become too rigid, they become fragile and break. Our social structures, cultures and organizations must feel solid and dependable on the one hand to inspire trust, but on the other, they need to flex with the evolving needs of an ever-changing and increasingly connected world.

Flexibility and balance are particularly important in terms of power structures to avoid hegemony and the breakdown of the rule of law. Moving away from rigid social divisions and polarization is key to ensuring dynamic balance and the health of society. This cannot occur without respect for basic human rights, which include the right to healthy living conditions and access to nature, good nutrition, access to education, freedom of speech, social justice, self-determination, cultural integrity, and diversity.

Diversity

Another principle of ecology that is critical to sustainability is diversity. The variety of life in nature contributes to the adaptability, resilience, and productivity of ecosystems. Genetic diversity is vital for the evolutionary process so that species can adapt to changing environments. Greater genetic diversity provides a larger pool of traits that can be selected for in the face of change. This means that biodiverse ecosystems are more stable and better able to withstand disturbances like invasive species or a changing climate and natural disasters. Biodiversity creates strong networks that can buffer against disruptions, hence maintaining ecological balance. Diversity in nature provides a wide range of ecoservices and increases the likelihood of finding sustainable alternatives in the face of resource scarcity or depletion.

Diversity is also critical to human health by providing us with a range of options for nutrition, medicine, livelihoods, and well-being. We need diversity in our gut microbiomes, in our food, in our plant medicines, and in our environment and green spaces so that we can maximize our physical and mental well-being. We also need diversity socially and in our personal relationships, as well as in our politics, cultures, and economics. Embracing diversity helps to dismantle systemic barriers, reduce inequalities, and promote social justice, fostering a more inclusive and equitable society. Embracing diversity promotes social inclusion and cohesiveness by fostering understanding and respect among individuals and communities. Sustainable societies are ones that encourage dialogue and ensure that all voices and perspectives are heard, leading to stronger and more harmonious social structures.

Diversity encompasses a range of dimensions, including race, ethnicity, culture, language, religion, age, gender, and sexual orientation. Drawing on a diverse range of perspectives ensures that we maximize our human potential, finding different ways to solve problems and view the world, which encourages us to open up to new ideas and possibilities. When people from different backgrounds collaborate, they bring unique insights and ideas, creating pioneering solutions to challenges. Good examples are social entrepreneurs, who often bring together diverse skill sets to create new business models that address social, economic, and environmental issues. Diversity is also a hot topic in corporate social responsibility debates, as businesses strive to encourage innovation by promoting equal opportunities for employment. By leveraging the different strengths and capabilities of their members, sustainable societies can foster economic competitiveness, productivity, and resilience, increasing prosperity.

Because diversity encourages innovation, creativity, flexibility and balance, this circles back to the need for interdependence and cooperation so that we avoid fragmented, polarized, and sclerotic social relationships. Diversity without an understanding of our innate interdependence only leads to prejudice, division, and conflict. By embracing and celebrating diversity, we can create societies that are socially, economically, and environmentally vibrant, leading to long-term sustainability and a better quality of life.

Growth and Development

Another key principle of ecology is growth. Growth and development are clearly central to the flourishing of life, yet as Capra and Luigi Luisi highlight, growth in nature is not linear or unlimited. Instead, different parts of natural systems develop and expand while other parts decline, die back, and are recycled back into the earth. This is the so-called circle of life. In the case of plants, when they are in their pioneering stage, growth is quantitative as the community seeds itself, colonizes a territory, and rapidly expands. As plants mature, there is a shift away from quantitative growth toward complexity and refinement, as the elegance of nature unfolds in partnership with the surrounding ecosystem. The authors liken this stage to the concept of "qualitative growth," which is growth that enhances the quality of life through the process of maintenance, and regeneration, which allows systems to stay in balance with the web of life.

If we are to accept that sustainability means meeting human needs without undermining nature's inherent ability to sustain life, this means avoiding breaching ecological thresholds by respecting planetary boundaries and the limits to growth. However, the notion that there are limits to growth flies in the face of traditional neo-classical economics, which unquestioningly sees all growth as good. This is perhaps the biggest flaw in our current political thinking because it is predicated on the idea that economic growth can carry on ad infinitum as long as we use resources more efficiently.

In the global political economy, national prosperity is measured by Gross Domestic Product (GDP), or the volume of goods and services bought and sold. However, this ignores the social and environmental costs of doing business. Countries use GDP as a measure of standards of living, but GDP does not account for the vast environmental degradation that occurs because of production, which in turn reduces the quality of life and general well-being of society. A famous study by Daly and Cobb (1987)[457] found that economic growth in the US in the 1960s caused welfare per capita to increase, but further economic growth in the 1970s and 1980s actually caused overall welfare to decline. They concluded that after a critical threshold, the negative aspects of affluence (such as environmental destruction, loss of community, increased materialism, and diminishing personal satisfaction from consumerism) start to outweigh the positive aspects so that continual economic growth results in a decline in quality of life.

The pursuit of unlimited economic growth is considered by many to be the root cause of our environmental crisis. Relentless growth has resulted in a "cowboy economy," so-called because the cowboys of the North American plains lived on a linear flow of inputs and outputs, from sources to sinks, taking what they wanted from the earth and throwing away the rest. In the cowboy economy, there was no need to recycle anything because resources were assumed to be so abundant. Now we are facing ecological catastrophe, we can clearly no longer afford to be cowboys.

In a systems view of life, a sustainable community is one that aspires to qualitative rather than quantitative growth. In stark contrast to the quantitative GDP model favored by most economists, qualitative growth in human communities requires balancing material and economic concerns with ecological, social, cultural, and spiritual dimensions. There are now alternative models of economics that emphasize qualitative growth as a measure of sustainability, such as Green National Product, (Green GDP) that factor in the environmental consequences of economic growth and therefore offer a more realistic measure of the quality of life. Others include social dimensions, such as Kate Raworth's Doughnut Economics, as discussed in the last chapter. Another excellent example is the country of Bhutan's Gross National Happiness index. This index has four pillars: sustainable socioeconomic development, environmental conservation, cultural preservation, and good governance.

The wisdom of nature shows us that the biggest challenge for humanity is to shift toward a global economy based on a qualitative model, where the development of a sustainable community is life-enhancing—both for humanity and for nature. This means ensuring environmental protection, social justice, and human rights, as well as ethical behavior toward animals and all living creatures on the understanding that what we take from nature, we give back. A sustainable community thus aspires to development that is measured not solely on increasing levels of material consumption but by the health and well-being of its citizens (including physical, mental, emotional, and spiritual health), environmental health (including the quality of the soil, air, water, and natural habitats), and the health of society, (including measures of poverty, equity, education, literacy, and the richness of its culture and civic engagement).

Sustainable communities can only grow as far as the wider networks they are nested in allows, ensuring the limits to growth are not exceeded. "Good growth" involves renewable energies and zero emissions, rewilding and the restoration of nature, a circular economy, and production that internalizes ecological and social costs (for instance, by taxing environmental "bads" and subsidizing environmental "goods" so that consumer prices reflect the sustainability of products and services). "Bad growth" includes industrial processes that use fossil fuels, produce pollution and toxins, deplete natural resources, and degrade the environment.

Applied to individual health, good growth entails having one's physical needs met in a life-enhancing way through green lifestyles, sustainable nutrition, and a healthy work-life balance that includes plenty of time for rest and relaxation, exercise, and play. Sustainable health also involves understanding the potency of the mind-body-spirit connection and the personal development that can arise from overcoming life's challenges. It means cultivating good relationships and supportive social networks and nurturing a sense of community and belonging. We as individuals embody the same qualitative, multidimensional growth inherent in nature. Growth is never purely physical—it includes the kind of mental, emotional, and spiritual development that gives us a strong sense of contentment, well-being, and purpose in life. Spiritual connection is key to personal growth and unlocking our inner potential, which is the subject of the remaining chapters of this book.

CONCLUSIONS

The climate crisis is undoubtedly the most significant health threat humanity has ever faced, but it is also our greatest opportunity to redefine the economic, social, and ecological determinants of well-being to become life-enhancing rather than life-destroying. Sustainable communities are circular, renewable, and regenerative, honoring social and planetary boundaries with qualitative versus quantitative growth so that happiness—not just success—becomes the main goal of life. For our world to be truly sustainable, we need to recognize how individual, social, and environmental health are deeply interwoven together, like the roots of a mighty oak that has strong foundations able to withstand any storm. The wisdom of nature reminds us to respect our fundamental interdependence so that we nurture both ourselves and our planet with lifestyles that have reciprocity, diversity, flexibility, and balance at their core. Just as in nature, these principles make us highly adaptable, enabling us to dance with the challenges of life instead of becoming rigid and fragile, breaking at the slightest hint of change. By being eco-literate and applying nature's principles to human well-being, we can adopt a more sustainable approach that recognizes our innate connectivity in a systems view of health.

The Earth is what we all have in common.
—Wendel Berry

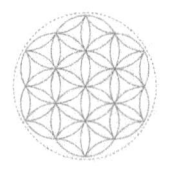

CHAPTER 13

SPIRITUAL CONNECTION

We are like islands in the sea, separate on the surface but connected in the deep.
—William James

In the next two chapters, we explore the importance of spiritual connection in a systems view of health. Here, we discuss the ancient idea that "we are one," delving into the mysterious world of quantum physics to find the essential unity of the universe as extolled by mystics throughout the ages. This idea of unity is causing a paradigm shift in Western thought, just as the global health and environmental crisis is encouraging a revision of the dualistic and polarizing perspectives of the past. The potential for a marriage of science and spirituality in the emerging systems paradigm sets the stage for the following chapter, where we discuss the link between spirituality, ecology, and human health, with a view to understanding humanity's role in preserving and sustaining the web of life.

THE UNITY OF THE UNIVERSE

Of all the forms of connection that are most fundamental to our well-being, it is perhaps our spiritual connection—or disconnection—that is having the greatest impact on our health. At the heart of the current malaise of chronic disease, environmental destruction, and social polarization in the world is a deep-rooted feeling of separation. People are unhappy, but they're not sure why; our lack of connection is causing us to experience reality in a fragmented and lonely way. We no longer see the sacredness of life; we do not believe that nature is to be revered or that our bodies are a temple. The natural world is valued simply as a resource to be used and then thrown away as part of an endless cycle of acquiring things in the pursuit of happiness.

In his acclaimed book *The Happiness Hypothesis*,[458] author Jonathan Haidt argues that humans have an innate desire for the divine; we need to feel a part of something larger than ourselves to know that we belong. He suggests that humans have a "divinity scale," according to which we perceive things to be more or less sacred. Even self-proclaimed atheists have places they consider to be sacred or special, such as where they got married or had their first kiss. Haidt asserts that special places, rituals, and awe-inspiring experiences make us feel happier because they allow us to feel more connected. In fact, establishing a relationship with something greater than ourselves is vital for the meaning of life. Yet many people, especially in the West, have an underlying sense that their lives are missing something because our culture does not really make room for sacred experiences. Our society has evolved to become fully practical, where everything is judged in terms of its instrumental value, and spiritual or religious sentiment is often frowned upon. There are plenty of scientific studies to bear this out; research shows mass consumption leads to lower levels of spiritual fulfillment and life satisfaction, because it simply creates more "wants," encouraging an addictive cycle of spending that feeds feelings of insecurity and discontent.[459]

Interestingly, though, at the frontiers of science, a nascent sense of the metaphysical is beginning to emerge, which is helping to change the Western worldview. Modern physics has opened the door to a quantum universe which can only be described as miraculous—and deeply mysterious. In the 1920s, the subatomic world encountered by the founding fathers of quantum physics was so puzzling that many of the early pioneers, such as

Niels Bohr, Werner Heisenberg, and Erwin Schrodinger, sought out the great spiritual traditions of the East and found some surprising answers. In the following discussion, we take a deep dive into the wacky world of quantum mechanics to see how science is converging on a view of reality that is remarkably akin to that of enlightened masters and sages throughout the ages.

Challenging Western Dualism

In Fritjof Capra's paradigm-shifting book *The Tao of Physics*,[460] which sold over a million copies worldwide in the 1970s, he describes how the Cartesian dualism of Western science gave rise not only to the blessings of classical physics and modern technology but also to the curse of environmental destruction and spiritual disconnection that defines our modern era. As discussed in Chapter 2, the worldview inspired by Descartes saw nature as consisting of two realms, matter and spirit, which existed independently of each other. Because the Church was so pervasive at the time of the scientific revolution, the narrative of science was founded on the division of body and soul, with the remit of scientists limited to the material realm lest they risk the wrath of powerful religious leaders who might have them executed for heresy. Galileo was put on trial for the "preposterous" idea that the Earth revolved around the sun, and Giordano Bruno was burned to death for having the audacity to champion his theory. This enmity resulted in a division between science and spirituality that persists to this day. For science, reality is defined by what is measurable, as perceived by the five senses. Rational objectivity rules supreme, banishing subjectivity, intuition, and spirituality from the pursuit of knowledge and worthy inquiry.

The schism that arose out of the Age of Reason has resulted in a dualistic perspective in Western thought that has caused us to feel separate from nature and the cosmos. So many of us see ourselves as isolated individuals living in a mechanical, random, and possibly even hostile universe. Nature has become objectified, seen as a resource to control and exploit rather than an organic, living organism we need to care for and sustain. Thankfully, however, this fragmented worldview is now coming full circle, not least because the advent of quantum physics has heralded a new vision of the cosmos as a dynamic web of infinite connection, complexity and harmony, where the parts cannot be separated from the whole.

We Are One

The idea that "we are one" has been expressed by saints and sages for millennia. Many of the world's greatest cultures, from the ancient Egyptians, Greeks, Aztecs, Chinese, and Indian civilizations to indigenous tribes around the globe, have conceived of the cosmos as inseparable, connected by a universal energy, spirit, or consciousness. In the West, before God and humankind were considered separate, Greek philosophy was in fact monistic (supporting the idea that reality is one organic whole). Heraclitus talked of "Logos" or universal divine reason, according to which all things were one. The Pythagorean school supported the idea of celestial unity and harmony, while the Neoplatonist school held that all reality could be derived from a single principle, "The One." The different mystery schools of the West have also variously emphasized oneness. For instance, the mystical branch of Islam, Sufism, teaches *wahdat-al-wujud*, which means "the Oneness of Being." The Kabbalah, the mystical arm of Judaism, teaches that there is only one reality, the infinite Ein Sof, which underlies all of creation.

The oneness of life is a particularly strong theme in Eastern spiritual traditions. The Vedic view (from which Hinduism is derived) is one of a dynamic and ever-changing world, which is a manifestation of "Brahman," the unmanifest, eternal cosmic consciousness of the universe.[461] Liberation, or "moksha," is to realize the unity and harmony of nature, understanding that all earthly phenomena are but divine expressions of Brahman. In the Vedic view, the true purpose of our lives is to transcend the idea that we are isolated egos and embrace this divine reality. We are enlightened when we experience our universal selves, when our individual consciousness dissolves into cosmic consciousness, and we become one with all that exists. Enlightenment is thus not simply an intellectual understanding of connection but a direct spiritual experience of unity.

Similarly, in Buddhism, there is a notion of oneness, as well as the constant flow and change of the manifest world.[462] As the Buddha said, "All things arise and pass away," and "He who experiences the unity of life sees his own self in all beings, and all beings in his own self." The Buddhist notion of nirvana is like that of moksha or liberation in Vedic texts, in which false notions of separateness vanish to reveal the oneness of life.

Likewise, in Taoism, the ultimate reality is called the *Tao* (or "the Way").[463] As with Vedic thought, there are two aspects of the Tao: the unmanifest, eternal aspect that is described as the "origin of all things" and the manifest aspect that is dynamic and ever-changing, known as the "Mother of ten thousand things." Eastern mysticism thus emphasizes both the inherent unity and dynamic nature of the universe.

Another common thread of Eastern traditions is the idea that enlightenment involves transcending the illusion of duality in the world. In the Taoist tradition, this is called "paradoxical unity," where the opposites of "yin" and "yang" merge to become one. Transcendence comes when you accept that the apparent polarity of life—mind and matter, light and dark, good and bad—are but two sides of the same coin, and that the cyclical nature of the universe means that one naturally waxes as the other wanes. The two aspects of reality transform themselves endlessly into one another; there is a constant merging and fusion of opposites in the harmony and rhythm of life. Rigidly attempting to adhere to one or the other pole does not work; the Tao is about finding the dynamic balance between the two.

This idea of duality in unity is also present in Vedic thought as "Purusha-Prakriti" (spirit-matter) or "Shiva-Shakti" (divine masculine-feminine).[464] The concept is not just limited to Eastern thought, though; Heraclitus wrote of a "dynamic unity" at the heart of the universe, in which "all is becoming" as opposites are united in a system of balanced exchanges. He proposed that there is a hidden connection behind all things, and therefore, aspects which are apparently "tending apart" are actually "being brought together."[465]

THE PARADOXICAL UNITY OF QUANTUM PHYSICS

Quantum physics also sees the universe as bound by a paradoxical unity. Physicists have been amazed to find that atoms and particles do not behave in the mechanical way that classical physics assumes they would, instead showing different—yet complementary—properties depending on the experimental context. Physics has revealed a quantum world that transcends dualistic thinking by being intimately entangled, where the whole is far more than the sum of its parts. As with Buddhist "koans,"[466] subatomic matter is a complete paradox, being both parts and wholes, particles and waves, form and empty space, subject and object, local and nonlocal, microcosm and macrocosm, matter and energy. To understand the unity behind these apparent opposites, let's look at each in turn.

Parts and Wholes

The mechanical worldview of mainstream science is atomistic; it sees nature as made up of elementary particles such as electrons that form the basic building blocks of the universe. However, the new paradigm gaining ground at the cutting edge of quantum physics sees the world as made up not of objects but of *relationships*. As Capra explains in the *Tao of Physics*, quantum theorists are exploring the idea that there are no basic building blocks in the universe, no elementary particles, laws, or equations. Because there are no fundamentals, nothing can be reduced or isolated; reductionist thinking is replaced with systems thinking. In this view, the relational nature of the universe means that parts are rather arbitrary distinctions because everything is ultimately one big, indivisible "whole." This quintessentially holistic perspective shares key characteristics with the ideas of Eastern philosophy.

In the quantum world, atoms are not discrete "things" per se but *probabilities of connections,* which means that they only exist as an *interaction*. This notion may at first be difficult to grasp, but the phrase "no man is an island" perhaps sums it up best. It means that "things" cannot exist independently but are in fact defined and determined by everything else in nature, so objects are really the product. Particles exist by virtue of their "self-consistency," or the degree to which they are in harmony with each other. Everything is in a process of synchronizing with everything else, and the synthesis of these relationships determines the overall structure of the web. Connections are thus primary, not objects, turning the mechanical view on its head and replacing the old metaphor of a machine with that of a network. Like the balance of yin and yang, there is a dynamic unity of opposites, so parts are really wholes, and objects are relationships.[467]

Waves and Particles

Wave-particle duality refers to the weird and wonderful property of subatomic matter where, at any given moment, it can appear like a wave or a particle. Where particles are hard, localized, and discrete, waves are fluid and spread out—so how can matter be both? Yet, at the subatomic level, this is exactly what occurs. Light is a classic example; when waves of light travel through space, they can also be observed as streams of photons. This is known as quantum "complementarity," which holds that matter has pairs of interrelated properties that cannot be observed simultaneously— so we see matter as either a wave or a particle, but we cannot see both at the same time. Physics thus appears to transcend dualistic notions such as particle and wave; like yin and yang, they are opposing aspects of a unified whole. Consequently, physicists have come up with a new term for subatomic matter: the "matter-wave."

Form Is Emptiness

Other paradoxes abound in modern physics. Studies have found that matter does not have the solidity assumed in classical physics but is in fact 99.9999999 percent empty space. This is due to the vast vacuum between nucleons and electrons. If the nucleus of an atom was magnified to the size of a golf ball, the whole atom would be the size of a sports stadium, and the electrons would be the size of little peas in the stands. It turns out that there is nothing really substantial about matter at all. This corresponds to the Buddhist philosophy that all things are essentially "empty," or, as the famous Heart Sutra describes, "form is emptiness and emptiness is form."

Stillness in Motion

There is also a unity between stillness and motion in the quantum universe. Physics highlights the fundamental "restlessness" of matter, revealing that a motionless object like a rock is in fact a hive of activity at the subatomic level. Matter is never still but always moving—rocks appear to be dead and inert but are in fact alive with dancing energy. Everything in the world is animated, reverberating in rhythmic patterns that move in harmony with nature. According to modern physics, nature is dynamic, in constant flow and motion. David Bohm, one of the founding fathers of quantum mechanics, famously described the universe as "the Undivided Wholeness in Flowing Movement."

Similarly, the Chinese sage Hong Ying-Ming said: "The stillness in stillness is not the real stillness; only when there is stillness in movement can a spiritual rhythm appear which pervades heaven and earth."[468]

Subject and Object: It's All in the Mind

The observer effect is perhaps the most striking example of paradoxical unity, dissolving the distinction between subject and object at the quantum level. The famous double-slit experiment shows that what you see depends on how you look at it. If an observer expects to see light as a particle, it will act like a particle (and only pass through one hole); if they expect a wave, it will act like a wave (and pass through two holes at the same time). As Wheeler's "delayed-choice experiment" shows, this even holds true if the observer postpones their prediction to the very last second. It is as if subatomic matter can read minds. This highlights that our experiences of reality can only ever be understood in terms of the interaction between the object and the observer; we always have an influence on what we are observing. As the great physicist Werner Heisenberg highlighted: "What we observe in nature is not nature itself, but nature exposed to our method of questioning."[469]

We can thus never speak about nature without speaking about ourselves.

As perplexing as this may seem, such experiments show that there is no objective reality out there, separate from us. Everything is a relationship and an interaction, so the observer effect is really a "participator effect," highlighting the inherent unity at the heart of the universe. According to the physicist John Wheeler: "We are not simply bystanders on a cosmic stage, we are shapers and creators living in a participatory universe."[470]

The rather earth-shattering implication of the observer effect is that reality is actually "all in the mind." The founding father of quantum physics himself, Max Planck, famously declared: "I regard consciousness as fundamental. I regard matter as a derivative of consciousness."[471]

This reflects the Eastern idea (described in the Tibetan Book of the Great Liberation)[472] that "matter is derived from mind, not mind from matter."

The slippery nature of objective reality is highlighted by the phenomenon of "quantum collapse." Experiments have shown that unobserved particles only show a potential to exist, expressed as a probability wave. Just like a wave, these unobserved particles are in fact in multiple places all at the same time (known as quantum superposition)—that is, until we take a peek, and the wave collapses into reality as a particle with a definite location—a "thing" with a place. Matter therefore only exists as a potential until we focus on it, and then our consciousness jolts it from an ethereal netherworld of possibility into definite reality—or, as mystics would say, from the unmanifest to the manifest.

The idea that there is no reality independent of our consciousness has been revelatory not just for the layperson (hence movies like Christopher Nolan's *Inception*) but for quantum physicists themselves. Einstein is famous for pointedly remarking "I like to think the moon is there even if I am not looking at it." As difficult as it is for us to imagine, quantum physics suggests that the very act of focusing our awareness is an act of creation itself. Yet the unity of opposites like existence and nonexistence, manifest and unmanifest, subject and object, are only paradoxical if one looks at things from a dualistic perspective. By seeing nature as a web of interaction, we transcend duality to see the unity.

To take the example of the moon, we can say that its existence is not as objective as we like to think it is because what we perceive is always mediated by our own consciousness. For instance, when we look at the moon, light enters the eye, which triggers chemical reactions in the retina; these create nerve impulses, which our brain then analyses to create our own idea of what is out there, seemingly separate from us. What we are seeing is thus not the moon itself but the image that appears in our mind of the moon. The poet Rumi put it succinctly: "The world exists as you perceive it. It is not what you see, but how you see it."[473]

This suggests that we can only ever experience our own nervous system—and, therefore, our own consciousness. As Max Plank suggested, consciousness is primary, and our experience of material reality is derived from that consciousness. Mind and matter, subject and object, are on a continuum, like two sides of a coin. We are, in effect, like a dog chasing its own tail—one imagining itself as two.

"Spooky Action at a Distance;" Local and Nonlocal Connection

The unity of the universe is further highlighted by the concept of "quantum entanglement." Because particles exist as a web of relationships, two can behave as one when they become an entangled system. For instance, if you split two entangled particles up and put them on opposite sides of the globe, changing the spin of one will automatically change the other. The apparent ability of matter to be instantaneously connected despite being separated by large distances (even billions of light years) is called "nonlocality," which Einstein called "spooky action at a distance," because it means that nature can interact even faster than speed of light. Matter is thus both locally discrete and nonlocally connected.[474]

Cosmologists theorize that prior to the Big Bang, all matter was compressed into a minuscule point of unimaginable density. Out of this tiny singularity, the Big Bang caused the entire universe to inflate to a size nearly an octillion (one with twenty-seven zeros after it) times bigger in less than a trillionth of a second. These cosmic origins suggest an extraordinary degree of "entanglement" within nature. In the words of Carl Jung, "synchronicity is an ever-present reality for those who have the eyes to see it."[475]

Space-Time

Einstein's theory of relativity is critical to understanding the unity of the universe in modern physics. In 1916, Einstein shook the world and forever changed the course of science by showing that time and space are not independent but interconnected in a four-dimensional continuum known as "space-time"—hence, you cannot speak of one without the other. Relativity theory highlights that depending on your position and speed, time will appear to move faster or slower relative to others in different parts of the universe. The "twin paradox" describes how an astronaut doing a round trip in space will age slower than his twin brother on Earth because the faster you move through space, the slower you move through time. This is called "time dilation," which means that (as aptly depicted in the movie *Interstellar*) the closer you move toward the speed of light, the nearer you get to time standing still.

Time is relative not just to speed but to gravity. Mass, time, and space are all connected; masses with a strong gravitational pull warp space-time, resulting in space being curved and time going slower around large objects like stars and planets. The bigger the mass, the stronger the pull of gravity, the slower time goes—reaching its most extreme near the event horizon of a black hole, where time begins to stand still. The effect of gravity also means that clocks at the top of Mount Everest go ever so slightly quicker than clocks at sea-level and people on the top floor of a skyscraper will age faster than those on the bottom (if only by a fraction of a nanosecond).[476]

Einstein refuted our everyday notions of time, writing that "people like us who believe in physics know that the distinction between past, present, and future is only a stubborn illusion."[477]

Likewise, the illusory and relative nature of space and time is reflected in the experiences of mystics. Zen Buddhist D. T. Suzuki explained that when one is enlightened, "there is no space without time, and no time without space." The thirteenth-century Japanese Zen master Dogen is famous for his explication of *uji* or "being-time," which means the complete oneness of time and space, where everything is found to be in the now. Dogen explained that: "it is believed by most that time passes; in actual fact, it stays where it is."[478]

This statement sounds puzzling to our analytical minds because it challenges our linear notions of time, but when viewed from the perspective of relativity, it makes more sense. Mystics describe higher states of consciousness that transcend time and space by moving into a vast and infinite present. The Buddhist teacher Lama Govinda says that the experience of meditation "becomes a living continuum in which time and space are integrated." In *The Power of Now*, Eckhart Tolle writes:

What you think of as the past is a memory trace, stored in the mind, of a former now. When you remember the past, you reactivate a memory trace—and you do so now. The future is an imagined now, a projection of the mind. When the future comes, it comes as the now. When you think about the future, you do so now. Past and future obviously have no reality of their own. Just as the moon has no light of its own, but can only reflect the light of the sun, so are past and future only pale reflections of the light, power and reality of the eternal present.[479]

Some traditional cultures also have a very different concept of space and time compared with Western notions. For instance, Australian Aboriginal people view reality as an eternal here and now. They talk of "dreamtime," a continuous "everywhen," that transcends linear notions of past, present, and future. They conceive of time circles where an individual is in the center and important events are placed closer in time relative to other events, regardless of the calendar date they took place.

Everything Is Energy

Along with space and time, mass and energy are also relative, as shown by the famous equation E=MC2. According to Einstein, "Everything is energy, and that's all there is to it." Matter and energy are thus different manifestations of the same thing. Once again, form is emptiness, and emptiness is form; the solidity and substance of our everyday reality is an illusion (or "maya" in Sanskrit) because what seems to be material is really an energetic vibration, albeit in a very condensed form. This is not to say that the material world is not real, but rather that reality is most definitely not what it appears. Matter, energy, space, and time are all relative aspects of the same underlying oneness.

The Microcosm and the Macrocosm

The unified view of nature revealed by modern physics is expressed in the following quote by David Bohm who said, "The universe and everything in it—including us—may, in fact, be part of a grand cosmic pattern where all portions are evenly shared by every other."[480]

According to quantum theory, not only is everything connected, but all particles are dynamically composed of each other, so in a sense, they contain or reflect one another. This corresponds to the idea that, to quote William Blake, there is "a world in a grain of sand and heaven in a flower." Bohm was the first physicist to suggest that the universe is in fact a great cosmic hologram, where the whole is enfolded in each part. The idea of a holographic universe has recently gained traction with the advent of string theory (discussed later in this chapter). Bohm posited that: "In some sense man is a microcosm of the universe; therefore, what man is, is a clue to the universe."

Spiritual traditions share a similar view. Christians believe that "God made man in his own image." Eastern traditions teach that the macrocosm is contained within the microcosm. Yogi Baba Muktananda famously said, "You are the entire universe. You are in all, and all is in you. Sun, moon, and stars revolve around you."[481]

Or, in the simple words of Eckhart Tolle: "You are the universe, expressing itself as a human for a little while."[482]

MAY THE FORCE BE WITH YOU

In perhaps the most revelatory parallel between science and spirituality, the "vacuum" of space in quantum field theory is similar to the concept of the unmanifest or "void" in Eastern mysticism, which is a state of pure cosmic consciousness. In classical physics, the vacuum is the absence of all matter and energy. However, quantum theory tells us that there is in fact no such thing as a vacuum—space is brimming with "virtual particles" that spontaneously dance in and out of existence (called "quantum foam"). What we think of as a void is actually full of tiny vibrations, which all together amounts to an infinite amount of energy. To give you an order of magnitude, the physicist Richard Feynman estimated that the energy of one cubic meter of "empty" space would be more than enough to boil all the oceans in the world.[483] This underlying quantum field—variously called the zero point field, the source field, the unified field, the ether—is in fact so lively that it contains infinitely more energy than all the solid and dark matter in the universe combined.

Like the mystics' description of unmanifest and manifest reality, Bohm called the quantum field the "implicate order," a hidden world of energy and information from which the "explicate order" of creation unfolds.[484] In the *Tao of Physics*, Capra describes the field as a "living void," fluctuating and pulsating in an eternal, rhythmic dance of creation as particles spontaneously appear and disappear at whim. The quantum universe is engaged in a perpetual cosmic jig that resembles the dance of Shiva in Hinduism, symbolising the cycles of birth and death, creation and destruction. In the words of Capra: "Shiva's dance is the dance of subatomic matter, the basis of all existence."[485]

The concept of space as a unified field of energy is echoed in the words of the great Chinese philosopher Chang Tsai, who said: "When one knows that the Great Void is full of chi [energy], one realizes that there is no such thing as nothingness."[486]

Science has thus proven the maxim that nature abhors a vacuum. The emptiness of space is not really a void at all but a primordial field of energy interweaving and interpenetrating every atom, organism, planet, and galaxy in the cosmos, connecting everything, everywhere, all at once (as in the film directed by "The Daniels"). This has profound consequences for the idea that "we are one," as it means there can be no such thing as division or separation.

Moreover, space is literally teeming with unmanifest potential; it is shimmering and reverberating with infinite energy, rather like the Force in Star Wars. This energy matrix forms the fabric of creation and provides the essence for all that exists. Like the concept of the Absolute in spiritual traditions, Einstein concurred that "there is no place in this new kind of physics for the field and matter, field being the only reality."[487]

In his distinguished book, *Science and the Akashic Field*,[488] systems theorist Ervin Laszlo propounds that the quantum field is also a fundamental field of information that creates the entire metaverse. Laszlo asserts that Indian sages call this the "Akasha," which holds the encoded memory of the entire universe—the source of all possible knowledge in the past, present, and future. The great Swami Vivekananda described it as "the omnipresent, all-penetrating existence. Everything that has form . . . is evolved out of this Akasha."[489]

In Hinduism, Jainism, and Buddhism, the Akasha is the universal medium, creating, containing, and connecting everything in nature. Like the Tao, it is the origin of all things, birthing all potentialities of existence—everything we can, and cannot, imagine. Omnipresent, omnipotent, and omniscient, it is the creative force of the universe, variously known as Brahman, Allah, Yahweh, or God.

A Living Universe

At the very least, if all matter, including empty space, is animated, then it is not a huge leap to say that the universe is very much alive. Far from being a dead machine, modern physics is revealing a living cosmos, a dynamic, harmonious, and highly ordered network that is self-organizing, self-referential, and self-actualizing. Whether one takes this a step further to say that the universe is self-aware is a matter of opinion, although according to Deepak Chopra, "a sizable quotient of very smart physicists believe that consciousness is an innate part of creation."[490]

For instance, Max Planck propounded that "all matter originates and exists only by virtue of a force . . . we must assume behind this force the existence of a conscious and intelligent mind. This mind is the matrix of all matter."[491]

CERN physicist John Hagelin, an expert on string theory, asserts that "the unified field is a nonmaterial, self-interacting, self-aware, dynamic field of intelligence, which is equivalent to saying that it is a field of universal consciousness. It has all the fundamental characteristics of consciousness."[492]

In this view, the universe is not a random configuration of stars and planets drifting aimlessly in space toward a ruinous end but a harmonious and mindful whole. Through the all-encompassing Akasha, Laszlo writes that "our brain/mind can access a broad band of information well beyond the information conveyed by our five sensory organs. We are, or can be, literally 'in touch' with almost any part of the world, either here on Earth or beyond the cosmos."[493]

This quantum nonlocality is exactly how, through the simple act of meditation, yogis have been able to intuit such rich metaphysical knowledge about the universe that predates the advances of modern science. When mystics say, "We are one," they are describing the idea that we are all part of a singular consciousness, a Divine Mind. This cosmic consciousness experiences itself in the myriad of different forms that make up the material universe—the "ten thousand things" that the Taoists talk of. Unity, in this sense, means more than just connection; it means oneness. Spiritual connection is thus really about discovering the essence of who we truly are, the universal consciousness emanating within us, the source of all that is. For those with a spiritual inclination, consciousness is therefore the missing link in our scientific understanding of the cosmos.

Heavenly Vibrations

Ever since Einstein defined the relative universe, science has been trying to reconcile the laws of our familiar Newtonian world with the paradoxical world of subatomic particles. Theorists are attempting to find a single equation that describes all the forces of nature, including gravity, thus combining classical and quantum physics in a unified "theory of everything." One such contender is string theory, which, like so many other concepts in physics, has parallels with ancient spiritual traditions.

String theory posits that the basic constituents of the universe are not discrete particles but tiny vibrating "strings" of energy, rather like extremely thin rubber bands. These resonant strings have their own characteristic frequency, like the different frequencies on the strings of a violin. Everything has its own unique vibration, and different frequencies give rise to different masses—each string makes its own tone, resonating with other strings to orchestrate the evolution of the cosmos. In *The Elegant Universe*,[494] acclaimed physicist Brian Greene writes: "What appears to be different elementary particles are actually different 'notes' on a fundamental string. The universe—being composed of an enormous number of these vibrating strings—is akin to a cosmic symphony."

A branch of string theory called M-theory posits that we exist simultaneously in two realms: the three-dimensional physical universe and the vast, invisible energy realm, which M-theorists call "the bulk," so named because it comprises the bulk of the cosmos. M-theory suggests that the bulk is so immense that an infinite number of parallel universes could exist within it. In fact, recent theories suggest that the Big Bang was not a one-off, but is rather a cyclical event, with ours being just the latest in a never-ending repetition of big bangs that give birth to new universes—akin to a universal heartbeat of expansions and contractions without end.[495] This multiverse, filled with super high-frequency strings, interpenetrates the physical 3D universe at every point, creating and sustaining the world we live in, including our physical bodies.

String theorists propose that while it is foundational to existence, we cannot see the energy realm because it is enfolded within the higher dimensions of space-time (the theory posits that there are ten or eleven dimensions; making the Star Wars notion of "hyperspace" a distinct possibility). In fact, without the energy realm, the material world would simply vanish in the blink of an eye, like a 3D movie screen that goes blank when the projector loses power.

In his acclaimed book *The Physics of God*,[496] Joseph Selbie renames the "bulk" as "the energy-verse," explaining that the material world is nothing but "a light show illusion," a projection of this deeper layer of reality. He asserts that various theories in physics provide evidence for the existence of the energy-verse, not only string theory but field theory's quantum vacuum, the background energy of Einstein's "cosmological constant" and the mysterious "dark energy" that (along with dark matter) is thought to make up 96 percent of everything in the universe. All these theories posit that the material universe is but a tiny component of the infinitely large energy-verse.

Selbie highlights that the energy-verse has some striking similarities with the depictions of the so-called astral or heavenly realms in spiritual traditions. String theory suggests that the different dimensions interpenetrate space-time so that these higher realms are enfolded within our material reality, occupying the same space. For the sake of ease, we can conceptualize the different dimensions as a loaf of sliced bread, each slice having its own distinctive properties and energy densities that vibrate at successively higher frequencies.

Selbie asserts that this is very similar to the descriptions of the celestial realms given by enlightened saints and sages throughout the ages. In Hinduism, there are reportedly seven "lokas" or upper worlds, each with its own properties and purposes, the material world being the first and grossest of all lokas, followed by progressively more luminous and refined worlds until one reaches the highest heaven of the Absolute. The Koran mentions the existence of seven celestial realms ("samawat"), and Muhammad allegedly journeyed through each samawat as he slept. In Judaism, the upper part of the universe is said to be made up of seven heavens or "shamayim." Buddhists similarly believe in a hierarchy of celestial realms, and Christianity makes many biblical references to multiple heavens. Like the energy-verse, the astral or heavenly realms are purported to be infinitely vast and subtle, containing the templates for all material existence. Selbie quotes two of the greatest sages in recent history regarding the astral plane.[497] First, Sri Yukteswar, who said, "The astral universe, made of subtle vibrations of light and color, is hundreds of times larger than the material cosmos," and Paramahansa Yogananda, (author of *Autobiography of a Yogi*), who said, "If you could perceive the astral world, you would know that it is infinitely more real than the earth-plane, which is just inert matter without the enlivening powers of the upholding astral world . . . . The blueprints of everything in the physical universe have been astrally conceived—all the forms and forces in nature including the complex human body, have first been produced in that realm where God's causal ideations are made visible in forms of heavenly light and vibratory energy."

The strings of the energy-verse vibrate at too high a frequency for either our senses or scientific instruments to detect—so string theory remains a theory for now. However, there is recent hope that gravitational wave detectors (which can discern ripples in space-time) might be able to perceive the extra dimensions of space that string theory proposes and thus give the model some legs. Sound cannot travel through a vacuum, but it can travel through the gravitational waves that form the fabric of space-time.

Thanks to the invention of gravitational wave detectors, we are now hearing the universe for the first time. So far, scientists have used these instruments to detect the vibrational hum of the sun, the chants of the solar system, and the chirping of black holes in far-flung regions of space. The Big Bang's ballad is still detectable as acoustic ripples, described by astronomers as a "descending scream, which builds to a deep roar and ends in a deafening hiss[498]" NASA has even posted "Song of Earth" on YouTube with the hauntingly beautiful sounds of our own planet.[499] The universe quite literally sings.

The ancients also understood the harmonic nature of the universe and used the power of sound as a direct link to the divine. They saw sound as vibration, which creates energy and matter. The importance of sound is reflected in the Sanskrit term *Nada Brahman* ("Sound is God") and can be found in Hinduism, Buddhism, Islam, Christianity, and Judaism. The Holy Bible states that "in the beginning there was the Word." The Vedic texts state that sound is the primordial creative principle and that all matter is based on the vibrations of Natural Law. Hindu, Buddhist, and Jain traditions use the seed mantra *Om* (pronounced "Aum") as a sacred sound of the universe. In Christian, Jewish, and Islamic cultures, *Amen* is symbolic of God and creation. The Tibetans believe F-sharp to be a sacred tone, while the Chinese call F-sharp *kung*, the great tone of nature. The ancient Greeks also understood the power of sound, with Pythagoras developing the theory of planetary vibrations in the "music of the spheres." Pythagoras asserted that the movement of celestial bodies such as stars and planets forms music, which, while not audible, could be heard by the soul.

Sound has been used in religious ceremonies since the dawn of time as a bridge to the celestial. The primordial sounds of Vedic mantras are said to vibrate with the resonance of the universe, stilling the mind and opening one up to higher consciousness. Sacred sounds are recited in Buddhist chants, Jewish hymns, and in the dances of Sufi whirling dervishes. The holy language of Sanskrit is called the "language of vibration" because it is said to mimic the primordial sounds of nature and allow a direct rather than symbolic communication with the universe. Shamans have known for millennia that songs and the strong repetitive beats of drums can induce altered states of consciousness, creating transcendent experiences. Sound and vibration are therefore key aspects of the harmonic unity of the cosmos for both scientists and sages alike.

MARRYING SCIENCE AND SPIRITUALITY

With all the parallels of quantum physics and ancient mysticism, science appears to be staring spirituality right in the face, despite its apparent aversion to the metaphysical significance of its findings. Einstein once said, "Science without religion is lame; religion without science is blind."[500]

Einstein did not believe they should overstep their remit (science being the pursuit of "facts," religion being a guiding hand in morality and values), but he did believe that both have an equally important role to play in understanding our world. After all, just like the Taoist concept of paradoxical unity, both are aiming to describe the same thing, just in different ways. To understand the nature of reality, science studies the world without, while spirituality studies the world within. Science uses sophisticated instruments, while spirituality uses practices such as meditation. As both inner and outer worlds are reflective of each other, they are equally valid ways of attempting to understand life. To quote the great philosopher Alan Watts: "For every outside there is an inside, and for every inside there is an outside, and although they are different, they go together."[501]

Just as there is ultimately no separation between subject and object, we can argue that there is no real duality between science and spirituality. Like yin and yang, they are simply two sides of the same coin. While many scientists are reticent about asserting notions of universal consciousness (at least publicly), the findings at the cutting edge of physics and cosmology have, at the very least, fostered a veneration for and connection with nature that is slowly filtering into the collective human mind. In the systems view, there is renewed hope that a marriage between science and spirituality can be made, as the revelations of the observer effect, quantum entanglement and the energy-verse return our worldview to one of unity, where nonlocal connection is an accepted reality and consciousness is central to the meaning of life.

PANTHEISM

The emerging cosmological paradigm described in this chapter is a possible way for more scientifically minded people to feel spiritually connected with and devotional to nature. The idea of universal consciousness is central to "panpsychism," which holds that everything is conscious, and "pantheism," which holds that everything in the universe is divine. As we have seen from our discussion of Eastern mysticism, pantheistic traditions see the world as composed of an all-encompassing, immanent divinity, therefore all things in nature are sacred.

Because the age-old intuitive understanding that "we are one" now has both spiritual and empirical significance, scientifically minded people can now get behind this idea with less concern that they might be considered "irrational." In fact, the World Pantheist Movement, started by the environmental writer Paul Harrison in 1997, holds as its core tenets a reverence for and feeling of unity with nature and the cosmos, an acknowledgment of and respect for the intrinsic value of all beings, a desire to live in harmony with nature, and a "respect for reason, evidence and the scientific method as our best way of understanding nature and the universe."[502] After all, if God is everything, one does not need to believe in contested religious concepts about the divine; one can merely have a deep appreciation for nature and a feeling of awe and wonder at the incredible beauty and complexity of our world.

CONCLUSIONS

This chapter has summarized a highly complex subject for an important reason: to highlight the remarkable paradigm shift occurring in Western thought as the spiritual fragmentation at the heart of our current health and environmental crisis is beginning to be acknowledged and healed. At the frontiers of science, a more holistic view of the world is emerging, as quantum physics reveals the essential unity of the universe as extolled by saints and sages throughout the ages. Instead of a machine, the new paradigm sees the world as a network, a grand cosmic web of nonlocal relationships that link everyone and everything in a dynamic, flowing whole. Reflecting the Taoist idea of paradoxical unity, the yang appears to have reached its peak in Western philosophy and is now waning in favor of the yin, such that spiritual notions of consciousness and connection are beginning to blossom amid the materialist and mechanistic views that have enthralled us for the past three hundred years.

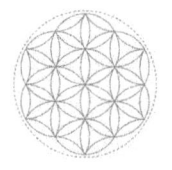

CHAPTER 14

SPIRITUALITY, ECOLOGY, AND HEALTH

The world is part of our own self, and we are a part of its suffering wholeness. Until we go to the root of our image of separateness, there can be no healing. And the deepest part of our separateness from creation lies in our forgetfulness of its sacred nature, which is also our own sacred nature.
—Thich Nhat Hanh

So, how do these revelations about the unity of the universe relate to health? This chapter answers this question by looking at the relationship between spiritual, ecological, and human well-being. The word "health" actually comes from the Old English word *hal*, which means "wholeness." Interestingly, it also comes from the same root that gives us the word *holy*. Health thus means wholeness and holiness. Wholeness is about connection, unity, and living in harmony with the web of life. There is a great spiritual, social, and environmental dimension to our health; it is folly to consider it as purely physical.

In the next section, we discuss the link between spirituality and ecological health, underlining the central role that environmental ethics plays in preserving nature. The interconnectedness of life is a key concept in both ecology and spirituality, making the environmental sciences (particularly "deep ecology") the perfect bridge between science and spirituality. We then look at the link between spirituality and human health. We explore the role of collective consciousness in the well-being of society, before delving into wellness at an individual level with specific spiritual healing modalities. We finish with a discussion of the meaning of our illnesses from a spiritual perspective and how our maladies can ultimately be seen as an opportunity for spiritual growth and transcendence.

SPIRITUALITY AND ECOLOGY

A pantheist worldview is one that is necessarily grounded in ecological awareness, for understanding that all things are divine gives one a strong incentive to be respectful of others and the planet. Perceiving the sacredness of life encourages us to care for all living beings, not just ourselves or our family and friends. Yet because our Western worldview is rooted in dualistic conceptions of heaven and earth, we implicitly tend not to see ourselves as divine. This fragmented view extends to everything in the material world, which is why so many people do not see nature as sacred or requiring preservation. As Karen Armstrong argues in her celebrated book *Sacred Nature*,[503] if we are to avoid environmental disaster, we not only have to change our behavior, we need to rekindle our spiritual bond with Mother Earth.

Understanding the ethical roots of our conflicted relationship with nature from a Taoist vantage point, we can see that the world today is extremely out of balance when it comes to the harmony of "yin and yang," or feminine and masculine energies. While yang is about "doing," yin is about "being." The feminine yin favors relationships and process over structure and form; it is all about cooperation, community, caring and conservation. Because yin is receptive and relational, it favors intuitive wisdom and "going with the flow" energy; yin is therefore responsible for keeping us integrated with the web of life in a flexible and adaptable way. Conversely, yang is all about action; it favors assertiveness, expansion, competition, and the pursuit of rational knowledge. As an active force, the yang gets things done in an efficient, orderly manner and is responsible for structure, progress, and evolution. However, while the shadow side of yin is the tendency to be passive and acquiescent, the shadow side of yang is a preoccupation with power, control, and domination.[504]

It is easy to see that our modern way of life is heavily biased toward the yang end of the spectrum, resulting in the alarming situation we find ourselves in now—a crisis of social, environmental, and ethical proportions. From a spiritual perspective, resolving the environmental crisis will require addressing this disharmony by connecting with the feminine principle: caring for, conserving, and cooperating with the natural world, not working against it out of a competitive and self-interested desire for perpetual expansion and unlimited economic growth.

A collaborative "share culture" is arguably the hallmark of a society that is connected and integrated with its environment—the indigenous tribes of the Amazon rainforest are a good example. Collaboration calls for empathy, solidarity, and, ultimately, love. In contrast, an overly competitive culture courts division and strife, which can ultimately lead to its downfall. Taken to the extreme, competitiveness and individualism leads to divisive "us and them" thinking, which results in dangerous power struggles, tribalism, nationalism, and even totalitarianism or terrorism, creating war and suffering on a grand scale.

Such dualistic thinking has also led to the extreme subjugation and exploitation of women for millennia. Male-dominated values have created patriarchal institutions and cultures, with devastating results for both society and the planet. This yin-yang imbalance has resulted in an overemphasis on wealth, power, and control based on fear, greed, and scarcity. The fallout is a lack of connection, compassion, and inclusiveness.

Just as spiritual awareness and ecological values go hand in hand, so do humanitarian ethics, as the oneness of life highlights the importance of appreciating and respecting one another, no matter our gender, creed, color, religion, or political affiliations. A spiritually mature and ethical approach to life is one that balances individual agendas with communal relationships, respecting the dignity of all the diverse people on the planet so that society can shift from polarization to unity.

Our overly yang society has created obsessive behavior patterns such as hypercontrol over surrender and flow, excessive doing and striving over relaxation and stillness, myopic linear analysis and reductionism over synthesis and systemic thinking. It is important to remember though, that in Taoism, neither yin nor yang is superior to the other. For instance, while being too yang can create feelings of separation, egotism, competitiveness, and emotional detachment, being too yin can create feelings of subservience, codependency, and passive aggression. Instead, we need to take a leaf out of the Taoists' book and find the dynamic balance between the two, achieving what is known as *wu-wei* ("effortless action"). Wu-wei arises when we feel spontaneous and inspired to act; life feels effortless because our activities are such a joy that they do not feel like work. According to Taoism, wu-wei can only occur when we balance the male "doing" energy with the female "being" energy so that we align ourselves with the natural flow of life, creating progressive change that is harmonious with the needs of the time.

Yin-yang balance is all about finding the harmony between the poles. In the world of knowledge, this means finding the balance between rational thought and intuitive wisdom, analysis and synthesis, learning and realization, scientific and spiritual perspectives. With regard to society and the environment, it means that the drive to expand should be tempered with the need for conservation, and that our competitive streak needs to be balanced with cooperation for the sake of the collective interest. From an individual perspective we need a balance of action and rest, doing and being, outward and inward pursuits. We require both self-assertion and humility, individualism and community, diversity and unity in order to survive and flourish.

This highlights the value of seeing both sides of the coin. Paradoxical unity is not about demonizing one pole over the other but transcending judgment to see the intrinsic value of all things. As William Shakespeare wrote: "For there is nothing good or bad, but thinking makes it so."[505]

Deep Ecology

The idea of intrinsic value is a strong theme in the global grassroots movement of Deep Ecology. Deep Ecology was founded by the Norwegian philosopher Arne Ness in the 1970s.[506] Ness greatly influenced environmental thought by making a dßistinction between "shallow" and "deep" ecology, the former being based on the instrumental value of nature and the latter being rooted in its intrinsic value. Ness argued that all living beings have a basic moral right to live and flourish and that we should value nature as more than just a resource for human use. Deep Ecology is essentially a spiritual philosophy because all life is considered intrinsically worthy and, therefore, sacred. While shallow ecology is anthropocentric, viewing humans as separate from and above nature, deep ecological values see humans as part of nature, positing us as just one strand in the web of life with no more importance than any other. Like the pioneering models of quantum physics, Deep Ecology takes a systems view by seeing the world as a network.

The idea of a hierarchy in nature is quite clearly a human construct. If we look at the workings of ecosystems, we see that bacteria and bugs are no more or less intrinsically valuable than animals further up the food chain. We apply our human-centered values to the natural world, not realizing their repercussions. We value the environment based on its usefulness to us, which implies that we are somehow superior to other creatures.

This anthropocentrism stems in part from the medieval Christian belief in "the great chain of being," which is very different from the view of the world as a network. This idea supposes a hierarchy of holiness as decreed by God. In the great chain of being, God and angels are at the top, then come humans, animals, and plants in descending order until we get to rocks and minerals at the bottom. This kind of hierarchical thinking has been prevalent in Western thought for hundreds of years, greatly amplified by the scientific view of nature as a machine. Our left-brained predilection for ordering and ranking things has created the perfect conditions for an exploitative human-centered ethic to arise in society. During the scientific revolution, the seventeenth-century attitude of "dominion" over the earth was augmented by the patriarchal image of nature as a female, who, according to Sir Francis Bacon, "must be taken by the forelock" so that science could "torture [her] secrets from her."

Nowadays, such disturbing ecological sentiment may be less explicit, but nevertheless, instrumental values abound in our dealings with nature. Living beings that are not considered useful to us (think ants or slugs) are generally not as highly regarded as animals that are (think birds and bees). We apply dualistic judgments all the time; creatures that are ugly (like toads or maggots) are not as valued as ones we consider beautiful (like horses or tigers). We apply dualistic notions of good and bad to nature without thinking; "pests" (like mosquitoes and flies) are bad, while "pets" (like cats and dogs) are good.

Yet, in nature, no such dualistic distinctions are made. There is no judgment or hierarchy; things are not useful or useless, beautiful or ugly, good or bad. They just are. Everything has its place in the ecosystem; bacteria at the bottom of the food web are just as important as the predators at the top. Because the ecosystem acts as a unit, all creatures have equal and intrinsic value. When we take a more transcendent view of the world and realize that nature is beyond dualistic judgment, life takes on a whole new meaning.

This kind of ethic implies a very different way of living as we move from an anthropocentric view of the world to a Deep Ecology view. When all things have intrinsic value, we live a life of reverence for the natural world, honoring the resources that nature provides us. We take only what we need, so sufficiency comes naturally. We harmonize with nature, and in doing so, our health flourishes because we are integrated and in sync with our environment. Our ethics and values therefore need to change from domination and control to cooperation and connection, from anthropocentric, patriarchal values to a harmonizing, ecological ethic that embraces a spiritual awareness of unity, emphasizing the sacredness of all creatures, great and small.

Ahimsa

Ahimsa, an ancient Indian principle of nonviolence to all living things, is a virtue of Hinduism, Buddhism, Sikhism, and Jainism.[507] The concept has reached an extraordinary pinnacle in the ethical philosophy of the Jains, whose diet is extremely strict to avoid harming any creature, extending even to microorganisms found in fermented food. Jains are vegans who go out of their way to avoid hurting even the smallest insects and make considerable efforts not to injure plants (such as root vegetables where the whole plant is dug up in the harvesting process). Their meticulous and exhaustive approach to applying nonviolence to everyday life, and especially to food, is a hallmark of Jain identity. While taking the principles of Deep Ecology this far may be considered too extreme for most, such ecologically minded spiritual communities certainly give us a high bar when it comes to adopting a more sustainable way of life.

SPIRITUALITY AND HUMAN HEALTH

As we covered in Chapter 10, studies show that a rich spiritual life is great for our physical and mental health. Spirituality can give us a sense of belonging and purpose, helping us to feel more connected and "whole." Spiritual contemplation may also foster altruistic behavior, inspiring us to be of service in some way. Cultivating love and connection with others encourages compassion and kindness, which is not only good for the health of society and the planet but for our individual health too. When we feel like there is purpose and meaning to our existence, life does not feel so mundane or senseless. It feels promising and abundant, which makes the joy of living so much more apparent. The feel-good factor of such connection is deeply nurturing for body, mind, and soul.

Contemplating our purpose in life entails believing in ourselves and knowing that we can create meaningful change in the world by spreading good things like love, compassion, and joy. A rich spiritual life also entails greater mindfulness as we realize our impact on others and try to balance our personal desires with the needs of the whole. Considering the impact of our words, thoughts, and deeds on others can expand our perspectives and inspire acts of kindness and tolerance. Simply put, it makes us more caring and less selfish.

Balancing our personal needs with the needs of others is something we learn from an early age, as it is a key aspect of creating healthy relationships.

We must learn to give and take if we are to get on in the world. Spiritual well-being involves considering the needs of others in relation to our own so that we are neither acting in blind self-interest nor only in the interests of the whole, suffering to serve and draining ourselves in the process. This balancing act between ego and universal interest is always a work in progress, but knowing where we are on the continuum and being able to adjust our actions accordingly is certainly a hallmark of emotional and ethical maturity.

Examples of kindness and compassion are not just about helping others or expressing love and affection but also about more difficult things like finding understanding amid conflict, seeing another person's point of view and overcoming judgment and enmity. It is about transcending duality to find unity. While this might seem challenging in our deeply divided world, it is essential for building a society based on mutual respect and harmony. There are many spiritual practices that cultivate this kind of heartfelt connection, from the well-known Buddhist loving-kindness meditation to praying for the welfare of others.

Distant Healing and the Power Of Prayer

In *The Physics of God*,[508] Joseph Selbie argues that across all religions, there are two key aspects of spiritual practice that result in transcendent experiences: stillness and inner absorption. This is why both meditation and prayer have been used throughout the ages to find enlightenment. Stillness limits physical stimuli, which slows down our nervous system and stops our mind from racing so that we can relax and find some inner peace. Inner absorption can lead to personal growth, as self-awareness can lead us to notice negative thought patterns and attitudes so we can create a change in behavior. As we saw in Chapter 9, over time, these changes can induce neuroplasticity, permanently rewiring the brain so that we experience the world in a more positive way.[509] Prayer and meditation thus hold the promise of profound inner growth and transformation.

Throughout human history, people have prayed to a higher power to find strength in adversity. Prayer is a practice woven with faith, spirituality, metaphysics, and psychology—a practice of going inward as well as outward. In an article for *Psychology Today*, author Michael Formica[510] argues that if prayer is simply intention (praying to the divinity within), God is an interior archetype. If prayer is directed outward (the divine "out there"), God is an exterior archetype. The various religious and spiritual traditions of the world tend to fall into one or other of these two categories or may be a blend of both. The major Western traditions such as Islam, Christianity, and Judaism are of the dualistic variety, so prayer tends to be directed outward. The mystic traditions such as the Sufis and Kabbalists focus on the God within, seeing the self as synonymous with the divine, and so prayer becomes a form of introspection and meditation. The Eastern traditions are more of a mixture; for instance, in Hinduism and Buddhism, meditation is interwoven with prayers to external gods and goddesses in their respective pantheons.

When it comes to health, studies have found that many people pray and meditate for healing, whether for themselves or for others. One study by Baylor University found that about 79 percent of Americans had prayed for their own health at some point in their lives, and over 87 percent had prayed for the healing of others.[511] Less than half of Americans have any religious affiliation, so people pray whether they consider themselves to be religious or not. The widespread use of prayer is significant because there is some evidence to suggest that "intercessory" (distant) prayer can have a healing effect not just on the person praying but on the person being prayed for.

The most well-known studies of the power of prayer in healing include Randolph Byrd's 1988 double-blind clinical trial of cardiac patients, who found that there was a significant difference in the quality of recovery among patients receiving prayer, including being less likely to have a heart attack, need antibiotics, or require ventilation.[512] This study was replicated by William Harris in 1999, who found similar results.[513] A 2000 meta-analysis of twenty-three studies on distant healing found that 57 percent had significant results supporting the positive impacts of distant prayer on health.[514] However, some studies have failed to find the same effect, giving rise to considerable controversy on the subject. There are major methodological issues that have caused much debate over the value of scientific research on the power of prayer, not least because the reliability of the data is hard to vouch for given that control groups may be prayed for by people outside the experiment, and patients may also pray for themselves.

Yet ancient wisdom has always understood the power of prayer, and—now that we understand a bit more about quantum nonlocality—it is perhaps not so difficult to believe that our healing thoughts and intentions toward others might have a positive effect on them. The physician Larry Dossey is one of the most vocal exponents of the power of prayer, viewing it to be so important that "not to employ prayer with my patients is the equivalent of withholding a potent drug or surgical procedure."[515] He has spent his career urging other medical practitioners to break out of the classical way of looking at space and time by heeding the effects of quantum nonlocality and distant healing in health. He states that "there are certain operations of consciousness such as those we see in distant healing and prayer, to which the categories of space and time simply do not apply. The new physics teaches us that 'non-local' is just a fancy word for 'infinite.' We have discovered a non-local or infinite quality of consciousness flowing from these [prayer] studies."

Mass Meditations: Can We Heal the World?

As we have seen in Chapter 10, meditation has a remarkable capacity to heal body, mind, and soul, causing many beneficial changes to produce health and well-being. Different meditative practices are associated with different brainwave activities, including alpha, delta, and gamma waves, which slow the mind down, de-excite the nervous system, and rejuvenate the physical body. Like prayer, meditation is a form of stillness and going within that can catalyze inner growth and personal transformation, cascading into many impressive health outcomes.

Meditation may not just be good for the individual meditating, however. Like prayer, mystics maintain that it has the power to transform the world, and now there is scientific evidence to back this up. The Maharishi Effect refers to the societal impact of mass meditation using a technique taught by the Maharishi Mahesh Yogi in the 1960s. The Maharishi proposed that by tapping into the field of universal consciousness, large groups meditating for peace could attune to the same frequency and create a nonlocal "field effect," which increased coherence in the environment. The Maharishi's Transcendental Meditation (TM) movement conducted over five hundred studies of group meditation all over the world during the 1980s and '90s, which showed an impressive impact on reducing conflict and suffering. A fascinating finding of these studies was the emergence of a threshold effect, whereby 1 percent of the population was found to be the critical mass needed to have a positive impact on society. Incredibly, this reduced to the square root of 1 percent (0.1 percent of the population) if meditators practiced a more advanced TM-Siddhi technique. This enabled a relatively small number of meditators (numbering just a few thousand) to have a measurable impact on cities around the globe.[516]

The evidence from this research was so compelling that over fifty empirical studies were published in numerous peer-reviewed scientific journals, suggesting a high degree of methodological rigor, data quality, and critical scrutiny. For instance, some twenty-two studies found a significantly positive effect on crime levels in numerous US cities. In one study, twenty-four cities found that crime rates dropped by 24 percent when enough people meditated together, and in a follow-up, another twenty-four cities had a 22 percent drop in crime as well as an 89 percent reduction in the overall crime trend.[517] Later studies also found similar effects. A 2016 study found that in a sample of 206 cities across the United States, Transcendental Meditation was linked with a 21 percent drop in homicide rates over three years from 2007–2010, reversing the previously rising trend from 2001–2006.[518] Other studies found a measurable effect on global conflict. When a thousand meditators met in Jerusalem and set the intention to resolve the war in Lebanon, fatalities fell by an astonishing 76 percent, and local crime decreased as well. Crime levels also dropped in Israel, as well as car and fire accidents. The chances of this occurring by statistical fluke were one in ten thousand.[519]

The Maharishi Effect remains controversial; critics accuse TM of cherry-picking data and lacking a causal basis for the effect. However, in her book *The Intention Experiment*[520] renowned journalist Lynn McTaggart argues that "the evidence is so abundant and the studies so thorough that it is difficult to dismiss them completely." Perhaps controversy is to be expected when the ramifications are so huge. The Maharishi Effect suggests that to make the prospect of world peace a reality, it would take seventy-nine million meditators around the world (that's less than the size of Germany) and, incredibly, a gathering of just under nine thousand if the more advanced Siddhi meditation technique were used.

Spurred on by such findings, daily mass meditations now occur all over the world. The Maharishi Effect has helped to create a groundswell of support for the idea that consciousness can create not just inner peace but world peace. We know that everything is energy, and if string theory is correct, everything in the universe is affected by vibration and resonance—including our collective thought patterns. In her article called "The Physics of Emotion"[521] neuroscientist Candace Pert asserts: "We're not just little hunks of meat. We're vibrating like a tuning fork—we send out a vibration to people. We broadcast and receive."

Our innate ability as quantum broadcasters suggests that large groups of meditators can alleviate stress in the collective consciousness by creating an energetic synergy that nonlocally enlivens our thoughts and actions toward peace. The old hippies may have been right—good vibes really can heal the world.

The Power of Collective Consciousness

While we have seen in Chapters 9 and 10 that our individual state of mind is a key factor in our own health, what studies of intercessory prayer and mass meditation highlight is that our *collective* consciousness has the potential to heal. The sociologist Emile Durkheim first coined the phrase "collective consciousness" in the 1900s to refer to the shared ideas, beliefs, and ethical perspectives that bind society together. With the advent of quantum physics, we now have a more "nonlocal" view of the term. Erwin Schrodinger famously said, "Mind—by its very nature—is a singular entity. I should say that the overall number of minds is just one."

Fritjof Capra asserts that "in the stratified order of nature, individual minds are embedded in the larger minds of social and ecological systems, and these are integrated into the planetary mental systems, which in turn must participate in some kind of universal or cosmic mind. The conceptual framework of the new systems approach is in no way restricted by associating this cosmic mind with the traditional idea of God. In this view, deity is not manifest in any personal form, but represents nothing less than the self-organizing dynamics of the entire cosmos."[522]

The Princeton Engineering Anomalies Research Lab has founded the Global Consciousness Project, which offers some interesting research on the power of collective consciousness.[523] The project uses random number generators (RNGs), which are basically electric coin-tossing machines that generate a series of random heads-and-tails outputs, converted into ones and zeros in the language of computers. Studies have shown that the "group mind" has a psychokinetic effect on these RNGs, so that big events such as the Olympic games, New Year's celebrations, or world tragedies like 9/11 create RNG outputs that are not statistically random. In the case of 9/11, the activity of the RNGs was normal in the days leading up to the catastrophe, but as a billion minds became focused on the horror, the machines became increasingly correlated—and stayed that way for two days afterward.[524] Data irregularities have also been seen around history-defining events such as the funerals of Princess Diana and Mother Theresa and the beginning of the COVID-19 pandemic.[525] Since 1998, there have been sixty-five sites of RNGs all over the world, which consistently show that strong collective emotion, either positive or negative, creates a measurable impact, although research has yet to explain why.[526] Whenever a mass consciousness forms in response to a global event, a correlation in RNG data is seen. Considering what we know about the Maharishi Effect, it begs the question of what could be achieved if we put our collective mind to it.

Lynne McTaggart writes: "A sizable body of research exploring the nature of consciousness, carried on for more than thirty years in prestigious scientific institutions around the world, shows that thoughts are capable of affecting everything from the simplest machines to the most complex living beings. This evidence suggests that human thoughts and intentions are an actual physical "something" with astonishing power to change our world. Every thought we have is tangible energy with the power to transform. A thought is not only a thing; a thought is a thing that influences other things."[527]

Spiritual Healing Therapies

Whether or not spiritual practices like prayer and meditation can be harnessed collectively to produce beneficial changes in society, there is certainly ample evidence to suggest that they have a positive impact on individual health, which is why they are sometimes included in integrative medical treatments. As we discussed in Chapter 10, Reiki, TCM, Ayurveda, shamanic healing, and numerous other spiritual healing modalities are now growing in popularity within complementary and alternative medicine.

Therapies involving energy medicine require us to think outside the box when it comes to scientifically validating its benefits for human health. Although some effects of Reiki and acupuncture are measurable, such as drops in heart rate and blood pressure, there are other more qualitative aspects that patients report, such as enhanced emotional well-being, self-esteem, and a sense of spiritual connection. Understanding these effects requires a different methodology than the randomized clinical trials that are usually used in medical research. Moreover, while science has shown that energy medicine can work, it does not yet know why—no technology exists to detect the existence of a subtle "energy body" with which they are purported to work. Luckily, this doesn't matter; aspirin was used for seventy years before science understood why it was effective.

In the absence of a biomedical model for understanding how spiritual therapies work, it is perhaps helpful to use a different lens for probing their efficacy. If string theory is correct in asserting that the material world is created and sustained by the "energy-verse," then invisible fields of energy surround and interpenetrate our physical body. Our physicality is thus inseparable from, and underpinned by, our energy body. In spiritual traditions, this energy body is variously called the astral, subtle or spirit body. In Eastern religions, the life force energy that sustains the physical body is called "prana" or "chi." Vedic, Buddhist, and Taoist philosophies have complex models of the subtle body, with energy centers called "chakras" or acupuncture points, connected by a series of channels called "nadis" or "meridian lines."

Musing on the implication of string theory for human health, Joseph Selbie writes: "[String theory] gives us a scientific framework to help us understand how subtle energy can exist . . . [which] is pretty much exactly the way astral or subtle energy is described by mystics . . . Our energy body . . . animates, controls, shapes, and continuously sustains the holographic projection our senses perceive as our physical body . . . in fact most of what matters to us—our vitality and life force, our feelings, our creative will, our personality and character, and our experience of happiness, love, or joy—is actually seated in our interpenetrating subtle energy body, not in the physical body at all."[528]

To elucidate the role of the energy body in an integrative model of health, celebrated physicist Amit Goswami writes about a model similar to the Vedic system of "koshas" in his bestselling book *The Quantum Doctor*.[529] Koshas in Sanskrit are "sheaths" that interpenetrate the physical body like the layers of an onion, or a Russian nesting doll that contains smaller and smaller versions of itself. The densest of these sheaths is the physical body, which is overlaid by the energy body, composed of "prana" (life force energy). The energy body holds the blueprint for the physical body and is the subtle realm on which energy medicine (such as Reiki and acupuncture) works. The next level is the mental body, representing our thoughts, emotions, and perceptions. Psychotherapy and mind-body medicine work well at this level. This is followed by the "wisdom body" (Goswami calls it the "supramental body"), which is the seat of our intuition, where our deeper and more subtle layers of thought occur. Spiritual therapies and other mind-body-spirit techniques might work effectively on this sheath. The final body is the "bliss body," the essence of our true nature, universal consciousness. In this most subtle of sheaths, the only healing required is to cast aside the illusion of separation and embrace oneness. It is at this level that the transcendent experiences of spiritual practice and meditation can help.

This provides us with a very different model of human health, one where an integrative approach to well-being is critical. Consciousness is primary in this model because it mediates all five bodies. Goswami argues that if our health problems originate in the energy body, then the physical treatments of conventional medicine are clearly going to be inadequate. At best, it may treat the bodily symptoms of the energetic imbalance, but until the energy body is healed, new physical symptoms will continue to emerge. This is also true of the mental and wisdom body; if our problems originate there, then treating the physical body will simply involve a whack-a-mole approach, which causes further health problems down the line. Goswami calls this a model of "downward causation" because problems in the higher subtle bodies will naturally flow downward to the grosser bodies, eventually causing symptoms in the physical body that cannot be healed until the problem further up is dealt with. This underlines the need for an integrative approach, so that we are not wasting our time healing symptoms rather than causes.

Goswami asserts that with such a complex model of health, we need to focus treatment on the higher planes, which allow healing to flow down to the lower planes automatically. Such downward causation may provide an explanation for so-called spontaneous healings of the physical body (described as "discontinuous quantum leaps" by Deepak Chopra in his book *Quantum Healing*[530]). However, healings that flow downward from the upper levels can also take time, so Goswami argues that a multi-level approach to health is needed. For instance, in the case of chronic illnesses such as cancer, you may be able to heal from the mental-emotional or energetic causes, but if it is already manifested in the physical body, then conventional medicine is essential to remove the tumor, which grows faster than the healing from the higher planes can keep up with. This highlights the importance of amalgamating both conventional and complementary approaches to health.

Another point that Goswami makes is that while medical doctors mistakenly assume that disease only manifests in the physical body, alternative medicine practitioners can also make a similar mistake, assuming that only certain bodies, such as the energy body, are affected. In reality, illness often manifests in all five bodies, and thus requires a truly systemic approach using multidisciplinary treatments to heal each layer simultaneously. While this model of the human body remains scientifically unverified, it nevertheless gives us a useful structure with which to make sense of all the different alternative healing modalities and how they can be integrated with conventional medicine to maximize benefits for body, mind, and spirit.

The Spiritual Meaning of Our Illnesses

An important aspect of holistic healing is to understand the root cause of our pain and disease from a spiritual perspective. We are encouraged to ponder the lessons that can be learned from our maladies so that we become aware of the imbalances in our lives and rectify them. What is our mind, body, and soul trying to tell us? This involves a journey of self-discovery that can be extremely transformative, not least because it causes us to slow down, go within, and gain perspective so that we can see our lives from a more transcendent viewpoint. Here, we can discover things about ourselves that we simply weren't aware of before, enabling us to heal those parts of ourselves that were hiding in the shadows. Illness can be created when we feel disconnected, when we are fearful or resistant to change, or when we don't want to accept situations or issues in our lives. When we drill down, we may find that it is only a negative thought or limiting belief about ourselves that has caused us to feel this way. Such beliefs can be released and transmuted to create healing on every level.

In Eastern philosophy, sickness and health are two sides of a coin. In paradoxical unity, they are both aspects of the relative world that are included in the perfection of a higher good. If health means wholeness, and we know that deep down, we are one, then we can see that we are perfect even when we are ill. However, if we feel we must prove ourselves somehow before we are worthy of being part of that higher good, then we can get stuck in a perpetual state of anxiety and stress, which ultimately creates disease. Fear is no more than resistance to a perceived threat, which is why it creates so much stress and suffering, creating a vicious circle of ill-health.

If sickness and health are two sides of a coin, then wellness requires surrendering to the process of illness, not fearing it. Illness is a natural part of life, after all, a symptom of flux and change. When we resist being sick, this creates suffering, but when we surrender and accept it, resistance—and therefore suffering—begins to dissolve. We become less rigid and more flexible, seeing illness as a natural part of the ebb and flow of life , and that trust may open us up to new ways of healing..Surrendering and going with the flow really means being one with life, which is what creates lasting health and happiness. Surrender may sound passive and meek, but it is in fact one of the most powerful things we can ever do. In the words of Eckart Tolle: "To be in alignment means to be in a relationship of inner non-resistance with what happens. It means not to label it mentally as good or bad, but to let it be. Does this mean you can no longer take action to bring about change in your life? On the contrary. When the basis for your actions is inner alignment with the present moment, your actions become empowered by the intelligence of Life itself."

Trust and surrender is true empowerment, for it can move mountains by giving birth to enlightened action. Surrender and empowerment, or strength in vulnerability, brings us back to the topic of yin-yang again. As a symbol of inner harmony and balance, the yin-yang emblem is genius for so many reasons. First, the dividing line is flowing to represent the fact that opposites are continually waxing and waning, merging and morphing into one another in the natural harmony and rhythm of life. Rigidly adhering to one or the other of the poles doesn't work; it's all about the balance. Second, the seed of the yin is contained within the yang, and vice versa. This is how they transform each other because in the darkness, just a pinprick of light will be illuminating, and similarly, a flash of darkness can be enough to dim the light. In the case of suffering and happiness, or sickness and health, the seed of health and happiness is in the suffering, because suffering can cause us to make positive life changes, and happiness comes when we have learned something worthwhile from the challenge. Similarly, the seed of suffering is in its opposite because we only need to think of losing our health or happiness to feel the pain of that loss. Just the thought of the other is enough to invoke the change.

From a spiritual perspective, we can conceive of disease and ill-health as holding a divine message for our growth and evolution, a blessing in disguise waiting for us to discover. When we are open to receiving the message, we can springboard ourselves to a new level, moving beyond suffering and pain to feel transcendent health and well-being. This can then ripple out to our relationships with others, to society, and to the environment, expanding out to a sense of unity with all life and the cosmos. In this way, our illnesses can be embraced as part of our hero's journey to remembering our own sacred nature, our wholeness, and holiness.

CONCLUSIONS

To summarize the main points of this chapter, understanding that "we are one" gives us a good reason to take care of our planet, for what we do to nature we essentially do to ourselves. Instead of seeing the natural world as a resource to exploit, we need to recognize that the web of life has intrinsic value, that it is sacred and needs to be cared for and sustained at all costs. As spiritual awareness and ecological values go hand in hand, so do humanitarian ethics, recognizing the importance of respecting human rights and the dignity of all the diverse people in the world.

Ultimately, spiritual health is about a profound sense of connectedness, combined with a respect for the well-being of other living beings and a desire to serve the greater good. Such feelings of belonging, compassion, and altruism give us a strong sense of purpose in life, helping us to feel happier and more fulfilled, which has a cumulative effect on all other aspects of health. Spiritual practices such as meditation and prayer can have numerous positive impacts, not just on individual health but potentially on societal well-being as well. A truly systemic model of health will thus incorporate spiritual healing modalities into its approach, considering them to be just as valid as more conventional therapies in supporting positive health outcomes.

Healing ourselves and our planet is ultimately about our path toward realizing our wholeness, our oneness. We can look upon our ills as having a divine message for us, one that ultimately leads to our own enlightenment. As we start to fully comprehend the interconnectedness of life, we begin to realize that everything we experience is an opportunity for growth and transcendence. Our journeys are ultimately helping us to remember our innate unity so that dualistic thinking is transcended in favor of nonjudgment and compassion for all living beings. Cultivating unity consciousness is key to finding the path back to a more sustainable way of living, where humanity thrives in dynamic harmony with the sacred web of life.

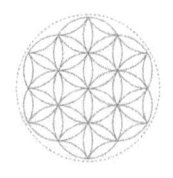

CHAPTER 15

CONCLUSIONS—TOWARD A SYSTEMS VIEW OF HEALTH

We know if we drop a stone in a pond, the ripples begin to move, and they move over the whole pond, reaching all the extremities. One slight stir in any part of the pond stirs the whole pond . . . . (similarly) every individual, by his every thought, word, and action, shakes the entire Universe.
—Maharishi Mahesh Yogi

We are in a time of intense turmoil and flux. This turmoil has the potential to transform us, if we let it. It is as if the world is going through a profound healing crisis, much like our bodies do when we are ill. During a healing crisis, all the toxins are pulled up to the surface to be felt and seen so that we often feel worse before we feel better. It is a necessary stage in the journey as we become aware of the mess we have created, not just for ourselves but for the planet. The toxic nature of old systems, structures, and patterns is being seen in the stark light of day, and it is difficult to stomach. Yet, this is all part of the healing process.

Once we accept this, we are in a position to work on the underlying causes of our health and planetary crises. We can delve deep into our inner recesses, unearthing the root causes of our stress, our disconnection, and our polarization. Only when we begin to heal those fragmented parts of ourselves can we begin to feel whole again, mending the fractures we have caused in the web of life.

Healing takes time, a great deal of self-belief, and a willingness to let go of the past. It involves moving beyond blame and shame, pointing the finger with outrage. It involves a willingness to be conciliatory and to partner with each other to move forward and do things in new ways. It involves understanding that there are some major challenges to overcome as deeply ingrained habits and belief structures come to the surface to be released and transformed. It is a process with lessons that need to be integrated before true healing occurs. It is up to us to determine how long the ride lasts, how much time it takes for us to shift ourselves and the collective consciousness of humanity. Mother Nature does not have long; she is asking us to shift quickly. We must take heart that we have all the know-how to make the transformations required. We simply need to let go of our fear and resistance to change as the new is birthed from the old.

This is not the time for handwringing or catastrophizing; instead, let us embrace this moment as a golden opportunity for growth and transcendence, a chance to shift to a new worldview that will create a healthier, more sustainable, life-enhancing existence. From this perspective, our pain can become our teacher, helping us to evolve and to rebalance with nature so that all life on Earth can flourish. We need to trust our journey, to be in a state of inner nonresistance so that we can bring forth the healing required in the world. This experience can be akin to a forest fire burning away all the dead wood, creating space for new growth. Crisis is always an opportunity, and we must seize the moment to cultivate a more systemic view of life.

Letting go of the past means doing away with the myopic reductionist perspectives that have dominated Western thought for hundreds of years. They are clearly no longer suitable for solving the severe systemic crisis we face. Old dualistic worldviews are based on outmoded notions, such as that mind is separate from matter, that we are isolated individuals living in a random, mechanical universe, that life is a competitive struggle for survival, that unlimited material growth is the key to happiness, and that nature is simply a resource to be exploited. It is time to clean up our concepts, our ideas—what Yuval Harare in *Sapiens*[531] calls our "imagined orders" that form our global systems and society. When we change our worldview, all else follows.

This is an invitation to embrace the new systems paradigm emerging at the forefront of science, which is based on the idea that the whole is far more than the sum of its parts. This perspective provides the salve needed to heal our overly yang society by emphasizing connection, giving primacy to the feminine yin values of cooperation and reciprocity to partner with the web of life. This new worldview embraces the unity of mind, body, and spirit, where individual health is seen as indivisible from the health of society and the planet. We are connecting the dots between our lifestyles and our illnesses, between unsustainable growth, social inequality, and ecological destruction. These things can no longer be seen in isolation; integrating them is essential for healing ourselves and our planet.

THE RIPPLE EFFECT

One of the most positive aspects of the interconnectedness of life is the potential for a ripple effect that enables vicious circles to be replaced with virtuous ones. Making even simple changes in one sphere can have major ripple effects in all the others. For instance, having a daily meditation practice can reduce our stress, which helps us to sleep better, eat well, and exercise more. Being well-rested and in better health gives us more adaptation energy to deal with further stress, which creates a virtuous circle. Looking after our health helps us to feel more relaxed, vibrant, and alive, increasing our levels of empathy and compassion for others. When we feel more socially and spiritually connected, our motivation to protect the planet increases. We don't have to overthrow the whole system to create change; we can make simple transformations in one area of our lives that influence all the other areas. These ripple effects can trigger a cascade of virtuous circles until a critical moment is reached where a new, more transcendent order emerges and previously inconceivable transformations occur, such as the Arab Spring and the Jasmine Revolution in Tunisia, the fall of the Berlin Wall, or the abrupt end of Apartheid.

This has enormous connotations; we no longer need to feel fearful and overwhelmed by the scale of the problems we face. The power of individual grassroots action is incredibly potent. The "3.5 percent rule" aptly highlights this; research by Harvard University shows that, statistically, it takes just 3.5 percent of the population to participate in a nonviolent political protest for the success of its aims to become inevitable.[532] In the UK, this would mean 2.4 million people, and in the US, 11.6 million. In smaller countries like New Zealand, it would require just 175,000 activists. Seemingly insignificant individual actions thus have the potential to trigger momentous breakthroughs for the collective. We really do have the power to make a difference, and every single choice we make is a vote for the world we wish to create.

The time-honored understanding that we are microcosms of the macrocosm means that when we heal ourselves, we have a healing effect on the planet. When we change our lives, we inspire others to follow our example and, in doing so, blaze new pathways and create chain reactions that transform the world. When we take small steps to care for our own health and well-being, we not only prevent illness and disease, but we also raise our game to maximize our human potential and those of others around us. When we do the right thing for ourselves, for our loved ones, and for the environment, we reinforce nature's potential to nurture and sustain life. This reverberates back to us so that bigger things can come our way, allowing us to flourish and thrive in a reciprocal network of giving and receiving. Like the roots of a forest, we are all intertwined, so everyone has a role to play in healing this beautiful planet of ours. We have all the tools we need for transformation; all it takes is one good thought, one positive choice, one right action to begin a virtuous circle.

SYSTEMIC PROBLEMS NEED SYSTEMIC SOLUTIONS

When we think about our global problems, we see very quickly that our solutions must be joined up; they need to solve several issues simultaneously. Yet these do not need to be conceived and implemented solely at the macro level—we can do simple things in our daily lives to create the changes we so desperately need. Here is a list of twenty actions that we can make as individuals—some may be familiar, others may be new, but they all have systemic impacts:

1. Eat more organic, seasonal whole foods from local farms that use regenerative agricultural methods. This has benefits for human and ecosystem health, as well as encouraging self-sufficiency in local economies and decentralization of global food systems.
2. Diversify your diet, which ensures diversity in your gut microbiome and in our crops, thus supporting the biodiversity of the planet and fair trade in the global food system.
3. Eat less meat (particularly beef), which can be beneficial for your health at the same time as dramatically lowering carbon emissions and the resource intensity of our food.
4. Buy oily fish or omega-3 supplements from sustainable sources, which support brain health and lower the risk of chronic disease. It also reduces overfishing and supports the jobs of local fishermen over large industrial fisheries.
5. Reduce, reuse, and recycle, which helps to create a circular economy. This stops resource depletion, limits waste, and reduces pollution, which is harmful to our health. Reducing food waste has a particularly big impact on reducing harmful greenhouse gas emissions.
6. Switch to green energy suppliers, divest from fossil fuel companies, insulate your house, and invest in solar panels. Swap to an electric car, and take a train rather than a flight to nearby holiday destinations. This helps to build a renewable energy economy that not only mitigates climate change but increases energy security (reducing reliance on foreign fossil fuels), promotes green jobs in local communities (as renewable energy infrastructure is homegrown), and improves health by reducing pollution.

7. Cycle or walk to work, which is a great form of exercise while lowering your carbon footprint. Reducing the demand for cars also addresses environmental and social impacts by reducing air pollution and smog, decreasing congestion and traffic accidents while increasing space for parks, playgrounds, and pedestrian zones. This, in turn, enhances street life and community, which all have a positive impact on human health and well-being.
8. Spend more time in nature, which is good for body, mind, and soul. Rekindling our bond with nature boosts health, helps to encourage greener lifestyles, heightens spiritual connection, and fosters community spirit as we are inspired to be kinder and more altruistic. Plant trees, spend time gardening, and let nature flourish by supporting rewilding projects and the greening of urban spaces.
9. Be a conscious consumer. Make educated choices about what you spend your money on. Purchase eco-friendly goods from green businesses, support social enterprises, and buy from companies that are transparent about their sustainability commitments. Boycott products that contribute to deforestation and pollution. Lease services such as electric cars or business equipment rather than buying them outright so that we can make the shift from ownership to service provision and help to dematerialize society. This supports the three sustainability pillars of people, planet, and profit.
10. Support "Green Zones" in low-income, high-pollution areas. This lowers carbon emissions, provides green jobs, and encourages social change, which addresses environmental and social injustice. This has a domino effect on health outcomes by reducing pollution and lifting communities out of poverty.
11. Support fair and equitable access to good quality housing, education, healthcare, and equal opportunities for employment. This improves the social determinants of health, which has a ripple effect on society and the planet.
12. Support the global civil society. Engage with local community

networks and citizen assemblies. Donate time, money, and energy to charities and nongovernmental organizations that matter to you. Deliberative democracy, promotion of civil rights, and a more humane, eco-literate society increases social cohesion and helps to protect people and the planet.

13. Engage in politics and vote for politicians who have sustainability and regeneration as their priority. Engage in nonviolent protest so that the 3.5% rule applies. Vote for female politicians and support female leaders, as women in charge are more likely to act on climate change.[533]

14. Support the education and empowerment of women, as this creates more equitable and just societies while slowing population growth, which in turn reduces poverty, resource depletion, and ecological destruction.

15. Put pressure on politicians and economists to replace GDP with qualitative growth indexes that focus on physical, mental, emotional, and spiritual well-being, as well as education, community, cultural diversity, ecological health, good governance, and quality of life.

16. Avoid online outrage and echo chambers by reading from a diversity of news sources and listening to other people's points of view with an open mind. This can help to heal social polarization, which reduces social stress and, in turn, boosts health. It may also foster more tolerant and united views about how to create the systemic changes we need in the world.

17. Support public health education in schools, the workplace, and in the media. Push for flexible work hours to encourage better sleeping habits or call for sleep pods in the office. Promote good nutrition in lunch canteens. Suggest meditation, yoga classes, or other deep relaxation techniques as part of the school curriculum.

18. Write to local politicians and start community initiatives to encourage joined-up thinking on public health policies. This could include ramping up the pressure on big corporations to

do something about environmental hazards, pushing for taxes on carbon emissions, junk food, and subsidies for organic, fair-trade products as well as building more eco-homes. It could also include more stringent food labeling laws, changes to work and school hours, funding for exercise and mindfulness-based stress reduction programs, or incentives to join nature-based initiatives such as forest bathing, green exercise and ecotherapy groups.
19. Support health professionals who care about lifestyle and preventive healthcare. Spread the word about integrative medicine and holistic health among family and friends.
20. Believe in the power of your mind, and see that medicine is not just a pill that you swallow, but a mindset you follow. The future of medicine is integrative; when we as individuals embrace a mind-body-spirit approach, it has the power to transform not just our own health but the health of the entire world.

These are just some examples of how we can address our health issues more holistically, causing grassroots changes in our social, economic, and ecological systems, which transform the global world order. When we start to find systemic solutions to the environmental and social crises we face, we create enlightened solutions to our health crisis. We can solve the climate crisis and social justice issues with the same solutions that bring our health back into alignment. All are interconnected.

SUSTAINABLE NUTRITION HAS THE POWER TO CHANGE THE WORLD

Creating sustainable communities based on a circular, renewable energy economy is central to ensuring the health of humanity and all life on the planet. Although much still needs to be done, the cost of renewable energy has now become so competitive that we can take heart in the huge momentum building behind the emergence of a global green economy. However, transitioning to green energy sources will undoubtedly take time. The most immediate way we can support our individual health and the environment is in fact with our food choices.

Nowhere is the interplay between human and planetary health more obvious than with our food, yet sustainable agriculture currently has less momentum than renewable energy because we have tended to put unhealthy food in one basket and climate change in another. The food we eat makes such a huge impact on the planet because it affects both carbon sources and sinks; it emits vast amounts of greenhouse gases while at the same time degrading the soil, forests, and oceans that sequester carbon from the atmosphere. Because there is less awareness of the impact of agriculture versus fossil fuels on the climate, the enormity of the effect we can have with even simple changes to our eating habits has yet to fully absorb into the popular mind.

With the right food choices, we can not only become healthier and happier human beings, but we can also change the face of agriculture, reducing soil degradation, deforestation, pollution, and the carbon intensity of farming to reverse climate change and biodiversity loss. We can maybe even change the balance of power within the global food system away from monocultures and monopolies and toward community-based sustainable farms, thereby reducing poverty and food insecurity in the Global South. Greater equality and empowerment in the South can, in turn, help to stem population growth and ecological degradation. Once again, all are interconnected, which means our actions at the individual level can have a wide-ranging effect on the entire world. In the same breath that we discuss renewable energy, we need to be talking about sustainable food choices, or we are missing a major part of the solution to our climate and health problems.

EMBRACING SUFFICIENCY

While reducing our consumption of unhealthy and environmentally damaging foods is a top priority, we also need to reduce our consumption in other areas to avoid coming up against planetary boundaries. This means addressing rampant consumerism and the idea that unlimited economic growth is not only feasible but desirable. Scaling back consumption in the West, where our basic needs are more than adequately met, will be crucial to reducing our impact on the environment while allowing for populations in the South to develop their economies so that poverty and suffering are alleviated. This kind of social justice is not only humane but critical to slowing population growth and reducing resource depletion and climate impacts.

Addressing overconsumption has well-being implications too. Not only will sufficiency be crucial to reducing the health fallouts from climate hazards, but it will also reduce health disparities related to social inequality and the growing gap between rich and poor. It can also greatly alleviate individual stress related to working overtime to pay for our high-consumption lifestyles. Sufficiency is deeply intertwined with stress management because our hectic, overstimulating consumer society is demanding in the extreme, and the stress of it all is making us chronically ill. Sufficiency is also intertwined with mental health because, as so many scientific studies have shown, consumerist lifestyles have a habit of making us feel less fulfilled, not more, which has a domino effect on our spiritual well-being. True satisfaction and inner contentment come from an inherent sense of having enough. In a society where we are conditioned to consume voraciously, it is easy to feel discontented when we are always wanting more. No matter how rich we are, so many of us choose to focus on what we lack, rather than what we have.

We need to get off the hamster wheel and out of the rat race because nature shows us that infinite growth is not only nonsensical but suicidal, causing us to overshoot the carrying capacity of the Earth. Moving away from materialism and focusing on what is really important in life, such as nurturing our health and well-being, our social relationships, and our spiritual connection, is an imperative that we can no longer afford to ignore. Along with green energy and sustainable agriculture, sufficiency is clearly something we need to engage with much more in political and popular debates.

A starting point in conversations about sufficiency might be to decouple it from the idea of "austerity" and instead reframe it as "simplicity." Let's take a leaf out of nature's book and slow things down. As Lao Tzu reminds us, "Nature does not hurry, yet all is accomplished." When we slow down, we relax and become more present. Calmer nervous systems allow us to enjoy the simple things in life, which means we are less likely to search for happiness outside of ourselves by accumulating more "stuff." When we feel peaceful in the moment, we can find joy in smallest of things like the warm sun on our face, the scent of a flower, or the sound of a child laughing. A litmus test of personal growth is our ability to enjoy these little things because simplicity can lead to an abiding sense of contentment that has nothing to do with material wealth and everything to do with a sense of inner abundance. When we have an abundance mindset, our benchmark of success is no longer confined to our income bracket or the size of our house. Instead it is about intangible things like vibrant health, psychological well-being, loving relationships, community spirit, and our connectedness with nature and the cosmos. From a societal perspective, replacing narrow quantitative indexes like GDP with qualitative growth models can help us move away from empty materialist lifestyles devoid of real meaning so that sufficiency becomes part of a philosophy of Gross National Happiness.

WE VOTE WITH OUR FEET

Every choice we make is a vote for the world we want to create. Every product we consume supports and reinforces the networks that are embedded within it, whether positive or negative. If we buy healthy, fair trade, eco-friendly goods and services, we are creating sustainable networks and structures that are in harmony with the ecology of the Earth. If we buy drugs and junk food, we are bankrolling those supply chains and all the ill-health and addictions that go with them. We create and recreate our world with every little action, every choice we make. Rather than finding this idea scary or overwhelming, let's embrace how empowered that makes us. When we make healthy choices, we have the feel-good factor of knowing we are bringing forth the world we want for ourselves and our children; we are manifesting good health and a sustainable society with every little transaction we make.

THIS IS AN "EVERYONE, EVERYWHERE MISSION"

Obviously, to create a sustainable world at the scale required, we need our leaders to be on board too. As citizens, we can vote for politicians who are serious about environmental action, social justice, and public health reform. Unfortunately, political intransigence and polarization can often lead us to feel hopelessly impotent when it comes to these big issues. Yet, because time is not on our side, we need major policy measures to address the enormous existential crisis we face. These policies need to be rapid, effective, wide-ranging and, most of all, joined up.

Transformations on this scale too often get stymied by political views about the role of "big government" in the affairs of people, with big government being associated with the left and small government the right side of the political spectrum. This explains why so many Republicans in the US have an aversion to the environmental agenda. Republicans are typically for deregulation and tax cuts, so when the Left proposes a carbon tax or clean energy standards, the Right often frames this as a potential power grab, a lefty attempt at authoritarianism and limiting individual liberties rather than a way to support sustainability. Republicans can thus be suspicious even when proposed policies are more conservative, such as environmental taxes that are revenue neutral or green incentives that are market-based—if they are proposed by Democrats. The fossil-fuel lobby has carefully manipulated this distrust to their benefit, fanning the flames of climate denial by perpetrating a misinformation campaign the likes of which Goebbels would be proud.

The only way we can circumnavigate this dualistic dynamic is to recognize that nature is our overarching support system and therefore it is in the undeniable interests of both the Left and the Right to protect it. For those on the Left, big government may seem like the best way to resolve the environmental crisis, while for those on the Right, protecting nature is best done through individuals and the market. Grassroots action in the manner of "think global, act local" is a way for those on the Right to feel more engaged with the environmental agenda, aligning it with their political values because they can exercise their individual right to choose green goods and services, as opposed to the government telling them to do so.

In reality, though, we need both individual and government action on the climate crisis. It is a bipartisan problem that needs bipartisan solutions. Time is running out, so we need action at every level: the local, national, and international. As Christiana Figueres highlights: "We can no longer afford to assume that addressing climate change is the sole responsibility of national or local governments, or corporations, or individuals. This is an everyone-everywhere mission in which we all must individually and collectively assume responsibility."[534]

The connectivity of our globalized world means that local grassroots action can have an impressive ripple effect, but action at the macro level undoubtedly gets things done in a hurry. The reoccurring theme in all of this is unity; finding common ground across the political spectrum has never been more important. We need to exercise our individual liberties by doing the right thing, at the same time as voting for governments that make doing the right thing easier. Finding ways to reach across the aisle and reconcile with each other is a crucial part of the healing process, leading us out of polarization toward unity. We cannot rely on the state alone to create this unity for us. Governments reflect the predominant worldview and values of society and, as such, can only guide us away from ecological disaster if we, as citizens, are prepared to cast aside our differences and embrace progressive change. If we want to create a more sustainable world, we need to cultivate unity, not division.

UNITY CONSCIOUSNESS

Quantum physics has shown us that we are not isolated beings living in a random, mechanical universe. Rather, we are part of a grand cosmic web of nonlocal connections that unite us with everything imaginable. We are sacred participators of the cosmos, cocreating our own reality so that every thought, every intention, every action we take in the present shapes our lives in the future. Every day, we recreate our minds and bodies with our expectations, beliefs and choices. We create our relationships with others, our communities, cultures, society, and even the very planet we live on.

We truly are cocreators of the Earth. As the Buddha once said: "All that we are, arises with our thoughts. With our thoughts we make the world."

Yet our current consciousness is manifesting grave problems for the planet because we have lost our sense of connection, the fifth—and most important—pillar of health. We feel disconnected from our biology and our ecology, from each other, and from the universe itself. We have stopped gazing at the starry skies at night or contemplating our navel. We no longer consider our place in the cosmos or recognize an underlying unity at the heart of all things. We do not see the oneness and sacredness of life.

The emerging systems view is a chance to reclaim this fifth pillar, to reconnect with that feeling of wonder and awe at our vast and interwoven universe. It is a chance to recognize the spiritual aspect of our existence, the unity within diversity, which is where the word "universe" comes from. When we feel this connection, we cultivate unity consciousness, which naturally engenders a reverence and respect for nature, human dignity, and the health of the planet.

When we care to think about it, the oneness of life means that we are transcendent beings, capable of doing things we never dreamed possible. Quantum physics has shown that we are both particles and waves, in one place and everywhere, all at the same time, united with all that exists. This nonlocal connection binds us irrevocably to every person, creature, and plant on the planet. We are both individuals and the collective, the microcosm and the macrocosm. There are no "others" in the world; we are all part of each other. What we do to nature, we do to ourselves. When we cut down the forest, we lose a part of ourselves. When we pollute the ocean, we pollute ourselves. When we fight our neighbor, we fight ourselves. Every action reverberates back to us like a boomerang. All is one reciprocal, indivisible whole.

Unity consciousness is the wellspring of three important aspects of individual and planetary health: progressive change, intuitive wisdom, and unconditional love. In terms of change, our oneness with nature highlights that we are dynamic beings in constant flux and flow, not rigid, inflexible creatures incapable of transforming. We adapt and evolve because it is in our very nature to do so. As humans, we have a particularly important role to play in the evolution of our planet, and transcending dualistic ideas is essential to ensuring that we progress in the right direction. When we truly comprehend the interrelatedness of our individual, social, and ecosystem health, when we see the indivisibility of mind, body, and spirit, we see that we are indeed all one. As the quote by Thich Nhat Hahn at the beginning of this chapter reminds us, true healing occurs when we remember the Earth's sacred nature, which is also our own nature. Previously insurmountable problems quickly resolve with this simple shift in perspective. This means we can create meaningful change simply by expanding our own hearts and minds to get in touch with who we truly are inside. When we shatter the illusion of separation and embrace our sacred nature, we heal at every level.

Unity consciousness is also how we come to embrace unconditional love. When we feel at one, love becomes unconditional because it is all-encompassing. Nothing is left out on condition of anything. When we connect at this very deep level, we can feel compassion for others even if they have done us harm in the past, because we see a bigger picture at play. With this love, we can overcome our differences and heal our individual and societal wounds. We can make good our relationship with the Earth. Healing our relationship with nature ultimately means healing our relationship with ourselves. We can start this process by cultivating self-compassion, self-love, and self-worth so that we are more compassionate, nurturing, and loving to others, extending out to the whole of humanity and all living beings on the planet.

Unity consciousness is also the source of our intuitive wisdom. Because we are one, we have the ability to tune in to everyone and everything instantaneously. We are like an antenna, capable of receiving all information but only listening to a very narrow range. When we quiet our minds, we can tap into the genius of existence because it is the very core of our being. Nature communicates with us; it is always reciprocating because *Tat tvam asi*—"We are it." This is what intuitive wisdom is: tuning in and allowing our right brains to glean the whole story, not just the select details the left brain wants to analyze and rationalize about. It is the big-picture view that lies at the heart of all things. We are indeed the universe seeing itself through human eyes. When we are still long enough to hear the rhythm of our breath, we intuitively know how to become whole again, to mend the fractured web of life. We are that web, the microcosm of the macrocosm, so when we connect to ourselves, we connect to it all.

Knowing that our every thought and action creates a ripple effect, we can use our intuitive wisdom to create health on every level. We can use mind-body practices such as meditation and mindfulness to feel our inner connectedness and release all the anxiety that comes from feeling separate, small, and disempowered. When we calm our nervous system, we become more in tune with ourselves and the natural world all around us. When we get "in sync," we can access our higher faculties and all the creative intelligence that we are capable of. This enables us to find more insightful solutions to our problems and, ultimately, fulfill our human potential in life. When we calm our busy minds, we cultivate a sense of inner peace and harmony that allows us to very naturally create peace and harmony in the world at large. As within, so without. Individual peace is the basis for world peace. The world is but a mirror of our own consciousness; therefore, we need look no further than our own hearts and minds to heal the planet.

Because unity is at its core, the systems view of health is ultimately about raising human consciousness. One might argue that it is all very well transforming ourselves, but what about the millions of people in the world who do not subscribe to this view? What about those who stoke division and strife at every turn by resolutely seeing the world in terms of *us* and *them*? While raising the consciousness of humanity might seem like a tall order, the Maharishi effect and the 3.5 percent rule show that we have a very real chance of evolving past our current problems if even just a few of us put our minds to it. As Mahatma Gandhi so poignantly highlighted, we need simply be the change we want to see in the world. The full quote is a wonderful reminder of just how empowered we are: "We but mirror the world. All the tendencies present in the outer world are to be found in the world of our body. If we could change ourselves, the tendencies in the world would also change. As a man changes his own nature, so does the attitude of the world change towards him. This is the divine mystery supreme. A wonderful thing it is and the source of our happiness. We need not wait to see what others do."

WE ARE THE CHANGE

We are the last generation that can make the transformations needed to avoid runaway climate change and seed a healthy, sustainable future. We have one last chance to put things right. The fate of all living beings is in our hands—not just the politicians, business leaders and billionaires of this world—but yours and mine, right here, right now. The stark truth is that our actions in the next few years will determine quite literally whether humanity and millions of other species on the planet get to live or die.

This is a heavy responsibility, but there is much reason to be optimistic. We have at our disposal all we need to transform our health, our society, and our planet—our creative minds, our intelligent bodies, and our ineffable spirit. In embracing this, we can become excited about what bright future we might create together. We are sacred souls of infinite love and scope, with the power to bring into existence something exquisitely bright and beautiful. When we shine our light, when we feel our profound connection with all things, we can create a verdant garden of Eden where humanity flourishes in dynamic balance with the entire web of life on the planet. All we need to remember is that everything we seek is already inside us.

You are not a drop in the ocean. You are the ocean in a drop.
—Rumi

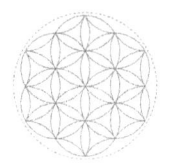

ACKNOWLEDGMENTS

I'd like to thank my dear husband and family, who patiently supported me in this huge endeavor, which took nearly three years to write. Much gratitude to Sue, my beta reader (and an excellent one at that), and to Anu whose unwavering faith and support has helped me to truly believe in myself. Most of all, thank you to Fritjof Capra for inspiring me to embark on such a sweeping systemic view of life—it has been quite the journey!

ENDNOTES

1 World Health Organization (2020) "World Health Statistics 2020: Monitoring Health for the SDGs," www.who.int (accessed 28 October 2020)
2 Bhattacharya, S. (2005) "Chronic Disease is Biggest Global Killer," https://www.newscientist.com/article/dn8099–chronic-disease-is-biggest-global-killer/ (accessed 23 November 22)
3 Rand Review (2017) "Chronic Conditions in America: Price and Prevalence," https://www.rand.org/blog/rand-review/2017/07/chronic-conditions-in-america-price-and-prevalence.html (accessed 4 January 2023)
4 Sagan, A. (2023) 'What is being done to respond to the risk of chronic disease and multi-morbidity in Czechia, Hungary, Poland and Slovakia' Frontiers Public Health, https://doi.org/10.3389/fpubh.2022.1082164 (accessed 9/11/24)
5 The Kings Fund (2012) "Long-Term Conditions and Multi-Morbidity" https://www.kingsfund.org.uk/projects/time-think-differently/trends-disease-and-disability-long-term-conditions-multi-morbidity (accessed 4 January 2023)
6 Hoffman, D (2022) 'Commentary on Chronic Disease Prevention in 2022" https://chronicdisease.org/wp-content/uploads/2022/04/FS_ChronicDiseaseCommentary2022FINAL.pdf (accessed 4 January 2023)
7 OECD.org (2017) "Obesity Update," https://www.oecd.org/els/health-systems/Obesity-Update-2017.pdf (accessed 23 November 2022)
8 Potsdam Institute for Climate Impact Research (2020) "Starved, Stuffed and Squandered; New Study Reveals Consequences of Decades of Global Nutrition Transition," https://www.pik-potsdam.de/en/news/latest-news/starved-stuffed-and-squandered-new-study-reveals-consequences-of-decades-of-global-nutrition-transition (accessed 25 January 2023)
9 Centers for Disease Control and Prevention (2022) "Chronic Health Conditions" https://www.cdc.gov/healthyschools/chronicconditions.htm (accessed 4 January 23)
10 Del Giudice F, etal. "The Association between Mortality and Male Infertility: Systematic Review and Meta-analysis," *Urology*, 2021 154:148–157, doi;10.1016/j.urology.2021.02.041

11 Davis, N. (2022) "Humans Could Face Reproductive Crisis as Sperm Count Declines, Study Finds" *The Guardian*, https://amp.theguardian.com/society/2022/nov/15/humans-could-face-reproductive-crisis-as-sperm-count-declines-study-finds (accessed 26 November 2022)
12 Nerurkar, A, and Davis, R. (2013) "When Physicians Counsel About Stress; Results of a National Study," *JAMA Internal Medicine*, 173(1):p76–77, https://jamanetwork.com/journals/jamainternalmedicine/fullarticle/1392494 (accessed 24 November 2022)
13 Salleh, M. (2008) "Life Event, Stress and Illness," *Malaysian Journal of Medical Science*, 15(4), p9–18
14 Singh, A (2019) "Stress: Prevalence and Correlates Among Residents of a Suburban Area" *Ind Psychiatry journal*, 28(1), p98–102
15 Newport, C. (2022) "What Hunter-Gatherers Can Teach Us About the Frustrations of Modern Work" *The New Yorker*, https://www.newyorker.com/culture/office-space/lessons-from-the-deep-history-of-work#:~:text=%E2%80%9CThe%20group%20engaged%20entirely%20in,gatherers%20enjoy%20more%20leisure%20time (accessed 7 August 2023)
16 Cilluffo, A and Ruiz, N. (2019) "World's Population is Projected to Nearly Stop Growing by the End of the Century" https://www.pewresearch.org/fact-tank/2019/06/17/worlds-population-is-projected-to-nearly-stop-growing-by-the-end-of-the-century/ (accessed 14 November 2022)
17 Figueres, C. and Rivett-Carnac, T. (2020) *The Future We Choose: The Stubborn Optimist's Guide to the Climate Crisis*, Manilla Press
18 Le Fanu, J. (2011) *The Rise and Fall of Modern Medicine*, Abacus
19 Capra, F. (1982) *The Turning Point: Science, Society and the Rising Culture*, Bantam Books
20 see Frances, A.J (2016) "We Have Too Many Specialists and Too Few General Practitioners" https://www.psychologytoday.com/gb/blog/saving-normal/201601/we-have-too-many-specialists-too-few-general-practitioners?amp (accessed 4 August 2023)
21 see Capra, F. (1983) *The Turning Point: Science, Society and the Rising Culture*, Flamingo
22 World Health Organization (2020) "WHO Report Highlights Global Shortfall in Investment in Mental Health" https://www.psychologytoday.com/gb/blog/saving-normal/201601/we-have-too-many-specialists-too-few-general-practitioners?amp (accessed 4 August 2023)

23   Lincare, Q. (2016) "How Western Medicine Lost Its Soul," 83(2); p 144–146, https://www.ncbi.nlm.nih.gov/pmc/articles/PMC5102204/ (accessed 4 August 2023)

24   Tai-Seale, M. et al (2007) "Time Allocation in Primary Care Office Visits," *Health Services Research* Vol 42(5), p1871–1894, https://doi.org/10.1111%2Fj.1475-6773.2006.00689.x (accessed 1 November 2023)

25   Dillon, S. (2018) "We Learn Nothing About Nutrition, Claim Medical Students," https://www.bbc.co.uk/news/health-43504125.amp (accessed 27 April 2023)

26   see National Library of Medicine (2007) "Understanding Emerging and Re-emerging Infectious Diseases"
https://www.ncbi.nlm.nih.gov/books/NBK20370/ (accessed 4 August 2023)

27   Balasubaramanian, C. (2022) "What is the Epidemiological Triad?" https://www.gideononline.com/blogs/epidemiological-triad/#:~:text=The%20epidemiological%20triad%20consists%20of,Environment (accessed 4 August 2023)

28   Barton, C. (2020) "Annual Revenue of Top 10 Big Pharma Companies," https://www.thepharmaletter.com/article/annual-revenue-of-top-10-big-pharma-companies#:~:text=According%20to%20market%20research%2C%20the,of%20sales%20(%24392.5%20billion).(accessed 26 April 2023)

29   Posner, G. (2020) *Pharma: Greed, Lies, and the Poisoning of America*, Avid Reader Press, Simon and Schuster

30   Ahramson, J. (2013) *Overdosed America: The Broken Promise of American Medicine*, Harper Perennial

31   Kassir, J. P. (2005) *On the Take: How Medicine's Complicity with Big Business can Endanger your Health*, Oxford University Press, USA

32   Angell, M. (2005) *The Truth About the Drug Companies: How They Deceive Us and What To Do About It*, Random House

33   Mitchell, A. et al (2022) "Industry Payments to Physicians are Kickbacks. How Should Stakeholders Respond?," *Journal of Health, Politics, Policy and Law* Vol 47(6), p815–833, https://pubmed.ncbi.nlm.nih.gov/35867550/ (accessed 2 November 2023)

34   Sismondo, S. (2021) "Epistemic Corruption, the Pharmaceutical Industry, and the Body of Medical Science," Frontiers, https://www.frontiersin.org/articles/10.3389/frma.2021.614013/full (accessed 4 August 2023)

35   Directorate General for Internal Policies (2012) "Disease Mongering (Pseudo-Disease Promotion)," https://www.europarl.europa.eu/RegData/etudes/note/join/2012/492462/IPOL-ENVI_NT(2012)492462_EN.pdf (accessed 4 August 2023)

36 Wouters, O. (2020) "Lobbying Expenditures and Campaign Contributions by the Pharmaceutical and Health Product Industry in the United States, 1999–2018," https://www.ncbi.nlm.nih.gov/pmc/articles/PMC7054854/

37 Telesford, I. et al (2023) "How has US Spending on Healthcare Changed Over Time?," https://www.healthsystemtracker.org/chart-collection/u-s-spending-healthcare-changed-time/, (accessed 27 April 2023)

38 Wager, E. (2022) "How Does Health Spending in the US compare to other Countries?," www.healthsystemstracker.com (accessed 13 September 2022]

39 Drouin, JP (20080 "Healthcare Costs: a Market-based Review," www.mckinsey.com (accessed 12 April 2021)

40 Karimi, A (2015) "Herbal Versus Synthetic Drugs: Beliefs and Facts," *Journal of Nephropharmacol*, 4(1); 27–30, https://www.ncbi.nlm.nih.gov/pmc/articles/PMC5297475/ (accessed 27 April 2023)

41 Medicines and Healthcare Products Regulatory Agency (2022) "Guidance on Adverse Drug Reactions," https://assets.publishing.service.gov.uk/government/uploads/system/uploads/attachment_data/file/949130/Guidance_on_adverse_drug_reactions.pdf (accessed 10 February 2023)

42 Light, D. (2014) "New Prescription Drugs: A Major Health Risk with Few Offsetting Advantages" www.ethics.harvard.edu (accessed 12 April 2021)

43 Light, D. W. (2014) "New Prescription Drugs: A Major health Risk with Few Offsetting Advantages," Harvard University Center for Ethics, https://ethics.harvard.edu/blog/new-prescription-drugs-major-health-risk-few-offsetting-advantages (accessed 4 August 2023)

44 Makary, M. (2016) "Medical Error—the Third Leading Cause of Death in the US," www.bmj.com (accessed13 April 2021)

45 World Health Organization (2019) "WHO Calls for Urgent Action to Reduce Patient Harm in Healthcare," www.who.int (accessed14 April 2021)

46 McGreal, C. (2018) "The Making of an Opioid Epidemic" *The Guardian*, https://amp.theguardian.com/news/2018/nov/08/the-making-of-an-opioid-epidemic (accessed 4 August 2023)

47 PEW Research Centre (2017) "Americans' Health Care Behaviours and Use of Conventional and Alternative Medicine," www.pewresearch.org (accessed 14 April 2021)

48 Conrady, D. and Bonney, A. (2017) "Patterns of Complementary and Alternative Medicine Use and Health Literacy in General Practice in Urban and Regional Australia," *Australian Family Physician*, 46(5), www.racgp.org.au (accessed 14 April 2021)

49 World Health Organization (2022) "WHO Establishes the Global Centre for Traditional Medicine in India" https://www.who.int/news/item/25-03-2022-who-establishes-the-global-centre-for-traditional-medicine-in-india (accessed 1 November 23)

50 Keefe, J. (2017) "Here Are The Therapies Offered By Top Hospitals," www.statnews.com/2017/03/07/alternative-therapies-chart/, (accessed 21 July 2022

51 Hart, J. (2018) "Complementary and Alternative Medicine Use and Initiatives in Europe" *Alternative and Complimentary Therapies*, 24(1), www.liebertpub.com (accessed 14 April 2021)

52 see Storr, W. (2015) "The Brain's Miracle Superpowers of Self-Improvement" https://www.bbc.com/future/article/20151123-the-brains-miracle-superpowers-of-self-improvement (4 August 2023)

53 Liu, L. et al. (2008) "Gene-Environment Interactions and Epigenetic Basis of Human Diseases" https://www.ncbi.nlm.nih.gov/pmc/articles/PMC2434999/ (accessed 4 August 2023)

54 see Enders, G. (2015) *Gut: The Inside Story of Our Body's Most Under-Rated Organ*, Scribe, UK

55 Johnson, J.R et. al (2014) "The effectiveness of integrative medicine on pain and anxiety in cardiovascular inpatients: a practice-based research evaluation," *BMC Complementary and Alternative Medicine*, 14 (1), p486–495

56 Lin, W.F. et al (2019) "Efficacy of complementary and integrative medicine on health-related quality of life in cancer patients: a systematic review and meta-analysis." *Cancer Management and Research*. 11, p6663–6680, www.pubmed.ncbi.nlm.nih.gov

57 Weil, A (2004) "Health and Healing: From Herbal Remedies to Biotechnology, a Survey of Alternative Healing in the Search for Optimum Health," Harvest publications

58 Capra, F. and Luigi Luisi, P (2014), *The Systems View of Life*, Cambridge University Press, UK

59 These tendencies tie in with the traditional Chinese notion of the balance of "yin and yang," such that "yang" (masculine) values are integrated with their "yin" (feminine) counterparts; competition is therefore balanced by cooperation, expansion with conservation, independence with community, structure with process, objects with relationships. This balance is critical to living systems, because it allows individual beings to flourish within communities that are well-integrated with their environment.

60 World Health Organization (2022) "Constitution of the World Health Organization," www.who.int (accessed 13 September 2022)

61 Capra, F. and Luigi Luisi. P. (2016) *The Systems View of Life: A Unifying View*, Cambridge University Press
62 Sapolsky, R. (1994) *Why Zebras Don't Get Ulcers*, Macmillan Press
63 Mujica-Parodi, L. et al. (2008) "Second-Hand Stress: Neurobiological Evidence for a Human Alarm Pheromone," *Nature Precedings*, doi.org/10.1038/npre.2008.2561.1 See also Anderson, J. R. (2008) "You Really Can Smell Fear, Say Scientists," www.theguardian.com/science/2008/dec/04/smell-the-fear-research-pheremone (accessed 20 September 2022)
64 Anchor, S. and Michelle, G. (2015) "Make Yourself Immune to Second-hand Stress," *Harvard Business Review*, www.hbr.org (accessed 26 September 2022)
65 LLacqua, A. (2018) "Lifestyle And Fertility: The Influence of Stress and Quality of Life on Male Fertility," Reproductive Biology and Endocrinology, 16 (115), https://doi.org/10.1186/s12958-018-0436-9 (accessed 26 September 2022)
66 see Hunter, P. (2012) "The Inflammation Theory of Disease," *The European Molecular Biology Organization*, 13 (11), pp 968–970, www.ncbi.nlm.nih.gov, doi:10.1038/embor.2012.142 (accessed 22 September 2022)
67 Yaribeygi, H. et al (2017) "The Impact of Stress on Body Function: a Review" *Experimental and Clinical Sciences Journal*, Vol 16, p1057–1072, www.ncbi.nlm.nih.gov, doi:10.17179/excli2017–480 (accessed 22 September 2022)
68 Williams, W. (2018) *The Effortless Mind: Meditation for the Modern World*, Simon and Schuster, UK
69 Mate, G. (2019) *When the Body Says No: The Cost of Hidden Stress*, Vermillion
70 Levitin, D. (2015) *The Organiezd Mind: The Science of Preventing Overload, Increasing Productivity and Restoring Your Focus*, Penguin Books
71 Demerouti, E. (2021) "New Directions in Burnout Research," *European Journal of Work and Organizational Psychology*, 30 (5), https://doi.org/10.1080/1359432X.2021.1979962 (accessed 22 September 2022)
72 Kelly, J. (2021) "Indeed Study Shows That Worker Burnout is at Frighteningly High Levels: Here Is What You Need To Do Now," *Forbes*, https://www.forbes.com/sites/jackkelly/2021/04/05/indeed-study-shows-that-worker-burnout-is-at-frighteningly-high-levels-here-is-what-you-need-to-do-now/?sh=24a4f85e23bb (accessed 22 September 2022)
73 Furman, et. al (2018) "Chronic Inflammation in the Etiology of Disease Across the Life Span" Vol 25, p1822–1832 https://www.nature.com/articles/s41591–019–0675–0 (accessed 12 December 2022)
74 Yong Tan, S. (2018) "Hans Selye (1907–1982): Founder of the Stress Theory," *Singapore Medical Journal*, 59(4), p170–171, doi: 10.11622/smedj.2018043, (accessed 26 September 2022)

75 see Huberman, A. (2023) *See, Breathe, Move*, Simon and Schuster, UK
76 Marchant, J. (2016) *Cure; A Journey into the Science of Mind and Body*, Canongate Books
77 McGonigal, K. (2015) *The Upside of Stress; Why Stress Is Good For You (and How to Get Good at It),"* Vermillion
78 Chatterjee, R. (2018) "*The Four Pillar Plan; How to Relax, Eat, Move and Sleep Your Way to a Longer, Healthier Life,*" Penguin Life
79 Chatterjee, R. (2018) *How to Make Diseases Disappear*, HarperOne
80 Jung, R.E and Vartanian. O. (2018) *The Cambridge Handbook of the Neuroscience of Creativity*, Cambridge University Press
81 Zabelina, D. et al. (2016) "Dopamine and the Creative Mind: Individual Differences in Creativity Are Predicted by Interactions Between Dopamine Genes DAT and COMT," *PLoS One*, 11(1), 10.1371/journal.pone.0146768,(accessed 27 September 2022)
82 see Abraham, A. (2018) *The Neuroscience of Creativity*, Cambridge University Press
83 Mendick, R (2011) "Brain Scans Reveal the Power of Art," https://www.telegraph.co.uk/culture/art/art-news/8500012/Brain-scans-reveal-the-power-of-art.html (accessed 4 October 2022)
84 Piechowski-Jozwiak, B. et al (2017) "Universal Connection through Art; Role of Mirror Neurons in Art Production and Reception," *Behavioural Sciences*, 7(2): 29, doi:10.3390/bs7020029 (accessed 4 October 2022)
85 see Gerritsen, R. et al. (2018) "Breath of Life: The Respiratory Vagal Stimulation Model of Contemplative Activity," *Frontiers in Human Neuroscience*, 12 (397), doi: 10.3389/fnhum.2018.00397 (accessed 22 September 2022)
86 Other ways to create vagal tone include massage, reflexology, exercise, and meditation
87 Sipperlin, A. (2016) "The Healing Power of Nature" Time.com (accessed 20 August 2021)
88 Engermann, K (2019) "Residential Green Space In Childhood Is Associated With Lower Risk of Psychiatric Disorders From Adolescence Into Adulthood," www.pnas.org, https://doi.org/10.1073/pnas.1807504116 (accessed 26 September 2022)
89 Nichols, W.J (2015) *Blue Mind: The Surprising Science That Shows How Being Near, In, Or Under Water Can Make You Happier, Healthier, More Connected, and Better at What You Do*, Back Bay Books
90 Weir, K. (2020) "Nurtured by Nature: Psychological Research Is Advancing Our Understanding of How Time in Nature Can Improve Our Mental Health and Sharpen Our Cognition," American Psychological Association, www.apa.org (accessed 26 September 2022)

91 Stellar, J. et al. (2015) "Positive Affect and Markers of Inflammation: Discrete Positive Emotions Predict Lower Levels Of Inflammatory Cytokins," *Emotion*, 15(2), p129–33
92 Mass, J. et al (2006), *Journal of Epidemiology and Community Health*, 60(7), p587–592, doi: 10.1136/jech.2005.043125 (accessed 26 September 2022)
93 Hansen, M. et al (2017) "Shinrin-Yoku (Forest Bathing) and Nature Therapy: A State-of-the-Art Review," *International Journal of Environmental Research and Public Health*, 14(8): 851, www.ncbi.nlm.nih.gov (accessed 21August 2021)
94 Wilkie, L. (2022) "The Complex Construct of Well-being and the Role of the Vagal Function," *Frontiers Integrative Neuroscience*, Vol 16, https://doi.org/10.3389/fnint.2022.925664
95 Kobayashi, L et. Al. (2009) "Effect of Phytoncide From Trees on Human Natural Killer Cell Function," *International Journal of Immunopathology and Pharmacology*, 22(4), p951–9, www.pubmed.ncbi.nlm.nih.gov (accessed 21August 2021)
96 Peterfalvi, A et. Al (2019) "Much More than a Pleasant Scent: A Review on Essential Oils Supporting the Immune System" *Molecules* 24(24), 4530, ncbi.nlm.nih.gov (accessed 21August 2021)
97 see McCraty, M. et al 2017() "Synchronisation of Human Autonomic Nervous System Rhythm with Geomagnetic Activity in Human Subjects," *International Journal of Environmental Research and Public Health*, 14(7):770, 10.3390/ijerph14070770 (accessed 26 September 2022)
98 Oschman, J. et al (2015) "The Effects of Grounding (Earthing) on Inflammation, the Immune Response, Wound Healing, and Prevention and Treatment of Chronic Inflammatory and Autoimmune Diseases," *Journal of Inflammation Research*, Vol 8; 83–96, doi:10.2147/JIR.S69656 (accessed 26 September 2022)
99 Dr Osansky (2015) "Earthing and Thyroid Health," www.endocrinesolutions.com (accessed 22August 2021)
100 The widespread use of DDT and its ill-effects led to the pivotal book *Silent Spring* by Rachel Carson, which inspired the emergence of the environmental movement in the 1960s.
101 Florida Atlantic University (2022) "Feeling Anxious Or Blue? Ultra-Processed Foods May Be to Blame" https://www.sciencedaily.com/releases/2022 August 20220825091343.htm
102 Poti, J et. Al (2018) "Ultra-processed Food Intake and Obesity: What Really Matters For Health—Processing or Nutrient Content?," *Current Obesity* report 6(4), p420–431
103 Zhou, Y. et al (2015) "The Food Retal Revolution in China and its Association with Diet and Health," *Food Policy* 1(55), p92–100

104 Beddington. J. et al (2020) "Future Food Systems: For People, Our Planet, and Prosperity," www.glopan.org (accessed 1 September 2021)

105 UNICEF (2019) "The Changing Face of Malnutrition: The State of the World's Children in 2019" www.features.unicef.org (accessed 10 September 2021)

106 Tian, X. and Wang, H. (2022) "Projecting National-Level Prevalence of General Obesity and Abdominal Obesity among Chinese Adults with Aging effects," *Front Endocrinol* (Lausanne), www.ncbi.nlm.nih.gov (Accessed 11 September 2022)

107 Pelc, Corrie (2022) "Ultra-processed Foods Linked to Heart Disease, Cancer, and Death, Studies Show", *Medical News Today*, https://www.medicalnewstoday.com/articles/ultra-processed-foods-linked-to-heart-disease-cancer-and-death-studies-show (accessed 13 December 2022)

108 (2019) "Ultra-processed Food Intake and Risk of Cardiovascular Disease: Prospective Cohort Study," *British Medical Journal*, 365:l1451, https://doi.org/10.1136/bmj.l1451 (accessed 12 December 2022)

109 Mancini, F. (2012) "The Truth About Food Additives; How They Threaten Your Health" www.theecologist.com (accessed 11 September 2021)

110 Jacob, L. (2020) "Fast Food Consumption and Suicide Attempts Among Adolescents Aged 12–15 Years From 32 Different Countries" *Journal of Affective Disorders*, Vol 266, p63–70 https://www.sciencedirect.com/science/article/pii/S0165032719325984 (accessed 15 November 2022)

111 Shuster, A. et al (2012) "The Clinical Importance of Visceral Adiposity: A Critical Review of Methods for Visceral Adipose Tissue Analysis," *The British Journal of Radiology*, https://www.ncbi.nlm.nih.gov/pmc/articles/PMC3473928/ (accessed 8 December 2022). See also Dryden, J. (2007) "Belly Fat May Drive Inflammatory Processes Associated with Disease", Washington University in St. Louis, https://www.medicalnewstoday.com/articles/ultra-processed-foods-linked-to-heart-disease-cancer-and-death-studies-show (accessed 13 December 2022)

112 Sales, V.M. et al (2017) "Epigenetic Mechanisms of Transmission Across Generations," *Cell Metabolism*, 25(3), p559–571, 10.1016/j.cmet.2017.02.016 (accessed 13 December 2022)

113 Madison, A. and Kiecolt-Glaser, J (2019) "Stress, Depression, Diet, and the Gut Microbiota: Human–Bacteria Interactions at the Core of Psychoneuroimmunology and Nutrition," *Current Opinions on Behavioral Sciences*, 28:p105–110, doi: 10.1016/j.cobeha.2019.01.011 (accessed 13 December 2022)

114 Renata. s et.al (2019) "Probiotics and Prebiotics: focus on psychiatric disorders—a systematic review," *Nutrition Reviews* 78(6), p437–450, www.academic.oup.com (accessed 21 September 2021)

115 Wang, H. and Lee In-Seon (2016) "Effect of Probiotics on Central Nervous System Functions in Animals and Humans: A Systematic Review," *Journal of Neurogastroenterology and Motility*, 22(4), p589–605 https://www.ncbi.nlm.nih.gov/pmc/articles/ (accessed 15 November 2022)

116 Wiertsema, S.et al (2021) "The Interplay Between the Gut Microbiome and the Immune System in the Context of Infectious Diseases Throughout Life and the Role of Nutrition in Optmising Treatment Strategies" *Nutrients* 9(13):886 https://pubmed.ncbi.nlm.nih.gov/33803407/ (accessed 18 November 2022)

117 Erdmann, J. (2022) "How Gut Bacteria Could Boost Cancer Treatments" https://www.nature.com/articles/d41586-022-01959-7 (November 2022)

118 Another healthy fat is ghee (clarified butter). Cooking with ghee is like a superfood for the gut. It stimulates digestive enzymes, acts as a prebiotic (feeding the microbiome), lubricates and strengthens the intestines, and is rich in omega-3 fatty acids which are absorbed directly to the liver (like carbs) which boosts metabolism and helps with weight loss. Ghee is like eating probiotics, prebiotics, and fiber combined, helping both digestion and immunity.

119 Guasch-Ferre, M. and Willett, W. C. (2021) "The Mediterranean Diet and Health; a Comprehensive Review," *Journal of Internal Medicine*, 290 (3) p549–566, https://onlinelibrary.wiley.com/doi/full/10.1111/joim.13333

120 Huggins Salomon, S. and Lawler, M. (2022) "8 Scientific Benefits of the Mediterranean Diet" www.everydayhealth.com (accessed 21 November 2022)

121 Dernini, S. et al. (2017) "The Mediterranean Diet with Four Sustainable Benefits," *Public Health Nutrition*, 20:1322–30

122 Schueller, G. (2020) "We Surveyed People on the Mediterranean Diet. Here's What They Say," www.health.usnews.com/wellness/articles/ (accessed 21 November 2022)

123 Enders, G. (2015) *Gut: The Inside Story of Our Body's Most Under-rated Organ*, Scribe, UK

124 Blaser, M. (2015) *Missing Microbes: How Killing Bacteria Creates Modern Plagues*, Oneworld Publication

125 Wook-Lee et. Al (2021) "Association Between Depression and Antibiotic Use: Analysis of Population-Based National Health Insurance Claims Data," BMC Psychiatry, 21, 536, https://doi.org/10.1186/s12888-021-03550-2 (accessed 18 November 2022)

126 Gallagher, S. (2019) "What Can Hunter-Gatherers Teach Us About Staying Healthy?" www.globalhealth.duke.edu (accessed 23 September 2021)

127 Harare, Y. (2011) *Sapiens: A Brief History of Humankind*, Random House Harper

128 Bailey, et. al (2015) "The Epidemiology of Global Micronutrient Deficiencies," *Annals of Nutrition and Metabolism*, https://www.karger.com/article/fulltext/371618 (accessed 13 December 2022)

129 World Health Organization (2022) "Anaemia" https://www.who.int/health-topics/anaemia#tab=tab_1 (accessed 13 December 2022)

130 see also Bjarnadottir. A. (2019) "7 Nutrient Deficiencies That Are Incredibly Common," https://www.healthline.com/nutrition/7-common-nutrient-deficiencies (accessed 7 December 2022)

131 Adeola, F. (2021) "Global Impact of Chemicals and Toxic Substances on Human Health and the Environment," *Handbook of Global Health*, Springer, www.link.springer.com (accessed 12 September 2021)

132 US EPA (1994) "National Human Adipose Tissue Survey (NHATS)," www.cfpub.epa.gov (accessed 10 September 2021)

133 Kalyabina, V. P. and Kratasyuk, V. A. (2021) "Pesticides: Formulants, Distribution Pathways and Effects on Human Health—a Review," https://doi.org/10.1016/j.toxrep.2021.06.004 (accessed 30 November 2022)

134 Mostafalou, S. (2013) "Pesticides and Human Chronic Diseases: Evidences, Mechanisms and Perspectives," Toxicology and Applied Pharmacology, 268(2), p157–77, www.pubmed.ncbi.nlm.nih.gov (accessed 21 October 2021)

135 National Institute of Environmental Health Sciences (2022) "Dioxins" https://www.niehs.nih.gov/health/topics/agents/dioxins/index.cfm (accessed 30 November 2022)

136 Filby, A. et al (2007) "Gene Expression Profiles Revealing the Mechanisms of Anti-androgen—and Estrogen-induced Feminization in Fish," *Aquatic Toxicology*, 81(2):219–31, https://pubmed.ncbi.nlm.nih.gov/17222921/ (accessed 25 January 2023)

137 Pivonello, C, et al (2020) "Bispheonal A: an Emerging Threat to Female Fertility," Reproductive Biology and Endocrinology, https://rbej.biomedcentral.com/articles/10.1186/s12958-019-0558-8 (Accessed 30 November 2022)

138 The Harvard Gazette (2018) "Study Tracks Mercury Sources in Seafood," https://news.harvard.edu/gazette/story/2018/02/harvard-study-tracks-methylmercury-in-seafood/ (accessed 30 November 2022)

139 Baranksi, M. et. al. (2014) "Higher Antioxidant and Lower Cadmium Concentrations and Lower Incidences of Pesticide Residues In Organically Grown Crops: A Systematic Review and Meta-Analysis," *British Journal of Nutrition*, 112(5), p794–811, www.pubmed.ncbi.nlm.nih.gov (accessed 21 November 2021)

140 IFOAM (2022) "Global Policy Toolkit on Public Policy Support for Organic Agriculture," https://www.ifoam.bio/our-work/how/regulation-policy/global-policy-toolkit (accessed 30 December 2022)

141 see UNEP (2021) "Why Climate Science Is Key to Protecting People and Planet" www.unep.org
142 Maynard, M (2018) "Veggies May Be Healthier, But in 2018, Americans Will Eat a Record Amount of Meat," www.forbes.com (accessed 12 September 2022)
143 ScienceDaily (2016) "Neu5Gc in Red Meat and Organs May Pose a Significant Health Hazard," Science Daily, https://www.sciencedaily.com/releases/2016/10/161019160201.htm (accessed 22 December 2022)
144 Pendick, D (2013) "New Study Links L-carnitine in Red Mead to Heart Disease," https://www.health.harvard.edu/blog/new-study-links-l-carnitine-in-red-meat-to-heart-disease-201304176083 (accessed 24 December 2022)
145 IACR (2014) "IARC Monographs Evaluate Consumption of Red Meat and Processed Meat," www.iarc.who.int (accessed 23 September 2021)
146 The World Health Organization (2015) "Cancer: Carcinogenicity of the Consumption of Red Meat and Processed Meat," https://www.nature.com/articles/d41586–022–01959–7 8 November 2022)
147 Katherine D. McManus (2019) "A Practical Guide to the Mediterranean Diet," https://www.health.harvard.edu/blog/a-practical-guide-to-the-mediterranean-diet-2019032116194 (accessed 24 December 2022)
148 see https://www.healthline.com/nutrition/grass-fed-vs-grain-fed-beef (accessed 10 June 2024)
149 Harari, Y (2019) *Sapiens: A Brief History of Humankind*, Vintage Classics
150 Hjalmarsdottir, F. (2018) "17 Science-Based Benefit of Omega-3 Fatty Acids," https://www.healthline.com/nutrition/17–health-benefits-of-omega-3#TOC_TITLE_HDR_4 (accessed 1 December 2022)
151 Hiroyasu, I. et al. (2006) "Intake of Fish and n3 Fatty Acids and Risk of Coronary Heart Disease Among Japanese," Ahajournals.org, https://www.ahajournals.org/doi/10.1161/circulationaha.105.581355 (01 December 2022)
152 Spencer, B. (2015) "A Few Mouthfuls of Oily Fish Once a Week Can Reduce the Risk of Dying from Cancer by 70%" https://www.dailymail.co.uk/news/article-3698188/amp/A-mouthfuls-oily-fish-day-reduce-risk-dying-bowel-cancer-70.html (accessed 1 December 2022)
153 Hjalmarsdottir, F. (2018) "17 Science-Based Benefit of Omega-3 Fatty Acids," https://www.healthline.com/nutrition/17–health-benefits-of-omega-3#TOC_TITLE_HDR_4 (accessed 1 December 2022)
154 Dhaka, V. et al (2011) "Trans Fat—Sources, Health Risks and Alternative Approach—a Review" *Journal of Food Science and Technology*, 48(5): 534–541, doi: 10.1007/s13197–010–0225–8

155 Astrup, A and Krauss, R. (2020) "Saturated Fats and Health; A Reassessment and Proposal for Food-Based Recommendations" *JACC State-of the-Art Review*, Cardiology, 76(7), p844–857 https://pubmed.ncbi.nlm.nih.gov/32562735/ (accessed 24 December 2022)

156 Wasink, B. (2011) *Mindless Eating: Why We Eat More than We Think*, Hay House

157 Saunders, J. (2023) "From Matchbox-sized Cheese to Meat No Bigger Than a Deck of Cards—What the Portions You Eat Should Really Look Like," *The Sun Newspaper*, https://apple.news/AuaciOPARQ5yPT4xKW1oZow (accessed 7 August 2023)

158 Anderson, J. (2020) "Harvard EdCast: The Benefits of Family Mealtime," www.gse.harvard.edu (accessed 12 September 2021)

159 see Harris. S (2018) "More Than Half of British Children Don't Use Cutlery at Home," www.dailymail.co.uk

160 HuffPost (2012) "Half of Young People Don't Know Butter Comes from Cows" https://www.huffingtonpost.co.uk/amp/entry/health-young-people-dont-know-butter-comes-from-cow_n_1593676/ (accessed 25 August 2023)

161 Harvard T.H Chan (2018) "The Power of a Family Meal," www.hsph.harvard.edu (accessed 12 September 2021)

162 Tapper, K (2022) "Mindful Eating: What we Know So Far," www.onlinelibrary.wiley.com (accessed 12 September 2022)

163 See Scritchfield, R (2017) *Body Kindness: Transform your Health From the Inside Out - and Never Say Diet Again*, Workman Publishing

164 Fung, J. (2016) *The Complete Guide to Fasting: Heal your Body Through Intermittent, Alternate Day, and Extended Fasting*, Victory Belt

165 Stephens, G (2020) *Fast, Feast, Repeat: The Comprehensive Guide to Delay, Don't Deny*, St Martin's Griffin

166 Ritchie, H. (2021) "How Much of Global Greenhouse Gas Emissions Come From Food?" https://ourworldindata.org/greenhouse-gas-emissions-food (accessed 22 November 2022)

167 Askew, K. (2021) "Crop Diversity Underpins Food Security: Scientists Flag 'Enormous' Diversity Loss," www.foodnavigator.com (accessed 11 November 2021)

168 see UNEP (2022) "New Report Reveals Devastating 69% Drop in Wildlife Populations," https://www.unep-wcmc.org/en/news/new-report-reveals-devastating-69-drop-in-wildlife-populations,(accessed 30 December 2022)

See also Garrington, D. (2019) "Plummeting Insect Numbers 'Threaten Collapse of Nature'," www.theguardian.com (accessed 11 November 2021)

169 Carson, R. (1962) *Silent Spring* Penguin Classics

170 see WHO (2022) "Pesticide Residues in Food" World Health Organization, https://www.who.int/news-room/fact-sheets/detail/pesticide-residues-in-food (accessed 30 December 2022)

See also Nelsen, A. (2022) "Pesticide Use Around World Almost Doubles Since 1990, Report Finds" *Guardian News*, https://amp.theguardian.com/environment/2022/oct/18/pesticide-use-around-world-almost-doubles-since-1990–report-finds (accessed 29 December 2022)

171 Leahy, S. (2018) "75% of Earth's Land Areas Are Degraded," https://www.nationalgeographic.com/science/article/ipbes-land-degradation-environmental-damage-report-spd (accessed 1 November 2022)

172 Shiva, V. (2016) *Stolen Harvest: The Highjacking of the Global Food Supply*, University Press of Kentucky

173 Shiva, V (2016) *Seed Sovereignty, Food Security: Women in the Vanguard of the Fight Against GMO's and Corporate Agriculture* Frog Ltd

174 VoedingsIndustrie (2022) "The Dutch Are Willing to Eat More Insects" https://vakbladvoedingsindustrie.nl/en/article/the-dutch-are-willing-to-eat-more-insects (accessed 21 November 2022)

175 WWF (2019) "Future 50 Foods," www.wwf.org.uk (accessed 21 September 2021)

176 Altieri, M (2019) *Agroecology; The Science of Sustainable Agriculture*, CRC Press, 2 edition

177 see Kogevinas, M. (2019) "Probable Carcinogenicity of Glyphosate" *British Medical Journal*, www.bmj.com (accessed 12 November 2019)

178 Peillex, C. and Pelletier, M. (2020) "The Impact and Toxicity of Glyphosate and Glyphosate-based Herbicides on Health and Immunity" *Journal of Immunotoxicology*, 17 (1), p163–174

179 Kirman, CR (2022) "Meta-analysis of Glyphosate and Non-Hodgkin's Lymphoma: Expert Panel Conclusions and Recommendations" *Journal of Toxicology and Risk Assessment*, 8(1), clinmedjournals.org (accessed 12 September 2022)

180 Gaines, M. (2022) "Roundup Lawsuit Update December 2022," *Forbes Advisory*, https://www.forbes.com/advisor/legal/product-liability/roundup-lawsuit-update/ (accessed 29 December 2022)

181 Gillan C. (2019) "How Monsanto Manipulates Journalists and Academics" *Guardian News*, https://amp.theguardian.com/commentisfree/2019/jun/02/monsanto-manipulates-journalists-academics (accessed 29 December 2022)

182 see IFOAM (2020) "Global Organic Area Continues to Grow," https://www.ifoam.bio/global-organic-area-continues-grow 30 December 2022)

183 USDA (2021) "Organic: A Thriving Agricultural Segment," https://www.usda.gov/media/blog/2020/10/28/organic-thriving-agriculture-segment (accessed 30 December 2022)

184 Eurostat (2022) "Organic Farming Statistics" https://ec.europa.eu/eurostat/statistics-explained/index.php?title=Organic_farming_statistics#Key_messages (accessed 30 December 2022)

185 Lori, M et al (2017) "Organic Farming Enhances Soil Microbial Abundance and Activity—A Meta-Analysis and Meta-Regression," *PLoS ONE* 12(7), www.journals.plos.org (accessed 21 November 2021)

186 EWG (2022) "EWG's 2022 Shoppers Guide to Pesticide in Produce," www.ewg.org (accessed 12 September 2022)

187 Monbiot, G. (2023) *Regenesis: Feeding the World Without Devouring the Planet*, Penguin

188 IPCC (2019) "Land Degradation in Climate Change and Land; an IPCC Special Report on Climate Change, Desertification, Land Degradation, Sustainable Land Management, Food Security, and Greenhouse Gas Fluxes in Terrestrial Ecosystems," .https://www.ipcc.ch/srccl/cite-report/Google Scholar (accessed 30 December 2022)

189 Regeneration International (2022) "Why Regenerative Agriculture Will Reverse Climate Change" www.regenerationinternational.org (accessed 12 September 2022)

190 Masters, N. (2019) "For the Love of Soil; Strategies to Regenerate Our Food Production System," Bowker

191 Bastin, Jean-Francois et al. (2019) "The Global Tree Restoration Potential" The global tree restoration potential - PubMed (nih.gov) (accessed 23 March 2023)

192 Vertical roots (2022) "The What and Why of Hydroponic Farming," https://www.verticalroots.com/the-what-and-why-of-hydroponic-farming/ (accessed 22 November 2022)

193 Gregory, A. (2022), "Antimicrobial Resistance a Leading Cause of Death Worldwide, Study Finds," The Guardian Newspaper 20 January, www.amp.theguardian.com

194 United Nations Environment Program (2021) "Why Climate Science Is Key to Protecting People and the Planet" www.unep.org/news-and-stories/story/why-climate-science-key-protecting-people-and-planet (accessed 10 May 2023)accessed

195 Schlosser, E. (2002) *Fast Food Nation: What the All-American Meal is Doing to the World*, Penguin

196 Hyman, M (2021) *Food Fix: How to Save Our Health, Our Economy, Our Community and Our Planet—One Bite At a Time* Yellow Kite

197 Saffron Foer, J (2011) *Eating Animals* Penguin

198 Twine, R. (2021) "Emissions from Animal Agriculture—16.5% is the New Minimum Figure," *Sustainability* 13(11), 6276, https://www.mdpi.com/2071-1050/13/11/6276/htm (accessed 5 December 20222)

199 Goodland, R. and Anhang, J. (2009) "Livestock and Climate Change" *World Watch* 22(6), p10–19, www.researchgate.net (accessed 21 November 2021)

200 Cowspiracy, (2022) "The Facts" https://www.cowspiracy.com/facts (accessed 18 November 2022)

201 Richie, H. (2019) "Half of the World's Habitable Land is Used for Agriculture" https://ourworldindata.org/global-land-for-agriculture (accessed 18 November 2022)

202 Carrington, D. (2021) "Amazon Rainforest Now Emitting More CO2 Than It Absorbs," www.theguardian.com (accessed 24 November 2021)

203 WWT (2019) "What Is the IUCN Red List and How Is It Used to Track Biodiversity Loss?," www.wwt.org.uk (24 November 2021)

204 Carrington, D. (2022) "Climate Crisis: Amazon Rainforest Tipping Point Is Looking, Data Shows," www.theguardian.com (accessed 25 April 2022)

205 Food and Agriculture Organization (2009), "How to Feed the World in 2050," www.fao.org (accessed 2 December 2021)

206 Carrington D. (2018) "Avoiding Meat and Dairy Is the 'Single Biggest Way' To Reduce Your Impact on Earth," www.theguardian.com (Accessed 25 November 2021)

207 see Food and Agriculture Organization (2019) "Water Scarcity—One of The Greatest Challenges of Our Time," www.fao.org (accessed 26 November 2021)

208 Science Daily (2010) "Groundwater Depletion Rate Accelerating Worldwide," https://www.sciencedaily.com/releases/2010/09/100923142503.htm (accessed 18 November 2022)

209 Petter, O. (2020) "Veganism Is 'Single Biggest Way' to Reduce Our Environmental Impact, Study Finds," www.independent.co.uk (accessed 10 December 2021)

210 IPCC (2019) "Special Report: Climate Change and Land," wwwipcc.ch (accessed 23 November 2021)

211 World Health Organization (2021) "Plant-based Diets and their Impact on Health, Sustainability and the Environment," https://apps.who.int/iris/bitstream/handle/10665/349086/WHO-EURO-2021-4007-43766-61591-eng.pdf?sequence=1&isAllowed=y 22 November 2022)

212 Anthony, A. (2021) "From Fringe to Mainstream: How Millions Got a Taste for Going Vegan" https://amp.theguardian.com/lifeandstyle/2021/oct/10/from-fringe-to-mainstream-how-millions-got-a-taste-for-going-vegan (accessed 22 November 2022)

213 Safran Foer, J (2019) *We are the Weather: Saving the Planet Begins at Breakfast* Hamish Hamilton
214 Carbon Brief (2020) "Interactive; What Is the Climate Impact of Eating Meat and Dairy?," www.interactive.carbonbrief.org (accessed 20 December 2021)
215 see Horton, H. (2022) "Replace Animal Farms with Micro-organism Tanks, Say Campaigners," *The Guardian Newspaper*, https://amp.theguardian.com/environment/2022/nov/12/replace-animal-farms-micro-organism-rewilding-food-precision-fermentation-emissions (accessed 5 December 2022)
216 World Economic Forum (2018) "90% of Fish Stocks are Used Up—Fisheries Subsidies Must Stop Emptying the Ocean" https://www.weforum.org/agenda/2018/07/fish-stocks-are-used-up-fisheries-subsidies-must-stop/ (accessed 18 November 2022)
217 CIWF (2021) "Murky Depths of the Scottish Salmon Industry Exposed in New Undercover Investigation," www.ciwf.org.uk (accessed 10 January 2022)
218 Compassion in World Farming (2019) "Wasteful and Unsustainable: The Use of Wild Fish to Feed Farmed Fish" https://www.ciwf.org.uk/media/press-releases-statements/2019/04/wasteful-and-unsustainable-the-use-of-wild-fish-to-feed-farmed-fish-is-causing-huge-environmental-and-social-damage 18 November 2022)
219 Corliss, J (2015) "Finding Omega-3 Fats in Fish: Farmed vs Wild," www.health.harvard.edu (accessed 11 January 2022)
220 Attenborough, D. (2022) "A Life on Our Planet," Ebury Press
221 Sears, B. (2004) "Simple Solutions for Global Wellness" in Church, D. and Gendreau, G., *Healing Our Planet, Healing Ourselves: The Power of Change within to Change the World*, Elite Books
222 World Trade Organization (2022) "Agreement of Fisheries Subsidies," https://www.wto.org/english/tratop_e/rulesneg_e/fish_e/fish_e.htm (Accessed 18 November 2022)
223 Bluefood.earth (2021) "Blue Food Assessment" https://bluefood.earth/science/ (accessed 5 December 2022)
224 OCEANA (2016) "More Fish, More Jobs, More Money," https://europe.oceana.org/more-fish-more-jobs-more-money/ (accessed 11 December 2022)
225 Marine Conservation Society (2022) "Good Fish Guide," https://www.mcsuk.org/goodfishguide/?sustainability=2 (accessed 7 December 2022
226 Christina Figueres and Tom Rivett-Carnac (2021) *The Future We Choose*, Manilla Press, exert from ch 3, p34–39
227 Walker, M. (2018) *Why We Sleep; The New Science of Sleep and Dreams*, Penguin Books

228 Huffington, A. (2017) *The Sleep Revolution: Transforming Your Life, One Night at a Time,* W. H. Allen
229 Duff, K. (2014) *The Secret Life of Sleep*, Oneworld Publications
230 Stevenson, S. (2016) *Sleep Smarter: 21 Essential Strategies to Sleep your Way to a Better Body, Better Health and Bigger Success* Rodale Books
231 Walker, M. (2018) *Why We Sleep: The New Science of Sleep and Dreams*, Penguin Books
232 Duff, K. (2014) "The Secret Life of Sleep," Oneworld Publications
233 Huffington, A. (2017) *The Sleep Revolution: Transforming Your Life, One Night at a Time,* WH Allen
234 see Dunster, G., Iglesia, L and Iglesia, H. (2018) "Sleep More in Seattle: Later School Start Times Are Associated with More Sleep and Better Performance in High School Students" *Science Advances*, Vol 4, No. 12 www.science.org
235 Kelly, P., Lockley, S.W., Kelley, J., and Evans, M. (2017) "Is 8:30 a.m. Still Too Early to Start School? A10:00 a.m. School Start Time Improves Health and Performance Of Students Aged 13–16," *Frontiers in Human Neuroscience*, https://doi.org/10.3389/fn-hum.2017.00588
236 Wang, C. (2021) "Association of Bedtime with Mortality and Major Cardiovascular Events; an Analysis of 112,198 Individuals From 21 Countries in the PURE Study" analysis, *Sleep Medicine*, Vol 80, pp 265–272 (https.//doi.org/10.1016/sleep2021.01.057)
237 Oxford University Press USA (2018) "Sleep Deprived People More Likely to Have Car Crashes," *ScienceDaily* www.sciencedaily.com/releases/2018/09/180918082041.htm
238 Von Schantz, M., Ong, J., Knutson, K. (2021) "Associations Between Sleep Disturbances, Diabetes and Mortality in the UK Biobank Cohort: A Prospective Population-Based Study," *Journal of Sleep Research*, Wiley online Library
239 Sandhu, A., Seth, M. and Hitinder, S. (2014) "Daylight Savings Time and Myocardial Infarction," www.openheart.bmj.com (http://dx.doi.org/10.1136/openhrt-2013-000019
240 Irwin, M. (1994) "Partial Sleep Deprivation Reduces Natural Killer Cell Activity in Humans" *Psychomed*, www.pubmed.ncbi.nlm.nih.gov
241 Walker, M. (2019) "Sleep is Your Superpower," *TED-Ed*, Youtube, June 3
242 Leprout, R and Van Couter, E. (2011) "Effects of 1 Week of Sleep Restriction on Testosterone Levels in Young Healthy Men" *The Journal of the American Medical Association (JAMA)*, 305(21):2173 DOI:10.1001/jama.2011.710
243 Bryant, E. (2021) "Lack of Sleep In Middle Age May Increase Dementia Risk," National Institutes of Health, nih.gov

244 National Institute for Sleep (2020) "Impairments due to sleep deprivation are similar to impairments due to alcohol intoxication" https://www.cdc.gov/niosh/work-hour-training-for-nurses/longhours/mod3/08.html
245 Cooper, C., Neufeld, E and Martin, J. (2018) "Sleep Deprivation and Obesity in Adults; A Brief Narrative Review," www.ncbi.nlm.nih.gov
246 Beccuti, G and Pannain, S. (2011) "Sleep and Obesity," *Current Opinion in Clinical Nutrition and Metabolic Care*, 14(4), p402–412, doi: 10.1097/MCO.0b013e3283479109 (accessed 27 September 2022)
247 see ScienceDaily (2019) "New Study Points to Another Possible Correlation Between Sleep and Overall Good Health," www.sciencedaily.com
248 Pacheco, D. and Lyo, J (2020) "Exercise and Insomnia" www.sleepfoundation.org (accessed 23 May 2022)
249 Pacheco, D. (2022) "How Can Exercise Affect Sleep?" www.sleepfoundation.org (accessed 27 September 2022)
250 Anwar, A. (2018) "How Poor Sleep Can Ruin Your Social Life" www.universityofcalifornia.edu (accessed 23 May 2022)
251 Hafner, M. et al (2016) "Why Sleep Matters—The Economic Cost of Insufficient Sleep; A Cross Country Comparative Analysis," www.rand.org/pubs/research_reports/RR1791.html
252 Pilcher, J. and Huffcutt, A. (1996) "Effects of Sleep Deprivation On Performance: A Meta-Analysis," Sleep, vol 19, issue 4, www.academic.oup.com, DOI: 10.1093/sleep/19.4.318) (accessed 22 March 2023)
253 "2008 Sleep in America Poll; Summary of Findings," www.sleepfoundation.org (accessed 22 May 2022)
254 See www.sleepfoundation.org/stages-of-sleep (accessed 2 August 2023)
255 Haidt, J. and Allen, N. (2020) "Scrutinizing the Effects of Digital Technology on Mental Health," www.nature.com (https;//doi.org/10.1038/d41586-020-00296) (Acccessed 25 May 2022)
256 Sample, I. (2017) "Having Trouble Sleeping? Grab a Tent and Go Camping, Suggest Researchers," www.theguardian.com (Accessed 28 May 2022)
257 Breus, M. (2018) "Sleep Better with These 7 Essential Oils," psychologytoday.com (accessed 29 May 2022)
258 Pacheco, D. (2021) "How Meditation Can Treat Insomnia" www.sleepfoundation.org (accessed 29 May 2022)
259 World Health Organization (2022) "The Global Health Observatory: Physical Inactivity," www.who.int/data/gho/indicator-metadata-registry/imr-detaild/3416 (accessed 12 September 2022)

260 British Heart Foundation; "Are you Sitting too Much?," *Heart Matters Magazine*, bhf.org.uk (accessed 12 September 2022)
261 BBC (2015) "Do You Really Need to Take 10,000 Steps a Day to Keep Fit," www.bbc.co.uk (Accessed 12 September 2022)
262 British Heart Foundation, (2022) "Are You Sitting Too Much?" *Heart Matters Magazine*, www.bhf.org.uk (accessed 12 September 2022)
263 Pratt, E. (2018) "Research Says Exercise Also Improves Your Gut Bacteria" www.healthline.com (accessed 12 September 2022)
264 ACS (2016) "Physical Activity Can Lower Risk of 13 Types of Cancer," www.amp.cancer.org (accessed 12 September 2022)
265 Warner, J. (2006) "Exercise Fights Fatigue, Boosts Energy," www.webmd.com (accessed 12 September 2022)
266 Reimers, C et al (2012) "Does Physical Activity Increase Life Expectancy? A Review of the Literature," www.pubmed.ncbi.nlm.nih.gov
267 McGonical, K (2020) *The Joy of Movement*, Avery Publishing
268 Williams, C. (2022) *Move! The New Science of Body over Mind*, Profile Books
269 Ratey, J. and Hagerman, E. (2010) *Spark: How Exercise Will Improve the Performance of Your Brain* Quercus
270 Reas, E. et al (2019) "Physical Activity and Trajectories of Cognitive Change in Community-Dwelling Older Adults: The Rancho Bernardo Study" *Journal of Alzheimer's Disease* 71(1), 109–118, www.ncbi.nlm.nih.gov (accessed 12 September 2022)
271 Alzheimers Society, "Physical Exercise and Dementia," www.alzheimers.org.uk (Accessed 12 September 2022)
272 Geneen, L. and Moore, A. (2017) "Physical Activity and Exercise for Chronic Pain in Adults: An Overview of Cochrane Reviews." CD011279. www.ncbi.nlm.nih.gov (accessed 12 September 2022)
273 Bergland, C. (2021) "Runners High Depends on Endocannabinoids (not Endorphins)," www.psychologytoday.com (accessed 12 September 2022)
274 McGonigal, K. (2021) *The Joy of Movement; How Exercise Helps us Find Happiness, Hope, Connection and Courage*, Penguin Publishing Group
275 Thomson Coon, J. et al (2011) "Does Participating in Physical Activity in Outdoor Natural Environments Have a Greater Effect on Physical and Mental Well-Being Than Physical Activity Indoors? A Systematic Review," *Environmental Science and Technology*, Vol 45, p 1761–1772
276 Logan, A. and Selhub, E. (2012) "Vis Medicatrix Naturae; does nature 'minister to the mind?'" *Biopsychosoc Med*, Vol 6 (3), www.pubmed.ncbi.nlm.nih.gov, (accessed 21 July 2022

277 Shin, J. C. et al. (2020) "Greenspace Exposure and Sleep: A Systematic Review," *Environmental Research*, Vol 182, www.pubmed.ncbi.nlm.nih.gov, (accessed 21 July 2022

278 Swain, F. (2013) "Fresh Air and Sunshine; The Forgotten Antibiotics," *New Scientist* https://www.newscientist.com/article/mg22029470-700-fresh-air-and-sunshine-the-forgotten-antibiotics/ (accessed 12 August 2024)

279 McGonnigal, K. (2020) *The Joy of Movement: How Execerise Helps us Find Happiness, Hope, Connection and Courage* Penguin Publishing Group

280 Denworth, L. (2023) "Brain Waves Synchronize when People Interact," *Scientific American*, https://www.scientificamerican.com/article/brain-waves-synchronize-when-people-interact/ (accessed 15 August 2024)

281 Chatterjee, R. (2018) *The Four Pillar Plan: How to relax, Eat, Move and Sleep Your Way to a Longer, Healthier Life*, Penguin Life

282 Brynie, F. (2012) "The Placebo Effect: How it Works" https://www.psychologytoday.com/gb/blog/brain-sense/201201/the-placebo-effect-how-it-works?amp, (accessed July 8, 2022

283 Cragg, J. J. et.al (2016) "Meta-Analysis of Placebo Responses in Central Neuropathic Pain; Impact of Subject, Study and Pain Characteristics," *Pain*, Vol 157 (3) p530–540

284 Marchant, J. (2016) *Cure: A Journey into the Science of Mind over Body*, Canongate Books

285 Watson, L (1974) *Supernature: A Natural History of the Supernatural*, Coronet Books

286 Wallis, C. (2018) "How Fake Surgeries Expose Useless Treatments" *Scientific American*, www.scientificamerican.com, (accessed 8 August 2022)

287 Wartolowska, K. et al (2014), "Use Of Placebo Controls In the Evaluation of Surgery: Systematic Review," *BMJ* 348:g3253, www.ncbi.nlm.nih.gov (accessed July 10 2022)

288 Mosely, et al. (2002) "A controlled trial of arthroscopic surgery for osteoarthritis of the knee," *New England Journal of Medicine*, 347(2), p81–88

289 Miller, F., Kallmes, D. and Buchbinder, R. (2011) "Vertoplasty and the Placebo Response," *Radiology*, 259(3): 621–625

290 Fassler, M. et al. (2010) "Frequency and Circumstances of Placebo Use in Clinical Practice—a Systematic Review of Empirical Studies" *BMC Medicine*, 8(15), https://doi.org/10.1186/1741-7015-8-15 (accessed 6 October 2022)

291 Dispenza, J. (2014) *You Are the Placebo: Making Your Mind Matter*, Hay House, UK

292 Zoffness, R (2019) "A Tale of Two Nails," www.PsychologyToday.com, (accessed 22 August 2022)

293 Hamilton, D. (2021) *Why Woo-Woo Works: The Surprising Science Behind Meditation, Reiki, Crystals and Other Alternative Practices*, Hay House, UK

294 Pert, C (1999) *Molecules of Emotion: Why You Feel the Way You Feel*, Simon and Schuster, UK (See also Denton, M. (2020) "The Miracle of the Cell," Discovery Institute)

295 Goswami, A. (2011) *The Quantum Doctor: A Quantum Physicist Explains the Healing Power of Integrative Medicine*, Hampton Roads Publishing Company

296 Dispenza, J (2009) *Evolve Your Brain: The Science of Changing Your Mind*, Health Communications Inc.

297 Cohen, B. (1991) *Multiple Personality Disorder from the Inside Out*, Sidran Press

298 Hamilton, D. (2018) *How Your Mind Can Heal Your Body*, Hay House, UK

299 Vincent Peale, N. (1990) *The Power of Positive Thinking* Cedar Books, Vermillion

300 Mate, G (2019) *When the Body Says No: The Cost of Hidden Stress*, Vermillion

301 Maruta, T. et al (2000) "Optimists vs Pessimists: Survival Rate Among Medical Patients Over a 30-Year Period" Mayo Clinic Proceedings, 75 (2), p140–143

302 Manninen et. Al (2017) "Social Laughter Triggers Endogenous Opioid Release in Humans," *Journal of Neuroscience*, 37 (25) p6125–6131, https://www.jneurosci.org/content/37/25/6125,(accessed 4 November 2022)

303 Giltray, E. et al (2004) "Dispositional optimism and all-cause and cardiovascular mortality in a prospective cohort of elderly Dutch men and women," *Arch Gen Psychiatry*, 61 (11), p1126–35

304 Seppala, E. (2013) "Compassionate Mind, Healthy Body', https://greatergood.berkeley.edu/article/item/compassionate_mind_healthy_body (accessed 17 March 2024)

305 HeartMath. Inc (2021) "The Science of HeartMath," https://www.heartmath.com/science/ (accessed 10 October 2022)

306 Ferrara, E. and Yang, Z. (2015) "Measuring Emotional Contagion in Social Media" *PLOS One*, 10 (11), www.sciencedaily.com (accessed 10 August 2022)

307 Alloway, T. (2022) "What 20 Seconds of Hugging Can Do For You," https://www.psychologytoday.com/gb/blog/keep-it-in-mind/202201/what-20-seconds-hugging-can-do-you?amp (accessed 10 October 2022)

308 Grimm, D. (2015) "How Dogs Stole Our Hearts," https://www.science.org/content/article/how-dogs-stole-our-hearts (accessed 12 October 2022)

309 Murray, D. (2019), "Falling in Love Is Associated with Immune System Gene Regulation," Vol 100, p120–126, www.sciencedirect.com, (accessed 10 July 2022

310 Kirschner, H. et al (2019), "Soothing Your Heart and Feeling Connected: A New Experimental Paradigm to Study the Benefits of Self-Compassion" *Clinical Psychological Science*, Vol 7 (3), p545–565, www.journals.sagepub.com, (accessed 10 July 2022

311 Frankl, V. (2004) *Man's Search for Meaning: The Classic Tribute to Hope from the Holocaust*, Rider

312 Merzenich, M. (2013) *Soft-Wired: How the New Science of Brain Plasticity Can Change your Life*, Parnassus Publishing

313 Doidge, N. (2008) *The Brain that Changes Itself: Stories of Personal Triumph from the Frontiers of Brain Science*, Penguin

314 Dispenza, J. (2009) *Evolve your Brain*, Health Communications Inc

315 Hebb, D. (1949) *The Organization of Behavior*, Wiley & Sons, NY

316 Lipton, B. (2015) *The Biology of Belief: Unleashing the Power of Consciousness, Matter and Miracles*, Hay House UK

317 see Fronsdal, G. (2006) "Dhammapada: A New Translation of the Buddhist Classic with Annotations" Shambhala Publications

318 Feltz, D. L. and Landers, D.M (1983) "The Effects of Mental Practice On Motor Skill Learning and Performance: A Meta-Analysis," *Journal of Sport Psychology*, 5, p25–57

319 Menzies, V. et al (2014), "Effects of Guided Imagery On Biobehavioral Factors In Women With Fibromyalgia," *Journal of Behavioral Medicine*, 37(1), p70–80

320 Rusch, H and Rosario, M (2018) "The Effect of Mindfulness Meditation on Sleep Quality: A Systematic Review and Meta-Analysis of Randomized Controlled Trials" *New York Academy of Sciences*, Vol 1445 (1), p5–16

321 Paolis D. G. et al (2019) "The Effectiveness Of Progressive Muscle Relaxation And Interactive Guided Imagery As A Pain-Reducing Intervention In Advanced Cancer Patients; A Multicenter Randomized Controlled Non-Pharmacological Trial," *Complementary Therapy Clinical Practice*, 34, p280 - 287

322 Trakhtenberg, E. C. (2008) "The Effects of Guided Imagery on The Immune System; A Critical Review," *International Journal of Neuroscience*, 118 (6), p839–55

323 Hamilton, D. (2018) *How Your Mind Can Heal Your Body*, Hay House UK

324 Mate, G. (2019) *When the Body Says No: The Hidden Cost of Stress*, Vermilion

325 Benson, H. and Klipper, M. (2000) *The Relaxation Response*, William Morrow and Company

326 Goleman, D. and Davidson, R. (2018) *The Science of Meditation: How to Change Your Brain, Mind and Body*, Penguin Life

327 Kingsland, J. (2018) *Siddhartha's Brain: The Science of Meditation, Mindfulness and Enlightenment*, Robinson

328 Anderson, et. al (2008) "Blood Pressure Response to Transcendental Meditation: A Meta-Analysis," *American Journal of Hypertension*, 21 (3), p310–316, www.academic.oup.com (accessed 20 September 2022)

See also Khoury, b. et al. (2013) "Mindfulness-Based Therapy: A Comprehensive Meta-Analysis," *Clinical Psychology Review*, 33(6), p763–771

See also Goyal, M. et al (2014) "Meditation Programs for Psychological Stress and Well-being," *JAMA Internal Medicine*, 174 (3), p357–368

329 see Ding-E Young, J. and Taylor, E. (1998) "Meditation as a Voluntary Hypometabolic State of Biological Estivation," *Physiology*, https://doi.org/10.1152/physiologyonline.1998.13.3.149, (accessed 28 September 2022)

330 Murnieks, C.Y and Haynie, M. (2020) "Close Your Eyes or Open Your Mind; Effects of Sleep and Mindfulness Exercises on Entrepreneurs' Exhaustion," *Journal of Business Venturing*, 35 (2)

331 May, C. J. et al (2019) "The Relative Impacts Of 15–Minutes Of Meditation Compared To a Day of Vacation in Daily Life: An Exploratory Analysis," *Journal of Positive Psychology*, 15(2), p278–284, https://doi.org/10.1080/17439760.2019.1610480, (accessed 3 October 2022)

332 Rusch, H. et al. (2018) "The Effect of Mindfulness Meditation on Sleep Quality: a Systematic Review and Meta-analysis of Randomised Controlled Trials," *The New York Academy of Sciences*, 1445 (1), p5–16, 10.1111/nyas.13996 (accessed 20 September 2022)

333 see Chowdhury, R. (2019) "16 Health Benefits of Daily Meditation According to Science," www.positivepsychology.com, https://positivepsychology.com/benefits-of-meditation/#practice (accessed 20 September 2022)

334 Kanchibhotla, D. et al. (2021) "Improvement in Gastrointestinal Quality of Life Index (GIQLI) Following Meditation" *Journal of Ayurveda and Integrative Medicine*, 12(1), p107–111, doi:10.1016/j.jaim.2021.01.006 (accessed 26 September 2022)

335 Ray, I.B et al. (2014) "Meditation and Coronary Heart Disease: A Review of the Current Clinical Evidence," *The Ochsner Journal*, 14 (4), p696–703, www.ncbi.nlm.gov (accessed 21 September 2022)

336 Hilton, L. et al. (2017) "Mindfulness Meditation for Chronic Pain: Systematic review and Meta-analysis" *Annals of Behavioural Medicine*, 51(2), p199–213, doi:10.1007/s12160-016-9844-2 (accessed 21 September 2022)

Ngamkham, S. et al. (2019) "A Systematic Review: Mindfulness Intervention for Cancer-related Pain," 6(2), p161–169, doi: 10.4103/apjon.apjon_67_18 (accessed 21 September 2022)

337 Meesters, A. et al. (2018) "The Effect of Mindfulness-Based Stress Reduction on Wound Healing: a Preliminary Study," *Journal of Behavioural Medicine*, 41, p 385–397, https://doi.org/10.1007/s10865-017-9901-8 (accessed 20 September 2022)

338 Chopra, D. and Tanzi, R.E (2013) *Super Brain: Unleashing the Explosive Power of Your Mind To Maximize Health, Happiness, And Spiritual Well-Being*, Rider

339 Blackburn, E. and Epel, E. (2017) *The Telomere Effect: A Revolutionary Approach to Living Younger, Healthier, Longer*, Grand Central Publishing

340 Luders, E. et al (2014) "Forever Young(er); Potential Age-Defying Effects of Long-Term Meditation on Grey Matter Atrophy," *Frontiers in Psychology*, 5:1551, doi:10.3389/fpsyg.2014.01551 (accessed 27 September 2022)

341 Zhang, Z. et al. (2021) "Longitudinal Effects of Meditation on Brain Resting-State Functional Connectivity," *Scientific Reporting*, 11, article 11361, www.nature.com, https://rdcu.be/cV1Vi (accessed 21 September 2022)

342 Williamson, W. (2019) *The Effortless Mind: Meditation for the Modern World*, Simon and Schuster, UK

343 see So, K.T and Orme-Johnson, D. (2001) "Three Randomised Experiments on the Longitudinal Effects of the Transcendental Meditation Technique on Cognition," Intelligence, vol 29, p 419–440, cited in Williams, W. (2018) *The Effortless Mind: Meditation for the Modern World*, Simon and Schuster, UK

344 Beaty, R. et al. (2018) "Robust Prediction of Individual Creative Ability From Brain Functional Connectivity." *Proceedings of National Academy of Sciences*, 115 (5), p1087–1092, https://doi.org/10.1073/pnas.1713532115 (accessed 20 September 2022)

Colzato, L. et al. (2012) "Meditate to Create: The Impact of Focused-Attention and Open-Monitoring Training on Convergent and Divergent Thinking," *Frontiers in Psychology*, vol 3, p116, 10.3389/fpsyg.2012.00116 (accessed 20 September 2022)

345 Holzel, B. K. et al. (2011) "Mindfulness Practice Leads to Increases in Regional Brain Gray Matter Density," *Psychiatry Research*, 191(1), p 36–43, doi: 10.1016/j.pscychresns.2010.08.006 (accessed 28 September 2022)

346 Esch, T. (2014) "The Neurobiology of Meditation and Mindfulness," in Schmidt, S. Walach, H. (eds) *Meditation-Neuroscientific Approaches and Philosophical Implications. Studies in Neuroscience, Consciousness and Spirituality*, vol 2, Springer, p153–173, https://doi.org/10.1007/978-3-319-01634-4_9

347 Pert, C. (2006) *Everything You Need to Know to Feel Go(o)d*, Hay House

348 Brewer, J. et al. (2011) "Meditation Experience Is Associated with Differences in Default Mode Network Activity and Connectivity," www.pnas.org, https://doi.org/10.1073/pnas.1112029108 (accessed 20 September 2022)

349 Bradt. S (2010) "About 47% Of Waking Hours Spent Thinking About What Isn't Going On," *The Harvard Gazette*, www.news.harvard.edu (accessed 3 October 2022)
350 Satpute, A. B. and Lindquist, K. A. (2019) "Trends in Cognitive Science," 23(10), p851–864, doi:10.1016/j.tics.2019.07.003 (accessed 28 September 2022)
351 Khoury, B. Sharma, M., Rush SE and Fournier, C., (2015) "Mindfulness-based Stress Reduction for Healthy Individuals; a meta-analysis," *Journal of Psychosomatic Research*, www.pubmed.gov (accessed 13 September 2022)
352 Huang, H. P., Wang, He Y., Shou, M. (2016) "A Meta-Analysis of The Benefits of Mindfulness-Based Stress Reduction (Mbsr) on Psychological Function Among Breast Cancer (Bc) Survivors." *Breast Cancer* 23 (4), p568 - 76
353 Van der Kolk, B. (2015) *The Body Keeps the Score: Mind, Brain and Body in the Transformation of Trauma*, Penguin
354 Cope, W. (2007) *The Wisdom of Yoga: a Seeker's Guide to Extraordinary Living*, Bantam Books
355 Broad, W. (2013) *The Science of Yoga: The Risks and Rewards*, Simon and Schuster
356 Chu, P., Gotink, R., Yeh, G. (2014) "The Effectiveness of Yoga in Modifying Risk Factors For Cardiovascular Disease and Metabolic Syndrome: A Systematic Review and Meta-Analysis Of Randomized Controlled Trials," *European Journal of Preventive Cardiology*, www.journals,sagepub.com (accessed 20 August 2022)
357 Bubnis, D. (2019) "What Are the Health Benefits of Yoga?" www.medicalnewstoday.com (accessed 20 August 2022)
358 Bhattacharya, K. and Small, B. (2021) "Effect of Yoga-Related Mind-Body Therapies on Cognitive Function In Older Adults; A Systematic Review with Meta-Analysis," *Archives of Gerontology and Geriatrics*, Vol 93, www.sciencedirect.com
359 Hagen, I. and Usha, S. Nayar (2014) "Yoga for Children and Young People's Mental Health and Well-Being: Research Review and Reflections on the Mental Health Potentials of Yoga," *Front Psychiatry* Vol 5 (35), www.ncbi.nlm.nih.gov (accessed 20 August 2022)
360 Zaccari, B., Callahan, M., and Loftis, J. (2020) "Yoga For Veterans With PTSD: Cognitive Functioning, Mental Health An,d Salivary Cortisol, Psychological Trauma," 12 (8), p913–917, www.ncbi.nlm.nih.gov (accessed 20 August 2022)
361 Nestor, J. (2021) *Breath: The New Science of a Lost Art*, Penguin Life
362 Townsend Willams, M. (2015) *Do Breathe: Calm Your Mind. Find Focus. Get Stuff Done*, The Do Book Co
363 15 Breathwork Benefits: "The Science Behind Breathing Practices" (2021), www.othership.us (accessed 20 August 2022)

364 Garg, R. et al (2016) "Effect of Left, Right, and Alternate Nostril Breathing on Verbal and Spatial Memory," *Journal of Clinical and Diagnostic Research*, 10(2): CC01– CC03, www.researchgate.net, 9accessed 16th July 20220

365 The Harvard Gazette, (2002) "Meditation Dramatically Changes Body Temperatures," www.news.harvard.edu (accessed 20 August 2022)

366 Lehrer, P., Kaur, K., Sharma, A., et al. (2020) "Heart Rate Variability Biofeedback Improves Emotional and Physical Health Outcomes," *Applied Psychotherapy and Biofeedback*, Sep 45(3), p109–129

367 Hauser, W., Hagl, M., Schmierer, A., and Hansen, E. (2016) "The Efficacy, Safety, and Applications of Medical Hypnosis: A Systematic Review of Meta-Analyses." *Deutsches Asteblatt International*, 113(17), 289

368 Sandoiu, A. (2018) "What Religion Does to the Brain," www.medicalnewstoday.com (accessed 21 August 2022)

369 Paiva, C. et al. (2012) "Association Between Prayer Activity, Inflammation, and Survival In Advanced Cancer Patients (ACPS), *Journal of Clinical Oncology*, 30(15), www.ascopubs.org (accessed 21 August 2022)

370 Koenig, H. et al. (2012) *The Handbook of Religion and Health*, Oxford University Press USA

371 Derbyshire, D. (2013) "Why Acupuncture Is Giving Sceptics the Needle," amp.theguardian.com, (accessed 12 July 2022)

372 Hao, J.J (2014) "Acupuncture: Past, Present and Future," Global Advanced Health Medicine, 3 (4), p6–8

373 Salehi, A. et.al (2015) "The Evaluation of Curative Effect of Acupuncture: A Review Of Systematic and Meta-Analysis Studies," *Journal of Evidence-Based Integrative Medicine*, www.journals.sagepub.com, (accessed 12 July 2022)

374 Holistic Health Oxford, (2017) "The World Health Organization Recommends Acupuncture For Over 100 Conditions" https://holistic-health.org.uk/world-health-Organization-recommends-acupuncture-100–conditions/amp/ (accessed 28 November 2023)

375 McManus, D. (2017) "Reiki Is Better Than Placebo and Has Broad Potential As a Complementary Health Therapy," *Journal of Evidence-based Complementary and Alternative Medicine*, 22(4), p1051–1057, www.ncbi.nlm.nih.gov

376 Demir Doğan M. (2018) "The Effect of Reiki On Pain: A Meta-Analysis," doi: 10.1016/j.ctcp.2018.02.020. (accessed 15 August 2024)

377 Beulke, SL et al (2019) "Reiki In The Relief of Chemotherapy-Related Biopsychoemotional Signs and Symptoms" *Cogitare Enferm*, www.dx.doi/10.5380/ce.v24i0.56694, (accessed 7 July 2022

378   Billot, M. et. Al (2019), "Reiki Therapy for Pain, Anxiety and Quality of Life," BMJ Supportive and Palliative Care, 9, p434–438
379   World Health Organization (2022) "Social Determinants of Health," https://scholar.google.co.uk/scholar?q=the+effects+of+social+exclusion+on+health&hl=en&as_sdt=0&as_vis=1&oi=scholart#d=gs_qabs&t=1690386990778&u=%23p%3DZN2GcqwFM68J (accessed 27 July 2023)
380   Bhandari, M. and Yasunubi, K. (2017) "What is Social Capital? A Comprehensive Review of the Concept," *Asian Journal of Social Sciences*, 37(3), p480–510
381   Valtorta, N. et al (2016) "Loneliness and Social Isolation as Risk Factors for Coronary Heart Disease and Stroke: Systematic Review and Meta-Analysis of Longitudinal Observational Studies" https://www.oecd-ilibrary.org/docserver/health_glance-2017-7-en.pdf?expires=1690547056&id=id&accname=guest&checksum=1E9D64CD33874149FFD05D187E947BEB (accessed 27 February 2023)
382   Singer, C. (2018) "Health Effects of Social Isolation and Loneliness," *Journal of Ageing Life Care*, Vol 28, p4–8
383   Blackpool et al (2018) "Loneliness is a Serious Public-Health Problem," *The Economist*, https://www.economist.com/international/2018/09/01/loneliness-is-a-serious-public-health-problem (accessed 26 September 2023)
384   University of Utah (2023) "The Impact of Social Media on Teen's Mental Health," https://healthcare.utah.edu/healthfeed/2023/01/impact-of-social-media-teens-mental-health#:~:text=Research%20has%20shown%20that%20young,for%20suicidal%20thoughts%20and%20behaviors (accessed 27 July 2023)
385   Haidt, J. (2021 "The Dangerous Experiment on Teenage Girls" https://www.theatlantic.com/ideas/archive/2021/11/facebooks-dangerous-experiment-teen-girls/620767/
386   Howarth, J. (2023) "Time Spent Using Smartphones (2023 Statistics)," https://explodingtopics.com/blog/smartphone-usage-stats# (accessed 27 July 2023)
387   Shriti, (2023) "Average Screen Time Statistics for 2023" https://elitecontentmarketer.com/screen-time-statistics/ (accessed 27 July 2023)
388   Vaishnavi, S.N. et al (2022) "Increased Screen Time as a Cause of Declining Physical, Psychological Health and Sleep Patterns: a Literary Review," https://www.ncbi.nlm.nih.gov/pmc/articles/PMC9638701/ (accessed 27 July 2023)
389   Orenstein, P (2021) *Boys & Sex; Young Men on Hook-ups, Love, Porn, Consent and Navigating the New Masculinity*, Souvenir Press
390   see Buettner, D (2020) "Blue Zones of Happiness; Lessons from the World's Happiest People" *National Geographic*

391 Shenassa, E.D, et. al (2007) "Dampness and Mold in the Home and Depression: An Examination of Mold-related illness and Perceived Control of One's Home as Possible Depression Pathways" *American Journal of Public Health*, https://www.ncbi.nlm.nih.gov/pmc/articles/PMC1994167/ (accessed 18 September 2023)

392 Braeger, E. (2023) "5,000 people died in damp and cold houses in 2023, new studies reveal," https://www.express.co.uk/news/uk/1809755/energy-bills-crisis-cold-home-deaths/amp (accessed 19 September 2023)

393 Santosa, A. et al. (2020) "Study Protocol; Social Capital as a Ressource for the Planning and Design of Socially Sustainable and Health Promoting Neighbourhoods—a Mixed Method Study," *Frontiers in Public Health*, https://www.frontiersin.org/articles/10.3389 (accessed 2 August 2023)

394 Stafford, M and McCarthy, M. (2006) "Neighbourhoods, Housing, and Health," in *Social Determinants of Health* by Marmot, M and Wilkinson, R (eds), Oxford University Press

395 Marmot, M. et al. (2020) "Marmot Review 10 years On," https://www.instituteofhealthequity.org/resources-reports/marmot-review-10-years-on/the-marmot-review-10-years-on-full-report.pdf (accessed 27 February 2023)

396 Luv, M. et al (2019) "The Impact of Increasing Education Levels on Rising Life Expectancy: A Decomposition Analysis for Italy, Denmark, and the USA" *Journal of Popular Sciences*, 75(11) https://doi.org/10.1186/s41118-019-0055-0

397 Luy, M. et al (2019) "The Impact of Increasing Education Levels on Rising Life Expectancy: A Decomposition Analysis for Italy, Denmark, and the USA" https://genus.springeropen.com/articles/10.1186/s41118-019-0055-0 (accessed 27 July 2023)

398 Kilfoyle, K. et. Al. (2016) "Health Literacy and Women's Reproductive Health; A Systematic Review" *Journal of Women's Health*, 25(12), https://www.ncbi.nlm.nih.gov/pmc/articles/PMC5175428/ (accessed 30 July 2023)

399 Cornett, A (2020) "Analysing the Relationship Between Female Education and Fertility Rate," https://www.drake.edu/media/departmentsoffices/dussj/2020documents/Cornett%20DUSSJ%202020.pdf (accessed 3 August 2023)

400 Upadhyay, U. et. al (2014) "Women's Empowerment and Fertility: a Review of the Literature," *Social Science and Medicine*, Vol 115, p111–120 https://doi.org/10.1016%2Fj.socscimed.2014.06.014 (Accessed 30 November 2023)

401 UN Women (2022) "Explainer: Why Women need to be at the Heart of Climate Action," unwomen.org (accessed 16 September 2022). See also Figueres, C. (2021) *The Future We Choose*, Manilla Press

402 World Health Organization (2013) "Social Determinants of Health: Key Concepts," https://www.ncbi.nlm.nih.gov/pmc/articles/PMC5175428/ (accessed 30 July 2023)

403   Bartley, M. et al (2006) "Health and Labour Market Disadvantage: Unemployment, non-employment, and job insecurity" in *The Social Determinants of Health* by Marmot, M and Wilkinson, R. Oxford University Press
404   Bartley, M. et al (2006) "Health and Labour Market Disadvantage: Unemployment, non-employment, and job insecurity" in *The Social Determinants of Health* by Marmot, M and Wilkinson, R. Oxford University Press
405   Fagin, L and Little, M (1984) *The Forsaken Families*, Penguin Books, Harmondsworth
406   Fox, A. and Shewry, M (1988) "New Longitudinal Insights into Relationship Between Employment and Mortality," *Stress Med* 4(1);p 11–19
407   Isaksson, K. (1989) "Unemployment, Mental Health and The Psychological Functions of Work In Male Welfare Clients in Stockholm," Journal of Health Soc Behav 35(3); p 213–34
408   Bartley, M. et al (2006) "Health and Labour Market Disadvantage: Unemployment, non-employment, and job insecurity" in *The Social Determinants of Health* by Marmot, M and Wilkinson, R. Oxford University Press
409   Aartsen, M et al (2017) "Social Pathway To Health: On The Mediating Role of the Social Network in the Relation Between Socio-Economic Position and Health," *SSM Popular Health*, https://www.ncbi.nlm.nih.gov/pmc/articles/PMC5769056/ (accessed 30 July 2023)
410   Baum, A. et al (1999) "Socioeconomic Status and Chronic Stress. Does Stress Account for SES Effects on Health?" *Annals of the New York Academy of Sciences*. 896, p131–44, doi:10.1111/j.1749–6632.1999.tb08111.x. (accessed 2 September 2023)
411   Plucinski, M. et al (2011) "Health Safety Nets Can Break Cycles of Poverty and Disease: A Stochastic Ecological Model," https://www.ncbi.nlm.nih.gov/pmc/articles/PMC3203484/ (Accessed 30 July 2023)
412   see Black, D. et. Al (1980) "Inequalities in Health; Report of a Working Party," Department of Health and Social Security, London
413   See Marmot, M. et al (1991) "Health inequalities among British Civil Servants; The Whitehall II Study" *The Lancet*, https://www.thelancet.com/journals/lancet/article/PII0140–6736(91)93068–K/fulltext (accessed 14 August 2023)
414   Sapolsky, R. (2018) "How Economic Inequality Inflicts Real Biological Harm," *The Scientific American*, https://www.scientificamerican.com/article/how-economic-inequality-inflicts-real-biological-harm/ (accessed 1 August 2023)
415   Marmot, M. (2015) *Status Syndrome: How your Place on the Social Gradient Directly Affects your Health,* Bloomsbury Paperbacks
416   Boyce, C. et. Al (2010) "Money and Happiness: Rank of Income, Not Income, Affects Life Satisfaction," *Psychological Science*, 21(4) https://journals.sagepub.com/doi/10.1177/0956797610362671 (accessed 1 August 2023)

417   World Bank (2018) "Nearly Half the World Lives on Less Than $5.50 A Day," https://www.worldbank.org/en/news/press-release/2018/10/17/nearly-half-the-world-lives-on-less-than-550-a-day (accessed 1 August 2023)

418   OECD (2021) "Average Wage" https://www.oecd-ilibrary.org/sites/210385a1-en/index.html?itemId=/content/component/210385a1-en#:~:text=Wage%20earnings%20across%20the%20OECD,Mexico%20at%20USD%206%20105 (accessed 1 August 2023)

419   United Nations (2020) "UNDESA World Social Report 2020; The Challenge of Inequality in a Rapidly Changing World," https://www.un.org/development/desa/dspd/world-social-report/2020-2.html

420   Neate, R (2017) "Richest 1% Own Half The World's Wealth, Study Finds" *The Guardian*, https://amp.theguardian.com/inequality/2017/nov/14/worlds-richest-wealth-credit-suisse (accessed 1 August 2023). Savage, M. (2018) "Richest 1% on Target to Own Two-Thirds of All Wealth By 2030," *The Guardian*, https://amp.theguardian.com/business/2018/apr/07/global-inequality-tipping-point-2030 (accessed 1 August 2023)

421   Phan, S. (2020) "Wealth Gap Widening For More Than 70% of Global Population, Researchers Find," https://www.theguardian.com/global-development/2020/jan/22/wealth-gap-widening-for-more-than-70-per-cent-of-global-population-researchers-find (accessed 1 August 2023)

422   Kawachi, I. and Kennedy, B.P (1997) "Health and Social Cohesion; Why Care About Income Inequality?" *British Medical Journal* 314(7086), p1037–1040, doi:11.1136/bmj.314.7086.1037

423   see Sapolsky, M. (2018) "How Economic Inequality Inflicts Real Biological Harm" *The Scientific American*, https://www.scientificamerican.com/article/how-economic-inequality-inflicts-real-biological-harm/ (accessed 1 August 2023)

424   Gao, L. et al (2022) "How Wealth Inequality Affects Happiness: The Perspective of Social Comparison" https://www.frontiersin.org/articles/10.3389/fpsyg.2022.829707/full (accessed 1 August 2023)

425   Phan, S. (2020) "Wealth Gap Widening For More Than 70% of Global Population, Researchers Find," The Guardian, https://www.thelancet.com/journals/lancet/article/PII0140-6736(91)93068-K/fulltext (accessed 14 August 2023)

426   Capra, F. and Luigi Luisi (2016) *The Systems View of Life: A Unifying Vision*, Cambridge University Press

427   WWF (2022), "The Effects of Deforestation" www.wwf.org.uk/learn-effects-of/deforestation (accessed 21 November 2022)

428 Food and Agriculture Organization (2020) "The State of the World's Forests," https://www.fao.org/state-of-forests/en/#:~:text=Between%202015%20and%202020%2C%20the,80%20million%20hectares%20since%201990. (accessed 23 June 2023)

429 See Intergovernmental Panel on Climate Change https://www.ipcc.ch/

430 See Brown, L (2011) *Plan B 4.0—Mobilising to Save Civilization*, W. W. Norton & Co.

431 Sea Level Change (2023) "How Long Have Sea Levels Been Rising? How Does Recent Sea-Level Rise Compare to That Over the Previous Centuries?" https://sealevel.nasa.gov/faq/13/how-long-have-sea-levels-been-rising-how-does-recent-sea-level-rise-compare-to-that-over-the-previous/#:~:text=Over%20the%20past%20100%20years,about%206%20to%208%20inches. (accessed 13 July 2023)

432 Dobson, J. (2019) "Shocking New Maps Show How Sea Level Rise will Destroy Coastal Cities by 2050" Shocking New Maps Show How Sea Level Rise Will Destroy Coastal Cities By 2050 (forbes.com) (accessed 13 July 2023)

433 Chersich, M. et.al (2022) "Increasing Global Temperatures Threaten Gains in Maternal and Newborn Health In Africa: A Review of Impacts and an Adaption Framew" ork,https://researchonline.lshtm.ac.uk/id/eprint/4667305/1/Chersich_etal_2022_Increasing-global-temperatures-threaten-gains.pdf (Accessed 23 October 2023)

434 World Meteorological Organization (2023) "Past Eight Years Confirmed to be the Eight Warmest on Record" www.public.wmo.int (accessed 31 March 2023)

435 Chen, H and Zhang, Xuebin (2022) "Influences of Temperature and Humidity on Cardiovascular Disease Among Adults 65 Years and Older in China," *Frontiers In Public Health* https://doi.org/10.3389%2Ffpubh.2022.1079722 (accessed 24 October 2023)

436 Thompson, R et al. (2018) "Associations Between High Ambient Temperatures and Heat Waves With Mental Health Outcomes: A Systematic Review" *Public Health*, pp161:171–191. doi: 10.1016/j.puhe.2018.06.008. Epub 2018 Jul 12. PMID: 30007545. (Accessed 24 October 2023)

437 See Rocklov, J. and Dubrown, R. (2020) "Climate Change: an Enduring Challenge for Vector-born Disease Prevention and Control" *Nature Immunology*, 21,p 479–483, https://doi.org/10.1038/s41590-020-0648-y

438 Bailey, M (2022) "Climate Change May Push the US Toward the 'Goldilocks Zone' for West Nile Virus," https://kffhealthnews.org/news/article/climate-change-may-push-the-us-toward-the-goldilocks-zone-for-west-nile-virus/amp/ (accessed 3 August 2023)

439   Ricco, M et al. (2022) "Dengue Fever in Italy: The 'Eternal Return' of an Emerging Arboviral Disease." *Tropical Medicine and Infectious Disease*, Vol 7(1) https://doi.org/10.3390%2Ftropicalmed7010010 (Accessed 24 October 2023)

440   World Health Organization (2017) "New Vector Control Response Seen as Game-Changer," https://www.who.int/news-room/feature-stories/detail/new-vector-control-response-seen-as-game-changer (accessed 31 March 2023)

441   University College of London (2021) "Fossil Fuel Air Pollution Responsible for 1 in 5 Deaths Worldwide," https://www.ucl.ac.uk/news/2021/feb/fossil-fuel-air-pollution-responsible-1-5-deaths-worldwide

442   Parikh, J et. Al (2003) "Cooking with Biofuels: Risk Factors Affecting Health Impact on Rural Women," https://www.jstor.org/stable/4413730 (accessed 31 March 2023)

443   Carbon Brief (2020) "Global Carbon Project: Coronavirus Causes 'Record Fall' In Fossil-Fuel Emissions in 2020" https://www.carbonbrief.org/global-carbon-project-coronavirus-causes-record-fall-in-fossil-fuel-emissions-in-2020/ (accessed 31 March 2023)

444   Alkousaa, R. and Abnett, K. (2023) "Shortfall in Climate Change Cash Grows Ahead of COP 28," https://www.reuters.com/business/environment/un-green-climate-fund-pledges-reach-93-bln-second-replenishment-round-2023-10-05/ (accessed 24 October 2023)

445   WWF (2021) "A Warning Sign; Where Biodiversity Loss Is Happening Around the World," https://www.worldwildlife.org/magazine/issues/summer-2021/articles/a-warning-sign-where-biodiversity-loss-is-happening-around-the-world

446   Johnson, M. (2021) "Biodiversity Loss in Amazon Rainforest" https://storymaps.arcgis.com/stories/81ee540b87914ad0baaa22305ce07c3c# (accessed 29 June 2023)

447   The Guardian (2019) "Plummeting Insect Numbers Threaten Collapse of Nature," https://amp.theguardian.com/environment/2019/feb/10/plummeting-insect-numbers-threaten-collapse-of-nature

448   Food and Agriculture Organization (2005) "Trade in Medicinal Plants," https://www.fao.org/3/af285e/af285e00.htm#:~:text=At%20present%2C%2080%20percent%20of,rely%20on%20plant%2Dbased%20medicines. (accessed 20 June 2023)

449   CDC (2020) "Mental Health, Substance Use and Suicidal ideation During the COVID-19 Pandemic," *US Morbidity and Mortality Weekly*, http://dx.doi.org/10.15585/mmwr.mm6932a1 (accessed 24 October 2023)

450   Looi, M. (2023) "Did Covid-19 Come From a Lab Leak in China?" *British Medical Journal*, 382, doi:https://doi.org/10.1136/bmj.p1556 (accessed 7 August 2023)

451 Capra, F. and Luigi Luisi (2016) *The Systems View of Life: A Unifying Vision*, Cambridge University Press
452 Brundtland, G.H (1987) "Our Common Future: Report of the World Commission on Environment and Development" http://www.un-documents.net/ocf-ov.htm (accessed 3 July 2023)
453 Norberg, J (2021) *Open: How Collaboration and Curiosity Shaped Humankind*, Atlantic Books
454 International Panel for Climate Change (2019) "Global Warming of 1.5C" https://www.ipcc.ch/site/assets/uploads/sites/2/2019/06/SR15_Headline-statements.pdf (accessed 6 July 2023)
455 University College London (2021) "Limiting Fossil Fuel Extraction to Meet 1.5C" https://www.ucl.ac.uk/news/2021/sep/limiting-fossil-fuel-extraction-meet-15degc#:~:text=This%20needs%20to%20be%2058,oC%20the%20desired%20target. (accessed 6 July 2023)
456 McLaren, L and Hawe, P (2005) "Ecological Perspectives in Health," http://dx.doi.org/10.1136/jech.2003.018044
457 Daly, H.E and Cobb, J.B (1987) *For the Common Good: Redirecting the Economy towards Community, the Environment, and a Sustainable Future*, Beacon Press, Boston
458 Haidt, J. (2021) *The Happiness Hypothesis: Ten Ways to Find Happiness and Meaning in Life*, Random House
459 Dittmar, H. et al. (2014) "The Relationship Between Materialism and Personal Well-Being: A Meta-Analysis" *Journal of Personality and Social Psychology*, 107(5): p870–924 https://www.researchgate.net/publication/267743492_The_Relationship_Between_Materialism_and_Personal_Well-Being_A_Meta-Analysis (accessed 20 October 2023)
See also De Angelis, T. (2004) "Consumerism and its Discontents," *American Psychological Association*, https://www.apa.org/monitor/jun04/discontents (accessed 14 November 2022)
460 Capra, F. (1975) *The Tao of Physics; an Exploration of the Parallels Between Modern Physics and Eastern Mysticsm*, Shambala Publications
461 see Maharishi Mahesh Yogi (1996) *The Science of Being and the Art of Living*, International SRM Publications
462 see Watts, A. (2021) *The Way of Zen*, Rider
463 see Dyer, W. (2007) *Change your Thoughts, Change your Life: Living the Wisdom of the Tao*, Hay House UK
464 see Kempton, S. (2013) *Awakening Shakti: The Transformative Power of the Goddesses of Yoga*, Sounds True

465   see Haxton, B. (2003) *Fragments*, Penguin Publishing Group

466   A "koan" is a paradoxical phrase, such as "the sound of one hand clapping," designed to arrest the thinking mind and force the student to slough reason in favor of sudden realization or enlightenment.

467   see Capra, F. (1992) *Tao of Physics*, HarperCollins Publishers

468   see Wong, E. (2015) *Being Taoist: Wisdom for Living a Balanced Life*, Shamballa Publications

469   see Gleiser, M. (2018) "How Much Can We Know?" https://www.nature.com/articles/d41586-018-05100-5 (accessed 23 October 2021)

470   see Folger, T. (2002) "Does the Universe Exist if We're not Looking?" https://www.nature.com/articles/d41586-018-05100-5 (accessed 23 October 2023)

471   see Chopra, D. (2019) "You Can't Get Around Consciousness," *New York Times*, https://www.discovermagazine.com/the-sciences/does-the-universe-exist-if-were-not-looking# (accessed 23 October 2023)

472   Evans-Wentz (1968) *The Tibetan Book of the Great Liberation; The Method of Realizing Nirvana Through Knowing the Mind*, Oxford University Press, USA

473   Khalili, N. (2020) *The Spiritual Poems of Rumi*, Wellfleet Press

474   Brubaker, B. (2021) "How Bell's Theorem Proved 'Spooky Action at a Distance' is Real" https://www.quantamagazine.org/how-bells-theorem-proved-spooky-action-at-a-distance-is-real-20210720/ (accessed 23 October 2023)

475   'Carl Jung (1960) *Synchronicity: an Acausal, Connecting Principle*, Princeton University Press, 2012 p.44

476   see Derbyshire, D. (2010) "How to Add 90 Billionths of a Second to Your Life . . . Live in the Basement: Scientists Prove Time Really Does Pass Quicker at a Higher Altitude," https://www.dailymail.co.uk/sciencetech/article-1314656/amp/Scientists-prove-time-really-does-pass-quicker-higher-altitude.html (accessed 23 October 2023)

477   Davies, P. (2014) "Time's Passage is Probably an Illusion" https://www.scientificamerican.com/article/time-s-passage-is-probably-an-illusion/ (accessed 23 October 2023_

478   Kim, H-J. (2000) *Eihei Dogen: Mystical Realism*, Wisdom Publications USA

479   Tolle, E. (2001) *The Power of Now: A Guide to Spiritual Enlightenment*, Yellow Kite

480   see Boh, D. (2002) *Wholeness and the Implicate Order*, Routledge

481   Russel, (2021) "The Primacy of Consciousness," https://www.peterrussell.com/SP/PrimConsc.php (accessed 23 October 2023)

482   Tolle, E. (2001) *The Power of Now*, Yellow Kite

483   Pilkington, M. (2003) "Zero Point Energy," www.amp.theguardian.com (accessed 14 September 2021)

484 see Joye, S.R (2020) *David Bohm's Implicate Order: New Frontiers in the Evolution of Consciousness*, The Viola Institute
485 Capra, F. (1992) *The Tao of Physics*, HarperCollins Publishers
486 Giles, H.A (2022) *Gems of Chinese Literature*, Legare Street Press
487 Bulyzhenkov, I. (2015) "Abstract: Continuous Material Space in the Nondual Field of Physics," CERN, https://indico.cern.ch/event/610415/contributions/2615023/attachments/1488616/2312948/0_Bulyzhenkov_05_06_17_Protvino.pdf (accessed 23 October 2023)
488 h Lazslo, E. (2004) *Science and the Akashic Field: An Integral Theory of Everything*, Inner Traditions Bear and Company
489 Swami Vivekananda (2008) *The Complete Works of Swami Vivekananda, Volume 3*, Kessinger Publishing
490 Chopra, D. (2019) "Why You Can't Always Believe Your Senses," https://deepakchopra.medium.com/why-you-cant-always-believe-your-senses-d511360397cd (accessed 12 September 2022)
491 see Borowski, S. (2012) "Quantum Mechanics and the Consciousness Connection" https://www.aaas.org/quantum-mechanics-and-consciousness-connection (Accessed 23 October 2023)
492 see chapter 11 in Spivack, B. (2020) *An Antidote to Violence: Evaluating the Evidence*, Changemakers Books
493 Lazslo, E. (2004) *Science and the Akashic Field: An Integral Theory of Everything*, Inner Traditions Bear and Company
494 Greene, B. (2000) *The Elegant Universe: Superstrings, Hidden Dimensions, and the Quest for the Ultimate Theory*, Vintage
495 Randerson, J. (2006) "One Big Bang, or Were There Many?" *The Guardian*, https://amp.theguardian.com/science/2006/may/05/spaceexploration.universe (accessed 2 September 2023)
496 Selbie, J. (2021) *The Physics of God: How the Deepest Theories of Science Explain Religion and How the Deepest Truths of religion Explain Science*, New Age Books, USA
497 see Selbie, J. "Heaven is a Hologram," https://www.crconline.org.uk/resources/articles/heaven-hologram, (accessed 26 July 2022)
498 see Whittle, M. (2004) 'Primordial Sounds: Big Bang Accoustics, University of Virginia https://www.markwhittle.uvacreate.virginia.edu/articles/griffith.htm, accessed 9/5/24
499 see NASA (2015) "Song of Earth," https https://youtu.be/UKd1cTeyuMU?si=dMJwS0tkm6pdzjG1, (accessed 28 March 2024
500 McGrath, A.E (2020) *Science & Religion: A New Introduction*, John Wiley and Sons
501 Watts, A. (1965) "Myth of Myself" https://www.organism.earth/library/document/

tao-of-philosophy-5 (accessed 23 October 2023)
502 see Harrison, P. (2021) "World Pantheism—Revering the Universe, Caring for Nature, Celebrating Life," www.pantheism.net, (accessed 26 July 2022)
503 Armstrong, K. (2023) *Sacred Nature: How We Can Recover Our Bond with the Natural World*, Vintage
504 See Cummings, A. (2021) *The Ultimate Guide to Yinyang: An Illustrated Exploration of the Chinese Concept of Opposites*, Watkins Publishing
505 MLA. Shakespeare, W. 1564–1616 author. *The Tragedy of Hamlet, Prince of Denmark* (Act II, scene II) London
506 see Naess, A. (2016) *Ecology of Wisdom*, Penguin Classics
507 See Altman, N. (2020) *Ahimsa: Dynamic Compassion: A Nonviolence Anthology*, Gaupo Publishing
508 Selbie, J. (2021) *The Physics of God: How the Deepest Theories of Science Explain Religion and How the Deepest Truths of Religion Explain Science*, New Page Books, USA
509 Goleman, D. and Davidson, R. (2018) *The Science of Meditation: How to Change Your Brain, Mind and Body*, Penguin Life
510 Formica, M. (2010) "The Science, Psychology and Metaphysics of Prayer," www.psychologytoday.com, (accessed 1 Aug 2022)
511 Goodrich, T. (2016) "Most Americans pray for healing: more than one fourth have practiced 'laying on of Hands' Baylor University study finds," www.baylor.edu, (accessed 1 [Aug 2022])
512 Byrd, R. (1988) "Positive Therapeutic Effects of Intercessory Prayer in Coronary Care Unit Population," South Med Journal, 81 (7) p826–829
513 Harris, W. (1999) "A Randomized, Controlled Trial of the Effects of Remote Intercessory Prayer on Outcomes in Patients Admitted to the Coronary Care Unit." https://pubmed.ncbi.nlm.nih.gov/10547166/ (accessed 15 August 2023)
514 Astin, J. A. et al (2000) "The Efficacy of 'Distant Healing': A Systematic Review Of Randomized Trials," Ann Intern Med, 132 (11), p903–10
515 Dossey, L. (1993) *Healing Words: The Power of Prayer and the Practice of Medicine*, Harper, San Francisco
516 see Aron, E. and Aron, A. (1986) *The Maharishi Effect: A Revolution Through Meditation*, EP Dutton
517 Dillbeck, N. C et al., (1999) "The Transcendental Meditation Program and Crime Rate Change in a Sample of 48 Cities," *Journal of Crime and Justice*, 1981(4), p 25–45

518   Dillbeck, M. et al., (2016) "Societal Violence and Collective Consciousness: Reduction of US Homicide and Urban Violent Crime Rates," *Sage Journals*, www.journals.sagepub.com (Accessed 14 September 2022)

519   Orme-Johnson, D. W. et al., (1988) "International Peace project in the Middle East: The effects of the Maharishi Technology of the Unified Field" *Journal of Conflict Resolution*, 32, 776–812. [Reprinted in R. A. Chalmers, G. Clements, H. Schenkluhn, and M. Weinless (Eds.), "Scientific Research on Maharishi's Transcendental Meditation and TM-Sidhi Programme: Collected Papers," Vol. 4 p2653–2678

520   McTaggart, L. (2008) *The Intention Experiment; Use Your Thoughts to Change the World*, HarperNonFiction

521   Freedman, J. (2007) "The Physics of Emotion" https://www.6seconds.org/2007/01/26/the-physics-of-emotion-candace-pert-on-feeling-good/ (accessed 4 October 2022)

522   Capra, F. (2019) "Turning Point: A Science of Living Systems" https://www.earthandspiritcenter.org/wp-content/uploads/2019/10/3-2-Turning-Point-A-Science-of-Living-Systems-Fritjof-Capra.pdf (accessed 19 September 2023)

523   see Nelson, R. (2020) "What is the nature of global consciousness?," www.noosphere.princeton.edu/science2.html, (accessed 21July 2022)

524   Nelson, R. (2001) "Formal Analysis September 11, 2001" https://noosphere.princeton.edu/911formal.html (11 December 2022)

525   Nelson, R. *1997b) "Multiple Field REG/RNG Recordings During a Global Event," https://noosphere.princeton.edu/ejap/diana/nelson_eJAP.htm (11 December 2022). See also Nelson, R. (2020) "Global Consciousness and the Coronavirus Crisis," https://noetic.org/blog/global-consciousness-and-the-coronavirus-crisis/ (accessed 11 December 2022)

526   Nelson, R. (2006) "The Global Consciousness Project," Journal of Science and Healing 2 (4), p342–51, www.researchgate.net/publication/6938639, (accessed 21 July 2022)

527   McTaggart, L. (2008) *The Intention Experiment: Use Your Thoughts to Change the World*, Atria Books

528   Selbie, J. (2018) "Science Confirms Ancient Spiritual Teachings—We Live in Two Bodies," www.scienceandnonduality.com, (accessed 1 Aug 2022)

529   Goswami, A. (2011) *The Quantum Doctor: A Physicist's Guide to Health and Healing*, Hampton Roads Publishing, USA

530   see Chopra, D. (2015) *Quantum Healing: Exploring the Frontiers of Mind-Body Medicine*, Bantam Books, New York

531   see Harare, Y. (2015) *Sapiens: A Brief History of Humankind*, Harper Collins, for a

discussion on "imagined orders" and how they have shaped human history.
532   Chenoweth, E. (2021) *Civil Resistance: What Everyone Needs to Know*, Oxford University Press, USA
533   Salamon, H. (2022) "The Effect of Women's Parliamentary Participation on Renewable Energy Policy Outcomes," https://ejpr.onlinelibrary.wiley.com/doi/10.1111/1475-6765.12539
534   Figueres, C. and Rivett-Carnac, T. (2020) *The Future We Choose: The Stubborn Optimist's Guide to the Climate Crisis*, Manilla Press

INDEX

3
3 R's, 202

A
Acid reflux, 59
Acupressure, 118
Acupuncture, 27, 28, 32, 118, 135, 164, 165, 247, 248, 298
Acupuncture, 164, 298
Acupuncturists, 32
Adaptation energy, 46, 155, 205, 256
Adrenal fatigue, 109, 128
Adrenaline, 40, 42, 50, 104, 109, 113, 115
Adverse drug reactions (ADRs), 22
Aerobic, 122, 123
Aeroponics, 89
Africa, 6, 182, 193, 303
Agricultural Era, 7
Agroecosystems, 87
Agroforestry, 88, 89, 90, 95
Ahimsa, 239, 308
AIDS, 10
Alcohol, 10, 59, 63, 108, 117, 290
Alexander technique, 27
Allergies, 6, 61, 164, 193
Allopathic, 27
Alzheimer, 5, 58, 105, 107, 124, 152, 169, 291
Amazon, 92, 197, 199, 205, 236, 287, 304

America, 6, 19, 56, 193, 197, 272, 274, 290
Amnesia, 22
Amygdala, 40, 41, 108, 153, 163
Anesthetics, 13
Anthropocene, 190
Anthropocentric, 238, 239
Anthropocentrism, 238
Antiandrogens, 67
Antibiotics, 9, 13, 17, 18, 21, 63, 85, 90, 96, 242, 292
Anti-inflammatory, 55, 61, 62, 70, 122
Antimicrobial, 90, 116, 127
Archaeological, 7
Arthritis, 135, 152, 157, 164
Artistic endeavors, 48
Asia, 6, 193
Asthma, 6, 61, 71, 193
Attention deficit hyperactivity disorder (ADHD), 6
Austerity, 44, 263
Australasian Integrative Medicine Association, 31
Australia, 28, 56, 86, 275
Australian bushfire disaster, 192
Autonomic nervous system, 50, 163
Avocado, 61, 72
Ayurveda, 118, 159, 163, 247, 295

B
Bangladesh, 10
Bankrupt, 23, 20, 82

Beef, 69, 92, 93, 94, 95, 258, 283
Berlin Wall, 22, 257
Big Bang, 221, 228, 230, 307
Biofeedback, 27, 28, 150, 160
Biology, 24, 16, 34, 63, 133, 139, 140, 267
Bloating, 59, 109, 121
Body-centered psychotherapy, 162
BPA, 66, 67
Brahman, 215, 226, 230
Brain tumors, 67, 116
Brazil, 37, 84
Breathwork, 27, 28, 49, 112, 134, 149, 150, 158, 159, 163, 318
Breathwork, 157, 158, 159, 297
Britain, 9, 169
British Civil Service, 181
Broccoli, 59
Brundtland Report, 200
Brussels sprouts, 72
Bubonic plague, 8
Buddhism, 216, 226, 230, 239, 242

C

Cadmium, 66
Canada, 56
Cannabis, 125
Canola, 71
Capra, 11, 21, 13, 14, 34, 35, 38, 190, 200, 201, 202, 205, 207, 214, 217, 225, 246, 271, 273, 276, 277, 302, 305, 306, 307, 309
Carbohydrates, 56, 58
Carbon farming, 88
Carbon footprints, 93, 94, 176
Cardiorespiratory, 119
Cardiovascular, 43, 53, 57, 58, 105, 106, 120, 192, 194, 276, 293

Caribbean, 6
Catastrophe, 83, 209, 246
Catastrophic, 64, 81, 189, 190, 204
Catastrophizing, 162, 255
Celestial unity, 215
Centers for Disease Control and Prevention (CDC), 6
Central nervous system, 30, 117
Chemical farming, 81, 86
Chia, 67, 72
Chikunga virus, 193
China, 10, 56, 57, 88, 92, 279, 303, 304
Chiropractic, 27, 118
Chiropractors, 32
Chlorella, 72
Cholera, 8, 9, 192
Cholesterol, 20, 58, 77, 120, 157
Christ, 8
Christianity, 229, 230, 242
Chronic, 12, 13, 21, 24, 5, 6, 9, 10, 12, 13, 17, 20, 21, 23, 25, 29, 35, 38, 39, 42, 45, 46, 47, 51, 53, 54, 57, 58, 62, 66, 67, 69, 70, 76, 85, 104, 105, 106, 117, 118, 119, 121, 122, 124, 152, 156, 159, 163, 164, 165, 169, 170, 175, 180, 192, 194, 213, 249, 258, 272, 318
Chronic obstructive pulmonary disease (COPD), 5, 194
Chronobiologist, 102
Circadian rhythms, 52, 53, 102, 104, 113, 203
Clickbait, 171
Climate crisis, 13, 21, 88, 185, 189, 190, 194, 196, 210, 261, 266, 318
Climbing, 119, 122, 135

Coca cola, 56
Cognitive, 50, 57, 58, 60, 62, 70, 112, 123, 124, 141, 151, 153, 157, 161, 169, 173, 177
complementarity, 218
complimentary and alternative medicine (CAM), 15
COP15, 97
Coronavirus pandemic, 194
Cosmologists, 221
Cosmos, 214, 215, 225, 226, 227, 228, 229, 231, 232, 246, 252, 264, 266, 267
COVID, 24, 5, 10, 45, 197, 199, 246, 304
Craniosacral therapy, 27

D

DDT, 55, 80, 81, 279
Deep Ecology, 238, 239, 240
Deforestation, 92, 302
Dementia, 58, 70, 107, 124, 152, 169
Descartes, 14, 214
Diabetes, 5, 6, 9, 31, 53, 58, 61, 62, 65, 67, 69, 70, 71, 76, 105, 106, 140, 152
Digestive, 41, 42, 57, 59, 61, 62, 67, 108, 109, 115, 121, 164, 281
Digital literacy education, 172
Dioxins, 66, 282
Diphtheria, 8, 13
Divine Mind, 227
Divinity scale, 213
Dualistic, 22, 133, 212, 214, 217, 218, 220, 235, 236, 239, 242, 253, 255, 265, 268

E

E.coli, 90
Eastern mysticism, 216, 224, 232
Ebola, 10, 197
Ecological, 24, 8, 10, 13, 25, 34, 35, 36, 55, 74, 90, 92, 168, 177, 187, 190, 191, 201, 202, 206, 208, 209, 210, 234, 235, 236, 238, 239, 246, 252, 256, 260, 261, 262, 266
Ecology, 24, 33, 34, 83, 94, 197, 200, 204, 206, 207, 212, 234, 235, 238, 264, 267
Ecotherapy, 127, 261
Edamame, 72
Egyptian dynasty, 7
Electromagnetic frequencies (EMFs), 52, 116
Elephant, 5
Embodied simulation, 48
Empowerment, 27, 33, 251, 260, 262
Empty calories, 57, 58
Emulsifiers, 57
Environmental Working Group, 87
Enzymes, 29, 41, 144, 281
Epidemiological triad, 19
Epigenetics, 26, 29, 30, 31, 144, 153
Ethanol, 59, 117
Eucalyptus, 51
European and British Society for Integrative Medicine, 31
European Food Safety Authority, 86

F

Facebook, 110, 184
Fahrenheit, 114
Feed livestock, 92, 96

Fiber, 56, 58, 61, 63, 64, 109, 281
Fibromyalgia, 146, 152
Fight- or-flight, 40
Finland, 7
Fish, 61, 62, 67, 70, 71, 72, 95, 96, 97, 98, 197, 258, 283, 288
Flax, 72
Forest bathing, 51
France, 56, 61, 86
F-sharp *kung*, 231

G

GABA, 60, 106, 125
gastroesophageal reflux disease (GERD), 20
Germany, 28, 86, 109, 245
Global inequality, 21
Glyphosate, 66, 85, 86
Gobbledegook, 74
Goji berries, 67
Goldilocks zone, 193
Greece, 33, 61, 173
Green Climate Fund (GCF), 196
Green National Product, 209
Green noise, 114
Greenhouse gases (GHGs), 81
Gross domestic product (GDP), 7
Guided visualization, 27
Gynecologic, 164

H

Habitat destruction, 178, 190, 197
Harmony, 22, 34, 42, 97, 128, 141, 215, 216, 218, 219, 232, 234, 235, 237, 241, 251, 253, 264, 269
Harvard, 76, 103, 146, 150, 153, 154, 159, 257, 275, 277, 282, 284, 297, 298

Headaches, 57, 136
Health disparities, 167, 180, 181, 195, 263
Heart attacks, 21, 43, 104, 105, 192, 318
Heatwaves, 192
Herbal medicine, 21, 32, 118
Herbalists, 32
Herbicides, 66
Hiking, 122
Himalayan mountains, 159
Hippocrates, 33, 36, 78
Hippocratic Oath, 33
Holistically, 21, 11, 132, 261, 318
Holographic universe, 224
Holotropic breathwork, 159
Holy Bible, 230
Homeopathy, 27, 28, 118
Homeostasis, 38, 42
Homo erectus, 7
Homo sapiens, 7, 70
Hormonal systems, 41
Hormone dopamine, 48
Horses, 239
Housing, 174, 176, 300
Human Genome Project, 29
Humanistic, 162
Humanistic therapy, 162
Hunter-Gatherer Era, 7
Hydroponics, 89
Hygiene, 9, 101, 108, 113, 118, 131, 177
Hyperactivity, 6, 57, 58
Hypercontrol, 237
Hyperventilating, 40
Hypervigilant, 40
Hypnosis, 27, 118, 134, 149, 150
Hypnotherapists, 160

I

Impoverished, 168, 181
India, 10, 83, 92, 156, 276
Industrial Revolution, 8, 10, 12, 22, 44, 204
Infectious diseases, 24, 5, 8, 9, 10, 18, 22, 30, 43, 175, 191, 193
Influenza, 8
Insomnia, 57, 104, 109, 113, 114, 117, 118, 146, 152
Instagram, 170
Interbrain synchrony, 128
Interconnectedness, 11, 12, 13, 22, 25, 234, 253, 256
Intergovernmental Panel on Climate Change (IPCC), 190
International Panel on Climate Change (IPCC), 87
International Union for Conservation of Nature (IUCN), 92
Irritable bowel syndrome (IBS), 59
Islam, 215, 230, 242
Italy, 61, 86, 173, 193, 300, 304

J

Jainism, 226, 239
John Hopkins University, 22
Judaism, 229, 230, 242

K

Keep Calm and Carry On, 41
Kidney beans, 72

L

L-carnitine, 69, 283
Liberation, 215, 220, 306
Light therapy, 27

Logos, 215
Luigi Luisi, 34, 35, 38, 200, 201, 202, 205, 207, 276, 277, 302, 305
Lungs of the earth, 92

M

Mackerel, 62, 71
Macrocosm, 11, 22, 217, 224, 257, 267, 269
Magic bullet, 19, 23
Maharishi Effect, 243, 244, 245, 246, 308
Malaria, 8, 193, 197
Malnourishment, 9
Malnutrition, 10, 57, 175, 191, 198
Manipulative, 27
Marine algae, 72
Marine Conservation Society (MCS), 98
Maternal mortality, 178
McDonalds, 56, 180
Measles, 8
Meditating, 21, 159, 243, 244, 318
Meditation, 27, 28, 29, 39, 47, 49, 53, 112, 115, 118, 134, 147, 149, 150, 151, 152, 153, 154, 155, 158, 160, 163, 223, 227, 231, 241, 242, 243, 244, 245, 247, 249, 252, 256, 260, 269, 278, 295, 318
Mediterranean diet (MedDiet), 61
Mercury, 66, 67, 72, 96, 282
MERS, 10, 91, 197
metabolism, 42, 77, 104, 120, 152, 159, 281
Mexico, 10, 19, 84, 302

Microbiome, 17, 26, 30, 31, 57, 59, 60, 61, 62, 63, 64, 65, 67, 80, 87, 109, 120, 121, 258, 281
Microcosms, 11, 22, 257
Microsleeps, 108
Middle East, 6, 193, 309
Mind-body interventions (MBIs), 150
Mindfulness, 27, 32, 39, 47, 48, 49, 52, 53, 126, 134, 149, 150, 155, 156, 240, 261, 269
Mindfulness-based stress reduction (MBSR), 28, 156
Miraculous, 131, 139, 165, 213
Modern Era, 9
Moksha, 215, 216
Monistic, 215
Monocrops, 80
Monsanto, 86, 285
Morphine, 23
Mosquitoes, 8, 193, 197, 239
Mushroom, 165
Mysterious, 212, 213, 229
Mystical arm of Judaism, 215

N

NASA, 230, 307
National Health Service, 164
National Institute of Health, 152
National Sleep Foundation, 101, 109, 110, 113, 114
Natural killer (NK) cells, 51
Natural Law, 230
Neoplatonist, 215
Nervous system, 40, 41, 42, 48, 49, 53, 59, 107, 126, 141, 151, 154, 155, 156, 158, 163, 221, 241, 243, 269
Netflix, 91, 171, 199
Neu5G, 69

Neurochemistry, 30
Neurogenesis, 123
Neuropeptides, 139
Neuroplasticity, 26, 29, 30, 31, 46, 112, 123, 133, 143, 145, 165, 241
Neuroscience, 26, 28, 48, 144
Neuroscience, 29, 278, 279, 289, 293, 294, 296
Neurosis, 164
Nike, 110
Nipah virus, 91
Non-Hodgkin lymphoma, 86
Nonlocality, 221, 227, 243
Nutritionists, 32, 69
Nutritious diet, 7, 30

O

Obese, 21, 5, 6, 57, 318
Obsessive- compulsive disorder (OCD), 61
Occupy Wall Street, 183, 184
Oddbox, 66
Olive, 61
Olympic games, 246
Omega-3, 55, 62, 70, 71, 72, 96, 258, 281, 283
Omega-3s, 71
Omega-6, 71, 96
Online community building, 172
Onus, 94, 98
Osteopathic manipulation, 27
Osteoporosis, 65, 122
Overcrowding, 175
Overexercising, 128
Oxygen, 40, 50, 120, 123, 204

P

Pacific, 6

Painting, 26, 48
Pandemics, 8, 91, 197
Panpsychism, 232
Paradoxical unity, 216, 217, 219, 231, 233, 250
Paradoxical unity, 237
Paradoxically, 57
Parasympathetic, 41, 42, 48, 126, 151, 158, 163
Pesticides, 55, 63, 66, 67, 80, 81, 82, 83, 85, 89, 90, 95, 96, 194
Pesticides, 66, 67, 85, 96, 282
Pharmaceutical, 23, 19, 20, 23, 82, 165
Physicist, 21, 219, 220, 224, 225, 227, 228, 248
Physics of Emotion, 245, 309
Phytoncides, 51, 116, 126
Pioneering, 13, 17, 23, 13, 29, 31, 34, 86, 101, 133, 139, 142, 143, 165, 202, 207, 238
Placebo-controlled dose reduction (PCDR), 137
Planet, 11, 12, 13, 21, 22, 23, 11, 31, 35, 36, 52, 54, 55, 63, 64, 74, 75, 78, 79, 80, 81, 83, 91, 95, 97, 132, 178, 185, 187, 190, 192, 194, 195, 196, 198, 200, 204, 211, 225, 230, 235, 236, 240, 252, 253, 254, 256, 257, 258, 259, 260, 261, 262, 266, 267, 268, 269, 270, 286, 318
Planetary boundaries, 12, 186, 187, 208, 210, 262
Plethora, 27, 28, 47, 51, 64, 83, 126, 133
Post-traumatic stress disorder (PTSD), 50, 156
Potbelly, 58

Poultry, 62
Poverty-stricken, 174, 195
Prefrontal cortex, 41, 136, 154, 157
Probable carcinogen, 106
Proteins, 29, 83, 95, 123, 139, 144
Psychiatrists, 16
Psychodynamic, 161
Psychokinetic effect, 246
Psychology, 26, 133, 139, 242, 273
Psychotherapists, 32, 48
Purusha-Prakriti, 216

Q

Qigong, 27, 32, 164
Quantum collapse, 220
Quantum foam, 225
Quantum mechanics, 214, 219
Quantum physics, 35, 212, 213, 215, 217, 220, 227, 231, 233, 238, 245
Quantum superposition, 220

R

Random number generators (RNGs), 246
Rebirthing, 159
Red meat, 62, 69
Reductionism, 14, 15
Reductionist, 21, 12, 13, 14, 15, 17, 25, 81, 131, 201, 217, 255, 318
Reference, 12, 22
Reflexology, 27, 118, 278
Regenerative organic certified (ROC), 87
Reiki, 27, 28, 118, 164, 165, 247, 248, 293, 298, 299
Rejuvination, 151
REM (rapid eye movement), 111
Respiratory problems, 57, 175

Rewilding, 88
Rheumatoid arthritis, 61
Rolf therapy, 27
Rumi, 221, 270, 306

S

Safflower, 71
Saints, 215, 229, 233
Salmon, 62, 70, 71, 95
Salmonella, 90
Samawat, 229
Sandalwood, 51, 116
Sanskrit, 155, 223, 230, 231, 248
SARS, 10, 91, 197
Scaremongering, 22
Seafood, 62, 70, 96, 282
Seaweed, 72, 84, 97
Seeds, 43, 61, 65, 67, 71, 72, 81, 82, 83, 87, 145, 196, 207
Segregated, 175
Self-esteem, 76, 125, 130, 154, 155, 158, 163, 168, 172, 179, 180
Serotonin, 48, 50, 52, 60, 70, 115, 125, 154, 163
Shinrin-yoku, 51, 127
Shiva, 83, 216, 225, 285
Shiva-Shakti, 216
Sikhism, 239
Skyrocketing, 23, 17, 45
Slow wave sleep—SWS, 111
Smallpox, 8, 9
Smoking, 44, 63, 112, 120, 169, 175, 177
Snapchat, 170
Social capital, 167, 168, 174, 177, 180
Social cohesion, 44
Social determinants, 167, 181, 187, 188, 259

Social Foundation, 186
Social isolation, 169, 173
Socioeconomic, 6, 167, 168, 179, 180, 181, 182, 184, 188, 199, 209
Socioeconomic status (SES), 179
Socio-economic strata, 5
Sodium nitrate, 57
Song of Earth, 230, 307
South Africa, 22, 84, 185, 318
Soybean, 71
Spain, 61, 86
Spiritual therapy, 163, 164
Spirituality, 24, 212, 214, 224, 231, 232, 234, 235, 241, 318
Spirulina, 72
Sprinting, 119
Stanford University, 150
Stubborn illusion, 222
Subatomic world, 213
Sufism, 215
Sunflower oil, 71
Surgeons, 15
Switzerland, 28, 164
Systems theorist, 21, 226
Systems view, 21, 23, 11, 13, 34, 35, 36, 37, 90, 132, 201, 209, 211, 212, 232, 238, 267, 269, 318

T

Taco Tuesdays, 76
Tao, 132, 214, 216, 217, 225, 226, 305, 306, 307
Taoism, 216, 237
Telomerase, 152, 153
Thailand, 37, 84, 86
Therapeutic touch, 27, 28
Thyroid disorders, 53
Tigers, 239

TikTok, 47, 170
Tobacco, 10, 69
Tofu, 72
Treatise, 22
Trout, 62, 70, 71, 95
Tuberculosis, 8, 9, 13, 91
Tummo technique, 159
Turmeric, 67
Typhoid fever, 8
Typhoon, 37

U

Uber, 110
Ulcers, 59
Unemployment, 175, 179, 199
UNICEF, 57, 280
United Nations Environment Program (UNEP), 68
Unmanifest, 215, 216, 220, 224, 225
US National Center for Complementary and Integrative Health, 31

V

Vacuum, 218, 224, 225, 229, 230
Vagus nerve, 48, 51, 158
Vedic view, 215
Vertebroplasty, 135
Vitamin B12, 65
Vitamin D, 127
Vivation, 159

W

Wahdat-al-wujud, 215
Walnuts, 72
War in Lebanon, 244
Water retention, 57

Web of life, 22, 10, 11, 13, 35, 38, 64, 80, 127, 189, 191, 197, 201, 204, 205, 208, 212, 234, 235, 238, 252, 253, 255, 256, 269, 270
Weight gain, 57, 59, 65, 72, 76, 108, 109, 170
West Nile virus, 193
Western, 5, 12, 13, 16, 17, 23, 24, 25, 33, 54, 55, 56, 57, 64, 65, 68, 70, 71, 78, 80, 84, 90, 212, 213, 214, 223, 233, 235, 238, 242, 255, 274
WhatsApp, 170
Wheatgrass, 67
Wonky veg box, 66
World Commission on Environment and Development, 200, 305
World Health Organization, 5, 36, 272, 273, 275, 276, 282, 283, 285, 287, 290, 298, 299, 300, 304
World Social Report, 182, 302

Y

Yoga, 27, 28, 32, 47, 49, 118, 124, 128, 134, 149, 150, 156, 157, 158, 260
Youtube, 289

Z

Zika, 193, 197
Zoonotic illnesses, 197